Mastering GameMaker: A Journey from Novice to Expert

Kameron Hussain and Frahaan Hussain

Published by Sonar Publishing, 2024.

MASTERING GAMEMAKER: A JOURNEY FROM NOVICE TO EXPERT

First edition. January 14, 2024.

ISBN: 979-8224908905

Written by Kameron Hussain and Frahaan Hussain.

Table of Contents

Puzzle Games

Simulation Games

Strategy Games

12.3 Case Studies: Notable Games in Each Genre

Action Game: "Hotline Miami"

Role-Playing Game: "Undertale"

Puzzle Game: "Hyper Light Drifter"

Simulation Game: "Spelunky"

Strategy Game: "Nidhogg"

12.4 Hybrid Genres and Innovative Design

Hybrid Genres Explained

Innovative Design Approaches

Implementing Hybrid Genres

Design Considerations

12.5 Trends and Future Directions in Game Genres

1. Virtual Reality (VR) and Augmented Reality (AR)

2. Hybrid Genres and Niche Experiences

3. Live Service and Games as a Service (GaaS)

4. Cooperative and Social Gameplay

5. Accessibility and Inclusivity

Chapter 1: Introduction to GameMaker

1.1 Understanding the GameMaker Landscape

Game development is an exciting and creative field that has seen remarkable growth in recent years. GameMaker, a powerful game development engine, has played a significant role in making game development accessible to a broader audience. In this section, we will delve into the GameMaker landscape to provide you with a foundational understanding of what GameMaker is and what it can offer.

What is GameMaker?

GameMaker is a versatile game development platform that allows individuals and small teams to create games without the need for extensive programming knowledge. It was created by Mark Overmars and later acquired by YoYo Games. GameMaker is known for its user-friendly interface, which makes it an excellent choice for beginners while still offering advanced features for experienced developers.

The Evolution of GameMaker

To appreciate the capabilities of GameMaker fully, it's essential to understand its evolution over the years. GameMaker has a rich history that dates back to the late 1990s when Mark Overmars first developed it as an educational tool. Since then, it has undergone significant transformations and enhancements, making it a powerful game development engine used by professionals worldwide.

Key Features and Capabilities of GameMaker

GameMaker boasts a wide range of features and capabilities that empower game developers to bring their ideas to life. Some of its key features include:

- **Drag-and-Drop Interface:** GameMaker provides an intuitive drag-and-drop interface for designing game logic and interactions, making it accessible to beginners.

- **Scripting:** For more advanced users, GameMaker offers its scripting language, GameMaker Language (GML). GML allows for complex game logic and customization.

- **Cross-Platform Development:** You can target multiple platforms with your games, including Windows, macOS, iOS, Android, and more, with a single codebase.

- **Asset Creation:** GameMaker includes tools for creating and managing game assets such as sprites, sounds, and backgrounds.

- **Physics Engine:** It has a built-in physics engine for simulating real-world interactions and behaviors.

- **Extensibility:** GameMaker can be extended with custom functions and libraries, enabling you to tailor it to your specific needs.

Setting Up Your GameMaker Environment

Before you dive into creating your first game with GameMaker, you need to set up your development environment. Here are the basic steps to get started:

1. **Download GameMaker:** Visit the official GameMaker website and download the version of GameMaker Studio that suits your needs. GameMaker offers both free and paid versions, with varying levels of functionality.
2. **Installation:** Follow the installation instructions provided on the website for your chosen platform (Windows or macOS).
3. **Account Creation:** Create a GameMaker account if required. Some features and services may be tied to your account.
4. **License Activation:** If you've purchased a paid version of GameMaker, you'll need to activate your license during the installation process.
5. **Getting Familiar:** Spend some time navigating the GameMaker interface to become familiar with its layout and features. We'll explore this further in Section 1.5.

With your GameMaker environment set up, you're ready to embark on your game development journey.

Navigating the GameMaker Interface

GameMaker's user interface is designed to be user-friendly and efficient. Here's a brief overview of the key components of the interface:

- **Workspace:** The workspace is where you'll create and edit your game's assets, scripts, and levels.

- **Resource Tree:** This panel on the left side of the interface contains all the resources used in your game, such as sprites, objects, and scripts.

- **Properties:** The properties panel allows you to view and modify the properties of selected resources or objects.

- **Code Editor:** If you're using GML for scripting, this is where you'll write and edit your code.

- **Game Window:** The game window displays your game as you develop it, allowing you to see how your changes affect gameplay in real-time.

- **Toolbar:** The toolbar contains various tools and shortcuts for common actions, such as saving your project or running your game.

This concludes our introduction to GameMaker and the essential steps for getting started. In the following chapters, we will delve deeper into the practical aspects of game development using GameMaker, building on the foundation we've established here.

1.2 The Evolution of GameMaker: A Historical Perspective

GameMaker's journey through the years has been marked by continuous growth and evolution. Understanding its history provides valuable insights into its development as a game creation tool. In this section, we'll explore the historical perspective of GameMaker, tracing its origins and highlighting key milestones along the way.

Early Origins

GameMaker's roots can be traced back to the late 1990s when Dutch computer scientist Mark Overmars developed the first iteration of the software. Overmars initially created GameMaker as an educational tool to teach students about game design and programming concepts. This early version of GameMaker, while rudimentary compared to today's standards, laid the foundation for what would become a powerful game development engine.

The YoYo Games Era

In 2007, GameMaker took a significant step forward when YoYo Games, a game development company founded by Sandy Duncan and David Soutar, acquired the rights to GameMaker. This acquisition marked the beginning of GameMaker's transformation into a commercially viable game development platform. Under YoYo Games' stewardship, GameMaker received substantial updates and improvements.

GameMaker Studio

One of the pivotal moments in GameMaker's evolution was the release of GameMaker Studio in 2012. GameMaker Studio represented a major overhaul of the software, introducing a more modern and streamlined development environment. It brought several key advancements, including:

- **Cross-Platform Support:** GameMaker Studio allowed developers to export their games to multiple platforms, including Windows, macOS, iOS, Android, and more, with ease.

- **Introduction of GameMaker Language (GML):** While earlier versions of GameMaker used a scripting language called Game Maker Language (GML), GameMaker Studio emphasized GML as the primary scripting language for advanced game development.

- **Improved Visual Editor:** The user interface received significant enhancements, making it more intuitive and efficient for developers.

GameMaker Studio 2

Building on the success of GameMaker Studio, YoYo Games released GameMaker Studio 2 in 2017. This iteration introduced several new features and improvements, including:

- **Layer-Based Workflow:** GameMaker Studio 2 introduced a layer-based approach to level design, simplifying the creation of complex game worlds.

- **Tilesets and Tilemap System:** The addition of tilesets and a tilemap system made it easier to create grid-based games, platformers, and RPGs.

- **Seamless 2D and 3D Integration:** GameMaker Studio 2 offered better support for 3D graphics, allowing developers to create games with 2D and 3D elements seamlessly.

- **Asset Browser:** A revamped asset browser made it easier to organize and manage game assets.

GameMaker Studio 2's Continued Evolution

Since the release of GameMaker Studio 2, YoYo Games has continued to refine and expand the engine. Regular updates have introduced features like a built-in code editor, enhanced debugging tools, and further improvements to the user interface. GameMaker Studio 2 has become a popular choice for indie developers, enabling them to create a wide range of games, from simple mobile titles to complex PC and console projects.

This historical perspective highlights GameMaker's remarkable journey from its educational origins to its current status as a versatile and professional game development engine. As you embark on your own game development journey with GameMaker, it's important to recognize the rich heritage and ongoing commitment to innovation that underpin this powerful tool. In the chapters ahead, we'll delve deeper into the practical aspects of using GameMaker to bring your game ideas to life.

1.3 Key Features and Capabilities of GameMaker

Understanding the key features and capabilities of GameMaker is essential as you embark on your game development journey. GameMaker offers a wide range of tools and functionalities that empower developers to create games of varying complexity. In this section, we'll explore some of the core features that make GameMaker a powerful and versatile game development engine.

1. Cross-Platform Development

GameMaker excels at cross-platform development, allowing you to target multiple platforms with a single codebase. Whether you want your game to run on Windows, macOS, iOS, Android, consoles, or even HTML5, GameMaker provides export options to reach your desired audience. This cross-platform support can save you valuable development time and resources.

2. User-Friendly Interface

One of GameMaker's standout features is its user-friendly interface. It offers a visual drag-and-drop system for designing game logic and interactions, making it accessible to beginners and those without extensive programming experience. However, for more advanced users, GameMaker provides the flexibility of scripting with GameMaker Language (GML), offering the best of both worlds.

3. GameMaker Language (GML)

GML is GameMaker's scripting language and a powerful tool for creating complex game logic and custom behaviors. GML is similar to other programming languages, making it easy for developers with programming experience to transition to GameMaker. With GML, you have full control over your game's behavior, enabling you to implement unique gameplay mechanics and features.

Here's a simple example of GML code to move an object horizontally:

```
// Create Event of the object

speed = 5; // Set the speed of movement

// Step Event of the object

if (keyboard_check(vk_right)) {

x += speed; // Move right

}

if (keyboard_check(vk_left)) {

x -= speed; // Move left
```

}

4. Asset Creation Tools

GameMaker provides built-in tools for creating and managing game assets such as sprites, sounds, and backgrounds. You can import image files, audio clips, and other resources directly into your project. The integrated sprite editor allows you to design and animate characters and objects without the need for external software.

5. Physics Engine

For games that require realistic physics simulations, GameMaker includes a built-in physics engine. This engine simplifies the implementation of physics-based interactions, such as collisions, gravity, and object dynamics. Whether you're creating a platformer or a puzzle game, the physics engine can enhance the realism and gameplay experience.

6. Extensibility

GameMaker's extensibility allows you to customize and extend its functionality. You can create custom scripts, objects, and libraries to tailor the engine to your specific needs. Additionally, the GameMaker Marketplace offers a wide range of assets and extensions created by the community, making it easy to enhance your game with pre-made resources.

7. Debugging and Testing Tools

Effective debugging and testing are crucial during game development. GameMaker provides a suite of debugging tools, including a debugger for GML scripts, a variable inspector, and real-time error reporting. You can step through code, inspect variable values, and identify and resolve issues efficiently.

8. Community and Support

GameMaker boasts a vibrant and active community of developers and enthusiasts. Online forums, tutorials, and documentation resources are readily available to help you overcome challenges and learn new techniques. YoYo Games, the company behind GameMaker, also provides official support and regular updates to improve the engine's performance and capabilities.

9. Publishing and Distribution

Once you've completed your game, GameMaker simplifies the process of publishing and distributing it. You can export your game to various platforms and distribution channels, including popular app stores and game marketplaces. GameMaker handles many of the technical aspects, such as building executable files and managing dependencies, allowing you to focus on delivering a polished gaming experience.

10. Community and Educational Impact

GameMaker has a significant presence in the education sector, making it an ideal tool for aspiring game developers and educators. Many educational institutions use GameMaker to teach game design and programming concepts. This educational support fosters a new generation of game developers and contributes to the growth of the game development industry.

These key features and capabilities illustrate why GameMaker has become a popular choice for game developers of all skill levels. Whether you're a beginner looking to create your first game or an experienced developer seeking a powerful and flexible game engine, GameMaker offers the tools and resources to bring your game ideas to life. In the following chapters, we'll explore these features in greater detail and guide you through the process of creating games using GameMaker.

1.4 Setting Up Your GameMaker Environment

Before you start creating your first game with GameMaker, it's crucial to set up your development environment correctly. Proper setup ensures that you have the necessary tools and configurations to work efficiently. In this section, we'll walk you through the essential steps to set up your GameMaker environment, whether you're using the free version or a paid edition.

1. Download and Installation

The first step is to download GameMaker from the official website (https://www.yoyogames.com/). GameMaker offers different editions, including a free trial and paid versions with varying features. Choose the version that suits your needs and click the download link. Follow the installation instructions provided for your specific platform (Windows or macOS). During installation, you may be prompted to create or log in to a GameMaker account if required.

2. License Activation (Paid Versions)

If you've purchased a paid version of GameMaker, you'll need to activate your license. This process typically involves entering a license key during installation or through the software's activation interface.

Ensure that you have your license key ready if you're using a paid edition.

3. Getting Familiar with the Interface

After installation and activation, launch GameMaker Studio. Take some time to explore the user interface to become familiar with its layout and features. Here's an overview of the key components:

- **Workspace:** This is where you'll create and edit your game's assets, scripts, and levels.

- **Resource Tree:** Located on the left side of the interface, it contains all the resources used in your game, such as sprites, objects, and scripts.

- **Properties:** The properties panel allows you to view and modify the properties of selected resources or objects.

- **Code Editor:** If you're using GML for scripting, this is where you'll write and edit your code.

- **Game Window:** The game window displays your game as you develop it, allowing you to see how your changes affect gameplay in real-time.

- **Toolbar:** The toolbar contains various tools and shortcuts for common actions, such as saving your project or running your game.

4. Creating a New Project

To start working on your game, you'll need to create a new project. Here's how to do it:

- Click on "File" in the menu bar.
- Select "New Project" to open the New Project dialog.
- Choose a project name and location for your game project files.
- Select the platform you want to target (e.g., Windows, macOS, Android, iOS).
- Choose a project template based on your game type or start from scratch.
- Click "Create" to generate your project.

5. Configuring Game Settings

Before diving into game development, it's essential to configure your game's settings, such as screen resolution, aspect ratio, and target platform settings. You can access these settings through the "File" menu under "Global Game Settings."

6. Adding Assets

GameMaker relies on assets like sprites, sounds, and backgrounds to build your game. You can import existing assets or create new ones using GameMaker's integrated editors. Import image files, audio clips, and other resources directly into your project by right-clicking the respective resource folder in the resource tree and selecting "Import."

7. Understanding the Resource Tree

The resource tree is where you organize and manage your game's assets. It includes folders for various resource types, such as sprites, objects, rooms, and scripts. As you create and import resources, you'll find them listed in their respective folders.

8. Saving Your Project

Frequent saving is a best practice to avoid losing progress. Use the "File" menu to save your project regularly. GameMaker projects have a ".yyz" file extension, and you can save them anywhere on your computer.

9. Exploring Documentation and Resources

GameMaker offers extensive documentation and online resources to help you learn and troubleshoot. Visit the official GameMaker documentation (https://docs.yoyogames.com/) to access tutorials, guides, and reference materials. Additionally, the GameMaker community is active on forums and social media, making it easy to seek help and share your progress.

10. Ready to Begin Development

With your GameMaker environment set up and your project created, you're ready to start developing your game. Depending on your game's complexity, you'll be working with assets, scripting, and level design. Subsequent chapters will guide you through each aspect of game development in GameMaker, helping you turn your ideas into playable games.

Setting up your GameMaker environment is a crucial foundation for your game development journey. Properly configured, you'll be well-equipped to bring your creative visions to life and explore the full potential of this versatile game development engine.

1.5 Navigating the GameMaker Interface

Now that you've set up your GameMaker environment, it's time to explore the GameMaker interface in more detail. Familiarizing yourself with the various components and tools of the interface is essential for efficient game development. In this section, we'll take a closer look at the key elements of the GameMaker interface and how they contribute to your game development workflow.

1. Workspace

The workspace is where you'll spend most of your time creating and editing your game. It's the central area of the interface where you can access and modify your game's assets, scripts, and levels. Here, you can visually design game rooms, place objects, and work on the overall structure of your game.

2. Resource Tree

Located on the left side of the interface, the resource tree is a crucial organizational tool. It contains all the resources used in your game, such as sprites, objects, sounds, and scripts. By expanding the folders in the resource tree, you can quickly access and manage these resources. Right-clicking on items in the resource tree allows you to perform various actions, such as importing assets or editing properties.

3. Properties Panel

The properties panel is context-sensitive and displays information and settings for the currently selected resource or object. Depending on what you're working on, the properties panel will show different options. For example, if you select a sprite, you'll see settings related to that sprite, such as its image and collision mask properties. This panel is where you fine-tune the attributes of your game elements.

4. Code Editor

If you're using GameMaker Language (GML) for scripting, you'll spend time in the code editor. This is where you write and edit your GML code. The code editor provides features like syntax highlighting, code completion, and debugging tools to streamline the coding process. GML scripts can be attached to objects and events to control their behavior.

Here's an example of a simple GML script that moves an object when a key is pressed:

```
// Step Event of the object

if (keyboard_check(ord("W"))) {

y -= 5; // Move upward

}
```

5. Game Window

The game window is a real-time preview of your game as you develop it. It shows how your game will appear and behave when played. This allows you to test your game and see the immediate effects of your changes. You can interact with your game directly in this window to check for bugs or fine-tune gameplay.

6. Toolbar

The toolbar, located at the top of the interface, contains various tools and shortcuts to perform common actions. Here are some of the functions you can access from the toolbar:

- **Save:** Save your project.
- **Run:** Launch your game for testing.
- **Debug:** Start debugging your game.
- **Create Object:** Quickly create a new game object.
- **Create Room:** Create a new game room.
- **Add Event:** Add an event to an object.

7. Object Properties and Events

In GameMaker, objects are central to gameplay. Each object represents an element in your game, such as a character, enemy, or item. Objects have properties and events that determine their behavior. For example, an object might have a "Create" event where you define its initial properties, and a "Step" event where you specify its ongoing behavior.

8. Room Editor

The room editor is where you design the layout and structure of your game levels or scenes. You can place objects, set their initial positions, define collision boundaries, and create the visual layout of your game world. GameMaker offers a grid-based system to help you align objects precisely.

9. Resource Creation and Import

GameMaker provides integrated tools for creating and importing game assets. You can create sprites, sounds, backgrounds, and more directly within GameMaker or import existing files. These assets can be used to build your game's visual and audio elements.

10. Scripts and Code Organization

Managing your scripts and code is essential for a well-structured project. GameMaker allows you to create and organize scripts for various purposes. You can reuse scripts across different objects and events to maintain clean and efficient code.

By becoming familiar with these key elements of the GameMaker interface, you'll be better equipped to navigate and utilize the tools at your disposal. In the upcoming chapters, we'll dive deeper into using these components to create, script, and design your games effectively.

Chapter 2: Your First GameMaker Project

2.1 Planning Your Game: Concept and Design

Before you dive into creating your first game with GameMaker, it's essential to lay a solid foundation through planning and design. Successful games start with a clear concept and a well-thought-out design. In this section, we'll explore the key steps in planning your game, from defining your game's concept to creating a design document.

1. Defining Your Game Concept

Every game begins with a concept, a fundamental idea that serves as the core of your game's identity. Your concept should answer essential questions:

- **Genre:** What genre does your game belong to? Is it an action game, puzzle game, platformer, or something else?

- **Theme:** What is the central theme or storyline of your game? What is the player's role in this world?

- **Objective:** What is the primary goal or challenge for the player to overcome? What defines success in your game?

- **Unique Selling Point (USP):** What makes your game unique and compelling? What sets it apart from other games in the same genre?

2. Creating a Design Document

Once you have a clear concept in mind, it's time to create a design document. A design document is a written plan that outlines the various aspects of your game, from gameplay mechanics to art style. It serves as a roadmap for your development process and can be a valuable reference as you work on your game. A typical design document includes:

- **Game Overview:** A brief description of the game, including its concept, genre, and target audience.

- **Gameplay Mechanics:** Detailed explanations of how the game will be played, including controls, objectives, and challenges.

- **Storyline and Narrative:** If your game has a storyline, outline the plot, characters, and any branching narratives.

- **Art and Visual Style:** Describe the art style, including character and environment designs, color palettes, and visual effects.

- **Sound and Music:** Specify the type of music and sound effects that will be used to enhance the game's atmosphere.

- **Level Design:** If applicable, outline the design of individual levels or game environments.

- **Technical Requirements:** List the platforms you intend to release the game on and any technical specifications or limitations to consider.

3. Storyboarding and Prototyping

Before you start coding, consider creating storyboards or prototypes to visualize your game's mechanics and flow. Storyboards are sketches or diagrams that illustrate key gameplay sequences and interactions. Prototypes are basic, playable versions of your game that help you test ideas and mechanics quickly. They can be created using placeholder assets and simplified gameplay.

4. Scope and Feasibility

It's crucial to manage the scope of your project to ensure it's achievable within your resources and timeframe. Be realistic about what you can accomplish, especially if you're working on your first game. Consider starting with a small, manageable project to gain experience and build confidence.

5. Iterate and Refine Your Design

Game design is an iterative process. As you work on your game, you'll likely encounter challenges and discover opportunities for improvement. Be open to refining your design based on playtesting and feedback. Playtest your game regularly to identify areas that need adjustment and fine-tuning.

6. Document Your Decisions

Throughout the planning and design phase, document your decisions and changes in your design document. This documentation helps maintain consistency and provides a reference point for your future development work.

7. Project Management Tools

Consider using project management tools and software to help you organize your tasks and stay on track. Tools like Trello, Asana, or even a simple to-do list can be valuable for tracking your progress and meeting milestones.

By carefully planning your game concept and design, you'll set yourself up for a smoother development process. Having a clear vision and documented plan will guide you as you move on to the next stages of creating your first GameMaker project, including asset creation, scripting, and level design.

2.2 Creating Sprites and Graphics

In the world of game development, sprites and graphics are the visual elements that breathe life into your games. These assets represent characters, objects, backgrounds, and everything the player interacts with. In this section, we'll delve into the process of creating sprites and graphics for your GameMaker project.

1. Understanding Sprites

Sprites in GameMaker are 2D images or animations used to represent game objects, characters, and more. They are essential for rendering visual elements on the screen. Here's how you can create and manage sprites in GameMaker:

- **Creating Sprites:** GameMaker provides a built-in sprite editor that allows you to draw or import images and create sprite assets. You can create a new sprite by right-clicking the "Sprites" folder in the resource tree and selecting "Create Sprite."

- **Importing Images:** If you have existing images for your game, you can import them into GameMaker by right-clicking the "Sprites" folder and selecting "Import." GameMaker supports various image formats, including PNG, JPEG, and GIF.

- **Sprite Properties:** After creating or importing a sprite, you can set properties such as its origin (the point around which the sprite rotates), collision mask, and frame speed (for animations) in the properties panel.

2. Creating Animations

Sprites are not limited to static images; they can also be used to create animations. Animations are sequences of images that give the illusion of movement. To create animations in GameMaker:

- **Sprite Frames:** In the sprite editor, you can add multiple frames to a sprite, each representing a different image. These frames are displayed sequentially to create animation.

- **Setting Speed:** You can control the speed of animation by adjusting the "Speed" property in the sprite's properties panel. This property defines how quickly the frames cycle.

- **Looping:** You can choose whether an animation loops continuously or plays once. This is determined by the "Loop" property.

- **Using Sprites in Objects:** To make use of your sprites in the game, you'll associate them with objects. In the object's properties, you can specify which sprite to use for the object's appearance.

3. Creating Tilesets

In addition to individual sprites, GameMaker supports tilesets, which are collections of tiles or small images used to create grid-based game worlds. Tilesets are commonly used in games like platformers and RPGs. Here's how to work with tilesets:

- **Creating Tilesets:** You can create tilesets by importing an image that contains multiple tiles, or by manually adding tiles to a tileset asset.

- **Defining Collision Masks:** For precise collision detection in tile-based games, you can define collision masks for each tile. This helps determine which parts of a tile are solid and which are passable.

- **Using Tile Layers:** In the room editor, you can create tile layers and use your tileset to populate the game world. This is particularly useful for designing levels efficiently.

4. Optimizing Graphics

Efficient use of graphics is essential for game performance. Consider the following optimization techniques:

- **Sprite Dimensions:** Keep your sprites at appropriate dimensions. Avoid using excessively large images when smaller ones will suffice.

- **Texture Pages:** Group multiple sprites into texture pages to reduce texture swaps, which can improve rendering performance.

- **Image Compression:** Use image compression techniques to reduce file sizes without sacrificing quality.

GameMaker provides options for texture group compression.

- **Minimize Overdraw:** Overdraw occurs when multiple objects overlap, and the engine must redraw pixels unnecessarily. Minimize overdraw to improve rendering efficiency.

- **Scaling and Resolution:** Consider supporting multiple screen resolutions and scaling your sprites appropriately to maintain visual quality on different devices.

Creating sprites and graphics is a creative and essential aspect of game development. Whether you're designing characters, objects, or environments, the visual elements of your game contribute significantly to its overall appeal. In the next section, we'll explore the basics of scripting and logic flow in GameMaker, allowing you to bring your game's elements to life with interactivity and behavior.

2.3 Basic Scripting and Logic Flow

In the world of game development, scripting is the backbone that adds interactivity and behavior to your game objects. GameMaker uses its scripting language called GameMaker Language (GML) to accomplish this. In this section, we'll explore the basics of scripting and logic flow in GameMaker.

1. Introduction to GameMaker Language (GML)

GameMaker Language (GML) is a custom scripting language designed specifically for GameMaker. It provides a versatile and powerful way to create behaviors and implement game logic. While GameMaker also offers a visual drag-and-drop system for beginners, GML allows for more advanced and precise control over your game.

Here's a simple example of GML code that moves an object to the right when the right arrow key is pressed:

```
// Step Event of the object

if (keyboard_check(vk_right)) {

x += 5; // Move to the right

}
```

2. Understanding Events and Actions

In GameMaker, game objects respond to events, such as key presses or collisions, by executing actions. Each object can have multiple events and associated actions. For instance, you can define what happens when an object collides with another object, when a key is pressed, or when the game starts.

To create an event and define actions for an object, follow these steps:

- Select the object in the resource tree.
- In the properties panel, click the "Add Event" button.
- Choose the type of event you want to respond to (e.g., "Keyboard," "Collision," "Mouse").
- Define the actions you want the object to perform when the event occurs.

3. Variables and Data Types

Variables are essential for storing and manipulating data in your game. GML supports various data types, including integers, strings, booleans, and arrays. You can create and use variables to keep track of scores, health, player positions, and more.

Here's an example of creating and using a variable in GML:

```
// Create Event of the object

score = 0; // Initialize a score variable

// Step Event of the object

if (collision) {

score += 10; // Increase the score when a collision occurs

}
```

4. Conditional Statements

Conditional statements allow you to make decisions in your code based on certain conditions. GML supports common conditional statements like "if," "else if," and "else." These statements help control the flow of your game's logic.

Here's an example of using conditional statements in GML:

```
// Step Event of the object

if (health <= 0) {

game_over = true; // Set a game over flag when health reaches zero

} else if (collision) {

health -= 10; // Decrease health on collision

}
```

5. Loops

Loops in GML allow you to repeat a set of actions multiple times. Common loops include "for" and "while" loops. Loops are useful for iterating through arrays, creating patterns, or executing actions a specific number of times.

Here's an example of a "for" loop in GML that creates a row of objects:

```
// Create Event of the object

for (var i = 0; i < 5; i++) {

instance_create(x + i * 32, y, obj_enemy); // Create five enemy objects in a row

}
```

6. Functions

Functions are blocks of reusable code that perform a specific task. You can create custom functions in GML to encapsulate complex behaviors and make your code more organized and modular.

Here's an example of creating and using a custom function in GML:

```
// Custom function to calculate the area of a rectangle

function calculateArea(width, height) {

return width * height;

}

// Step Event of the object
```

var area = calculateArea(10, 20); // Call the custom function to calculate the area

7. Debugging and Testing

Effective debugging is crucial during game development. GameMaker provides debugging tools to help identify and fix issues in your code. You can use the debugger to step through your code, inspect variable values, and track the flow of execution.

These are the fundamental concepts of scripting and logic flow in GameMaker using GML. As you become more comfortable with these concepts, you'll be able to create complex behaviors, implement game rules, and make your games interactive and engaging. In the following sections, we'll dive deeper into specific aspects of game development, including the game loop, debugging techniques, and more advanced scripting techniques.

2.4 The Game Loop: Bringing Your Game to Life

The game loop is at the heart of every video game, responsible for continuously updating the game state and rendering it to the screen. It ensures that the game world reacts to player input, moves objects, checks for collisions, and provides a real-time experience. In this section, we'll explore the concept of the game loop and how it functions within GameMaker.

1. Understanding the Game Loop

The game loop is a continuous cycle that consists of two main phases: updating and rendering. Here's how it works:

- **Updating:** In this phase, the game processes user input, updates the game state, checks for collisions, handles AI behavior, and performs other essential calculations. This phase ensures that the game's logic is up to date.

- **Rendering:** After updating, the game renders the current state of the game to the screen. It draws objects, characters, backgrounds, and any other visual elements based on their updated positions and properties.

2. Step Events and the Game Loop

In GameMaker, objects have "Step Events" that allow you to define what happens to them during each iteration of the game loop. These events are crucial for controlling the behavior of game objects over time. You can access the Step Event of an object by selecting it in the resource tree and clicking on the "Add Event" button in the properties panel.

Here's an example of using the Step Event to move an object:

```
// Step Event of the object

x += 5; // Move the object to the right by 5 pixels each frame
```

3. Game Speed and Framerate

The game loop's speed is determined by the frame rate, which is the number of frames (individual images) displayed per second. GameMaker allows you to set the frame rate for your game, typically at 30 or 60 frames per second (FPS). A higher frame rate results in smoother animations but requires more processing power.

You can set the frame rate in GameMaker's global game settings under the "Main" tab. Keep in mind that maintaining a consistent frame rate is crucial for a smooth gaming experience.

4. Delta Time

Delta time (Δt) is a critical concept in game development and the game loop. It represents the time elapsed between frames. By using delta time in your calculations, you can ensure that your game's behavior remains consistent, regardless of the frame rate. It prevents objects from moving too quickly on faster systems and too slowly on slower ones.

Here's how you can incorporate delta time into a simple object movement:

```
// Step Event of the object

var speed = 5; // Define the speed

x += speed * delta_time; // Move the object based on delta time
```

5. Managing Game State

The game loop also plays a role in managing the game's state. You can use variables and conditions to control different phases of the game, such as the main menu, gameplay, pause screens, and game over screens. By changing the game state within the game loop, you can switch between these phases seamlessly.

6. Optimizing the Game Loop

Efficient code is crucial for maintaining a high frame rate and smooth gameplay. To optimize your game loop, consider the following tips:

• Minimize unnecessary calculations and checks.

• Group objects that share similar behaviors to reduce redundant code.

• Use collision checks wisely, focusing on objects that are likely to collide.

• Limit the use of expensive functions or operations inside the loop.

7. Testing and Debugging

Testing and debugging your game loop are essential to identify and fix issues. GameMaker provides debugging tools, including breakpoints and variable watches, to help you track down problems in your code. Regular testing allows you to fine-tune gameplay and ensure that everything works as intended.

The game loop is the engine that powers your game, making it responsive and interactive. Understanding how it functions and how to work within it is fundamental to successful game development. As you continue to build your GameMaker project, you'll refine and expand upon the concepts introduced in this section, creating engaging and dynamic gameplay experiences.

2.5 Debugging and Testing Your First Game

Debugging and testing are crucial aspects of game development, ensuring that your game functions correctly, behaves as expected, and is free of errors and glitches. In this section, we'll explore the importance of debugging and testing in your GameMaker project and introduce you to some essential debugging techniques.

1. The Role of Debugging

Debugging is the process of identifying, diagnosing, and fixing issues or bugs in your game's code. These issues can range from logical errors that cause unexpected behavior to syntax errors that prevent your game from running.

Debugging is a systematic approach to problem-solving in game development. It involves examining code, tracking the flow of execution, and testing different scenarios to identify and resolve issues. Effective debugging saves time and ensures that your game runs smoothly.

2. Debugging Tools in GameMaker

GameMaker provides several built-in debugging tools to help you identify and fix issues in your game:

- **Debugger:** The GameMaker debugger allows you to pause your game's execution, inspect variable values, and step through your code line by line. You can set breakpoints to stop the game at specific points for detailed examination.

- **Output Console:** The output console displays messages and error information generated by your game. It's a valuable resource for tracking runtime errors and warnings.

- **Error Messages:** GameMaker provides informative error messages that pinpoint issues in your code. Pay attention to these messages as they guide you to potential problems.

- **Variable Watch:** You can watch specific variables in the debugger to monitor their values as your game runs. This helps you track how variables change during gameplay.

3. Common Debugging Scenarios

Here are some common debugging scenarios you might encounter during game development:

- **Logic Errors:** Logic errors occur when your code doesn't produce the desired outcome. To debug logic errors, review your code carefully, use the debugger to step through it, and check the values of variables and conditions.

- **Syntax Errors:** Syntax errors are typically typos or mistakes in your code that prevent it from running. GameMaker highlights syntax errors in the code editor, making them easy to spot and fix.

- **Runtime Errors:** Runtime errors occur while the game is running and can lead to crashes or unexpected behavior. Use the debugger and error messages to identify the source of runtime errors.

- **Performance Issues:** Debugging isn't just about fixing errors; it's also about optimizing your game's performance. Use profiling tools in GameMaker to identify bottlenecks and optimize your code.

4. Testing Your Game

Testing is the process of playing your game to evaluate its gameplay, identify issues, and gather feedback. Effective testing ensures that your game is enjoyable, balanced, and free of critical bugs. Here are some key aspects of testing:

- **Functional Testing:** This type of testing focuses on verifying that all game mechanics and features work as intended. Test every aspect of gameplay, including controls, interactions, and objectives.

- **User Interface Testing:** Check the user interface for usability and clarity. Ensure that menus, buttons, and HUD elements function correctly and are easy to navigate.

- **Balance Testing:** Balance is crucial in games. Test the difficulty level, pacing, and progression to ensure that the game is challenging but not frustrating. Collect feedback from playtesters to fine-tune the balance.

- **Compatibility Testing:** Test your game on different devices and screen resolutions to ensure compatibility. Address any issues related to screen size, aspect ratio, and input methods.

- **Regression Testing:** After making changes or fixes, perform regression testing to ensure that new issues haven't been introduced. Revisit previously tested areas of your game to confirm they still work as expected.

- **Player Feedback:** Gather feedback from playtesters and players. Their insights and suggestions can help you identify issues you might have missed and improve the overall player experience.

5. Iterative Development

Debugging and testing are iterative processes. As you identify and fix issues, your game becomes more stable and polished. It's common to go through multiple rounds of debugging and testing throughout the development cycle, especially as you add new features and content.

Remember that debugging and testing are integral parts of game development, and they contribute to the quality and success of your game. Dedicate time to these activities, and don't be discouraged by challenges. With practice, you'll become a more effective debugger and tester, leading to the creation of enjoyable and bug-free games.

Chapter 3: Advanced Graphics and Animation

3.1 Detailed Sprite Creation and Editing

In game development, creating visually appealing sprites is essential to make your game engaging and immersive. In this section, we will dive into the art of detailed sprite creation and editing using GameMaker. Detailed sprites enhance the quality of your game's characters, objects, and environments, making them more visually captivating.

1. Choosing the Right Tools

Before you begin sprite creation, it's crucial to choose the right tools for the job. GameMaker provides a built-in sprite editor that is suitable for basic sprite creation and editing. However, for more complex and detailed sprites, you might consider using external graphic design software such as Adobe Photoshop, GIMP, or Aseprite.

External software often provides more advanced features, layer support, and specialized tools for pixel art, which can significantly improve the quality and efficiency of your sprite creation process.

2. Pixel Art Techniques

Pixel art is a popular style for sprite creation, known for its retro charm and precise control over each pixel. Here are some pixel art techniques to enhance the detail and aesthetics of your sprites:

- **Pixel Placement:** Pay attention to the placement of each pixel. Make deliberate choices to convey texture, shading, and shape accurately.

- **Anti-Aliasing:** Use anti-aliasing sparingly to smooth jagged edges and create smoother transitions between colors. Avoid excessive anti-aliasing, as it can blur details.

- **Dithering:** Dithering is a technique where you alternate pixels of two colors to create the illusion of a third color. It's useful for creating gradients and texture.

- **Limited Color Palette:** Restrict your color palette to a limited number of colors to maintain a cohesive and retro look. Choose colors thoughtfully to evoke the desired mood and atmosphere.

- **Reference Images:** Use reference images or concept art as a guide when creating detailed sprites. Reference images can help you capture real-world details and proportions accurately.

3. Layering and Depth

For more complex sprites, especially characters or objects with multiple parts, consider using layers to organize and control different elements. Layers allow you to work on individual components separately and then combine them to create a cohesive sprite.

For example, when creating a character sprite, you might have separate layers for the body, clothing, accessories, and facial expressions. This approach makes it easier to modify and animate specific parts of the sprite while maintaining consistency.

4. Animation Frames

Detailed sprites often require multiple animation frames to convey movement and actions effectively. When animating sprites, consider the following:

- **Frame Consistency:** Ensure that the level of detail and style remains consistent across all animation frames. Slight variations are acceptable for conveying movement, but major discrepancies can be distracting.

- **Smooth Transitions:** Animate transitions between frames smoothly to create fluid movements. Pay attention to easing in and out of different poses to avoid abrupt changes.

- **Idle Animations:** Even when a character or object is idle, subtle animations can add life and detail. These might include idle breathing, swaying, or blinking.

5. Resolution and Scaling

Consider the target resolution of your game when creating detailed sprites. If your game supports multiple resolutions, create sprites at a higher resolution to ensure they look sharp on larger screens. GameMaker provides functions to scale sprites appropriately for different screen sizes.

When scaling sprites, use techniques like nearest-neighbor scaling to maintain the pixel art aesthetic. Avoid bicubic or bilinear filtering, which can blur pixel art when resizing.

6. Exporting and Importing Sprites

Once you've created detailed sprites, export them in a suitable file format (e.g., PNG) with a transparent background. GameMaker supports various image formats for importing sprites. When importing, consider configuring settings like the collision mask, origin point, and frame speed to ensure the sprite behaves as expected in the game.

Creating detailed sprites is both an art and a skill that can greatly enhance the visual appeal of your game. Take your time to refine and perfect your sprites, and don't hesitate to seek feedback from others to help you improve. Detailed and well-crafted sprites can set your game apart and captivate players with their visual richness.

3.2 Animating Characters and Objects

Animation breathes life into characters and objects in your game, making them dynamic and engaging. In this section, we'll delve into the art of animating characters and objects using GameMaker. Animation is a key element of visual storytelling in games, and it plays a crucial role in conveying actions, emotions, and interactions.

1. Sprite Sequences and Frames

In GameMaker, animations are created by defining sequences of frames within a sprite. Each frame represents a different image, and when these frames are displayed sequentially, they create the illusion of movement. Here's how you can work with sprite sequences and frames:

- **Creating Animation Sequences:** To create an animation sequence, you'll typically have a single sprite that contains multiple frames. In the sprite editor, you can add frames and arrange them in the desired order to create animations.

- **Setting Frame Speed:** You can specify the frame speed for each animation sequence. The frame speed determines how quickly the frames cycle. For example, a frame speed of 15 means that 15 frames are displayed per second.

- **Looping Animations:** You can control whether an animation sequence loops continuously or plays once. Looping animations are often used for actions like walking, while non-looping animations are suitable for one-time actions like jumping.

2. Keyframe Animation

Keyframe animation is a technique where you define specific frames (keyframes) that represent critical moments in an animation. GameMaker allows you to implement keyframe animations by:

- **Adding Keyframes:** In the sprite editor, you can add keyframes at important points in the animation. These keyframes define the main poses or states of your character or object.

- **Tweening:** Between keyframes, GameMaker can automatically generate intermediate frames using tweening. Tweening ensures smooth transitions between keyframes and creates the illusion of fluid motion.

Here's a simplified example of keyframe animation code in GameMaker:

```
// Create Event of the object
```

```
image_speed = 0.2; // Set the animation speed

// Step Event of the object

if (animation_index == spr_player_walk) {

// Check if the animation is the walking animation

if (image_index >= 3 && image_index <= 7) {

// Between keyframes 3 and 7, play a footstep sound

audio_play_sound(snd_footstep, 1, false);

}

}
```

3. Animation Control

Controlling animations in response to game events and player input is crucial. You can use GameMaker's scripting language (GML) to manage animation transitions and timing. Here are some common techniques:

- **Changing Animations:** Use GML to change the current animation sequence based on game events. For example, switch from a "walking" animation to a "jumping" animation when the player presses the jump button.

- **Pausing Animations:** You can pause animations or freeze specific frames to create dramatic effects. For example, you can pause an explosion animation briefly to emphasize the impact.

- **Blending Animations:** When transitioning between animations, blend the current animation with the next one to create seamless transitions. This technique is especially useful for character movements and transitions.

4. Sprite Sheets

Sprite sheets are large images that contain multiple sprites or frames in a grid pattern. They are commonly used for characters, objects, and items that require various animations. GameMaker allows you to import sprite sheets and create animations from them.

To work with sprite sheets in GameMaker:

- **Importing Sprite Sheets:** Import a sprite sheet image and configure the grid settings to define the dimensions of each frame. GameMaker will automatically split the sprite sheet into individual frames.

- **Creating Animations:** Once the sprite sheet is imported, you can create animations by defining sequences of frames within it. Assign specific sequences to objects or characters as needed.

5. Optimizing Animations

Efficiency is crucial when working with animations to ensure smooth gameplay and minimal resource consumption. Consider the following optimization techniques:

- **Limiting Frame Count:** Avoid excessive frame counts for animations. Use the minimum number of frames needed to convey the action effectively.

- **Texture Pages:** Group animations that share the same texture or sprite sheet into texture pages. This reduces texture swaps and improves rendering performance.

- **Animation Pools:** Use object pooling techniques to manage and reuse animated objects efficiently, especially for objects that frequently appear and disappear.

- **Frame Compression:** Compress sprite frames to reduce file sizes without sacrificing quality. GameMaker provides options for texture group compression.

- **Sprite Scaling:** When scaling sprites, consider using nearest-neighbor scaling to maintain the pixel art aesthetic. Avoid bicubic or bilinear filtering.

Animating characters and objects is a creative and technical challenge in game development. It requires attention to detail, timing, and an understanding of how animations contribute to the player's experience. By mastering animation techniques in GameMaker, you can bring your game's characters and objects to life, enhancing player immersion and enjoyment.

3.3 Backgrounds and Scenery Design

In the world of game development, backgrounds and scenery play a crucial role in setting the stage, creating atmosphere, and immersing players in the game's environment. In this section, we'll explore the art of designing backgrounds and scenery using GameMaker, with a focus on creating captivating and visually appealing game worlds.

1. Layered Backgrounds

Layered backgrounds are a common technique used to create depth and parallax effects in 2D games. Parallax scrolling gives the illusion of depth by moving background layers at different speeds as the player character or camera moves. Here's how to create layered backgrounds in GameMaker:

- **Background Layers:** Divide your background into multiple layers, each with its own sprite or image. For instance, you might have a distant mountain layer, a midground forest layer, and a foreground tree layer.
- **Layer Movement:** In GameMaker, you can control the movement of each layer independently. You can use the view_xview and view_yview variables to determine the camera's position and adjust the background layers' positions accordingly.

Here's an example of code to create a simple parallax scrolling effect:

// Step Event of a background object

x = view_xview * 0.5; // Adjust the horizontal position based on camera movement

y = view_yview * 0.2; // Adjust the vertical position based on camera movement

2. Tilesets for Seamless Environments

Tilesets are a versatile tool for creating seamless and detailed game environments. A tileset is a collection of tiles or small images that can be arranged to create larger backgrounds or levels. GameMaker supports tilesets through its tile layer system.

To work with tilesets effectively:

- **Create Tilesets:** Design tilesets that contain various tiles representing ground, walls, platforms, and decorative elements. Ensure that the tiles align seamlessly to avoid visible seams when they are placed next to each other.

- **Tile Layers:** Use GameMaker's tile layer system to paint tiles onto the game world. You can define collision properties and depth for each tile layer, allowing for dynamic interactions with the player character.

- **Auto-Tiling:** Consider using auto-tiling features in GameMaker to automatically select the appropriate tile based on its surroundings. Auto-tiling simplifies level design and ensures a consistent look.

3. Parallax and Lighting Effects

Adding parallax and lighting effects to backgrounds and scenery can greatly enhance the visual appeal of your game. Here are some techniques to consider:

- **Parallax Lighting:** Combine parallax scrolling with lighting effects to create dynamic environments. For example, a torch's light can illuminate nearby objects while casting shadows in the background.

- **Particle Systems:** Implement particle systems for effects like falling leaves, rain, or snow. These dynamic elements add life to your backgrounds and can be controlled to match the game's mood.

- **Dynamic Weather:** Change the appearance of backgrounds based on in-game weather conditions. For instance, a rainy day might make surfaces appear wet, and fog can obscure distant scenery.

4. Optimizing Backgrounds

Efficient background design is essential to maintain smooth gameplay and optimal performance. Here are some optimization strategies:

- **Texture Compression:** Compress background textures to reduce memory usage and load times. Use the appropriate texture groups and formats for different backgrounds.

- **Background Streaming:** Load and unload background assets dynamically as the player progresses through the game. This minimizes memory usage and speeds up level loading.

- **Collision Detection:** Minimize the use of collision detection with background elements that don't interact with the player or game objects. Use efficient collision masks where needed.

- **Background Animation:** Limit the use of animated backgrounds to scenes where they contribute significantly to the atmosphere. Animated backgrounds can be resource-intensive.

- **Texture Atlases:** Use texture atlases to group multiple background textures into a single image, reducing the number of draw calls and improving rendering performance.

Designing backgrounds and scenery is an art that requires attention to detail, creativity, and an understanding of how visual elements contribute to the overall game experience. By mastering these techniques in GameMaker, you can create captivating and immersive game worlds that enhance player engagement and enjoyment.

3.4 Particle Systems and Special Effects

Particle systems and special effects are powerful tools in game development for adding visual flair, realism, and immersion to your games. In this section, we'll explore how to create and use particle systems and special effects in GameMaker to enhance your game's graphics and gameplay.

1. Understanding Particle Systems

A particle system is a technique used to simulate and render a large number of small, individual graphical elements (particles) that collectively create dynamic and complex visual effects. Particle systems are commonly used for effects like explosions, fire, smoke, rain, and more.

In GameMaker, you can create and control particle systems using built-in functions and features. Here are the key components of a particle system:

- **Emitter:** An emitter is a source from which particles are generated. You can define the emitter's position, shape, direction, and rate of particle emission.

- **Particles:** Particles are individual graphical elements that make up the effect. Each particle has properties like position, velocity, size, color, and transparency. Particles can have various behaviors, such as fading out, scaling, or rotating.

- **Particle System Properties:** You can control various properties of the particle system, including the lifespan of particles, their initial and final appearance, and how they interact with the environment.

2. Creating Particle Systems

To create a particle system in GameMaker, follow these steps:

1. **Define an Emitter:** Create an object that will act as the emitter for the particle system. This object will determine where and how particles are generated.
2. **Configure the Particle System:** In the object's Create Event or a specific event where you want to trigger the effect, use functions like part_system_create() to create a new particle system and part_system_position() to set the emitter's position.
3. **Define Particles:** Use functions like part_type_create() to define the properties of the particles, such as their appearance, behavior, and lifespan.
4. **Start Emitting Particles:** Trigger the emission of particles using functions like part_emitter_burst() or part_emitter_stream() in response to specific game events.
5. **Update and Draw Particles:** In the object's Step Event, update the particle system using part_system_update(). In the Draw Event, use part_system_draw() to render the particles.

Here's a simplified example of creating a particle system for an explosion effect:

```
// Create Event of an explosion object

part_sys = part_system_create();

// Step Event of the explosion object

if (explosion_triggered) {

part_emitter_burst(part_sys, x, y, pt_explosion, 100);

}

// Draw Event of the explosion object

part_system_draw(part_sys);
```

3. Customizing Particle Behavior

GameMaker provides a wide range of functions to customize the behavior and appearance of particles within a particle system. You can control properties like:

- **Position:** Set the position of the emitter and individual particles to determine where the effect occurs.

- **Velocity:** Define the initial speed and direction of particles to control their movement.

- **Size and Scale:** Adjust the size of particles over their lifespan to create effects like growing or shrinking.

- **Color and Transparency:** Change the color and transparency of particles to achieve various visual effects.

- **Rotation:** Apply rotation to particles to simulate spinning or swirling motion.

- **Lifespan:** Set the duration of each particle's existence, determining how long it remains visible in the effect.

- **Collision and Physics:** Enable collisions between particles and game objects or apply physics forces to particles for realistic behavior.

4. Performance Considerations

While particle systems can add stunning visual effects to your game, it's essential to consider performance implications. Here are some tips for optimizing particle systems:

- **Particle Count:** Limit the number of particles in a system to avoid overwhelming the game engine. Use fewer particles when targeting lower-end devices.

- **Texture Atlas:** Combine multiple particle textures into a texture atlas to reduce texture swaps and improve rendering performance.

- **Collision Detection:** Be mindful of particle collisions with game objects. Excessive collision checks can impact performance.

- **Particle Recycling:** Reuse particles when they expire rather than creating new ones, reducing memory usage.

- **View and Culling:** Disable particle systems that are not within the player's view to save processing power.

- **Profile and Test:** Use GameMaker's profiling tools to identify performance bottlenecks in your particle systems and optimize accordingly.

Particle systems and special effects are valuable assets in game development, allowing you to create visually stunning and dynamic gameplay experiences. By mastering the use of particle systems in GameMaker, you can elevate your game's graphics and immerse players in captivating and engaging worlds.

3.5 Optimizing Graphics Performance

Optimizing graphics performance is a critical aspect of game development, as it ensures that your game runs smoothly and efficiently on a wide range of devices. In this section, we'll explore various techniques and strategies for optimizing graphics performance in GameMaker.

1. Sprite Optimization

Sprites are a fundamental element of 2D games, and optimizing them can significantly impact performance. Here are some sprite optimization techniques:

- **Texture Groups:** Group similar sprites into texture groups to reduce texture swaps during rendering. This minimizes the performance overhead of switching textures frequently.

- **Texture Compression:** Compress sprite textures to reduce memory usage and loading times. GameMaker provides options for texture compression in various formats.

- **Texture Atlas:** Combine multiple sprites into a single texture atlas to reduce the number of draw calls. This optimization technique is especially beneficial for mobile devices.

- **Sprite Scaling:** When scaling sprites, use nearest-neighbor scaling for pixel art to maintain the intended aesthetic. Avoid bicubic or bilinear filtering, which can blur pixel art.

2. Background Optimization

Backgrounds and scenery are essential for creating immersive game worlds. Here's how to optimize them:

- **Background Streaming:** Load and unload background assets dynamically as the player progresses through the game. This reduces memory usage and speeds up level loading.

- **Parallax Layers:** Use parallax scrolling for backgrounds to create depth without the need for additional sprites. Optimize parallax layers by reusing textures.

- **Background Compression:** Compress background images to minimize storage requirements and reduce loading times. Balance compression with image quality.

3. Particle System Optimization

Particle systems can add visual flair to your game, but they can also impact performance. Consider the following optimizations:

- **Particle Count:** Limit the number of particles in a system to avoid overwhelming the game engine. Use fewer particles on lower-end devices.

- **Texture Atlas:** Combine multiple particle textures into a texture atlas to reduce texture swaps and improve rendering performance.

- **Particle Recycling:** Reuse particles when they expire instead of creating new ones. This reduces memory usage.

- **View and Culling:** Disable particle systems that are not within the player's view to save processing power.

4. Shader Optimization

Shaders can enhance visual effects, but poorly optimized shaders can be a performance bottleneck. Here's how to optimize shaders:

- **Shader Complexity:** Keep shader code as efficient as possible. Minimize unnecessary calculations and conditionals.

- **Shader Passes:** Avoid using multiple shader passes unless necessary. Each pass adds computational overhead.

- **Shader Switching:** Minimize the frequency of switching shaders during gameplay. Group objects with the same shader for efficient rendering.

- **Shader Variables:** Reduce the number of uniform variables in shaders. Limit unnecessary data transfers between the CPU and GPU.

5. Memory Management

Efficient memory management is crucial for graphics performance:

- **Texture Memory:** Monitor and manage texture memory usage. Unload textures that are no longer needed to free up memory.

- **Texture Page Size:** Adjust the texture page size in GameMaker settings based on your game's requirements. Larger page sizes can improve performance but may increase memory usage.

6. Profiling and Testing

Regular profiling and testing are essential for identifying performance bottlenecks and areas that need optimization. Use GameMaker's built-in profiling tools to measure and analyze the game's performance.

- **Frame Rate Monitoring:** Monitor and maintain a stable frame rate. A consistent frame rate provides a smoother gaming experience.

- **Device Testing:** Test your game on a variety of devices to ensure it performs well across different hardware configurations.

- **Benchmarking:** Use benchmarking tools to measure and compare performance improvements when implementing optimizations.

- **Player Feedback:** Gather feedback from players to identify performance issues and prioritize optimizations.

Optimizing graphics performance is an ongoing process in game development. By implementing these techniques and regularly profiling your game, you can ensure that it runs smoothly and provides an enjoyable experience for players on various platforms and devices.

Chapter 4: Game Mechanics and Control Systems

4.1 Designing Intuitive Control Schemes

Designing intuitive and responsive control schemes is a fundamental aspect of game development. Player input is the bridge between players and the game world, and a well-designed control system can enhance the overall gaming experience. In this section, we'll explore the principles and strategies for creating control schemes that feel natural and enjoyable to players.

1. Understanding Player Input

Before diving into control scheme design, it's essential to understand the types of input devices players will use to interact with your game. Common input devices include:

- **Keyboard and Mouse:** The traditional input method for PC games, offering precise control and a wide range of keys for various actions.

- **Gamepad/Controller:** Widely used for console and some PC games, providing analog sticks, buttons, and triggers for versatile input.

- **Touchscreen:** Found on mobile devices, touchscreen input relies on taps, swipes, and multi-touch gestures.

- **Motion Controls:** Utilizes accelerometers and gyroscopes in devices like the Nintendo Switch Joy-Cons or VR controllers for immersive interaction.

Consider the target platform and input devices your game will support when designing your control scheme.

2. Player-Centric Design

A player-centric approach is crucial when designing controls. The goal is to create controls that feel intuitive and comfortable for players. Here are some principles to consider:

- **Minimize Learning Curve:** Keep the control scheme simple and easy to learn, especially in the early stages of the game. Introduce more complex actions gradually.

- **Consistency:** Use consistent button layouts and input mappings to avoid confusion. For example, if a button is used for jumping in one part of the game, it should have a similar function throughout.

- **Responsive Feedback:** Provide immediate visual and auditory feedback to confirm that a player's input has been recognized. This feedback helps players feel in control.

3. Customization and Accessibility

Recognize that players have diverse preferences and needs when it comes to controls. Consider offering customization options that allow players to tailor the control scheme to their liking. Additionally, prioritize accessibility by providing alternative input methods and options, such as remappable keys, adjustable sensitivity, and accessibility-friendly control options.

4. Test and Iterate

Testing and iteration are essential for refining your control scheme. Conduct playtesting sessions with a diverse group of players to gather feedback on the controls. Pay attention to any common issues, frustrations, or suggestions and use this feedback to make improvements.

5. Input Handling in GameMaker

In GameMaker, you can handle player input using the keyboard_check(), mouse_check_button(), and gamepad_button_check() functions, among others. Here's a simplified example of how you can check for keyboard input in GameMaker:

```
// Check for the "W" key to handle player movement

if (keyboard_check(ord("W"))) {

// Move the player character up

y -= move_speed;

}
```

To handle gamepad input, you can use functions like gamepad_button_check():

```
// Check for the A button on a gamepad

if (gamepad_button_check(0, gp_face1)) {

// Perform a jump action

perform_jump();
```

```
}
```

Remember that GameMaker also provides event-based input handling through the Key Press and Key Release events, which can be useful for specific actions or interactions.

6. Designing for Different Genres

The control scheme should align with the genre and gameplay mechanics of your game. Different genres may require unique control schemes. For example:

- **Platformers:** Typically involve movement, jumping, and interacting with objects. Responsive and precise controls are critical.

- **First-Person Shooters (FPS):** Require precise aiming and shooting controls, often using a combination of mouse and keyboard or gamepad.

- **Real-Time Strategy (RTS):** Utilize mouse-based controls for selecting units, issuing commands, and managing resources.

- **Racing Games:** Emphasize steering, acceleration, and braking controls, often using analog input for smooth handling.

- **Puzzle Games:** Focus on mouse or touchscreen interactions for manipulating objects or solving puzzles.

Adapt your control scheme to match the specific demands of your game's genre.

7. Documentation and Tutorials

Provide clear and concise in-game documentation and tutorials to help players understand the control scheme. Offer tooltips, hints, or interactive tutorials that guide players through the basics and advanced controls.

8. Platform Considerations

Keep in mind that the platform your game is released on may influence control design. Mobile games with touchscreen controls, for example, should prioritize simplicity and touch-friendly interfaces, while console games may leverage the capabilities of gamepad controllers.

Designing intuitive control schemes is a balance between player expectations, game genre, and the capabilities of the chosen input devices. By focusing on player-centric design, customization, and thorough testing, you can create control schemes that enhance the player experience and make your game more enjoyable to play.

4.2 Physics and Collision Detection

Physics and collision detection are core components of many games, determining how objects interact with each other and the game world. In this section, we'll delve into the principles of physics simulation and collision detection in GameMaker, which are essential for creating realistic and engaging gameplay experiences.

1. Physics Simulation

Physics simulation in games aims to replicate real-world physics behaviors to make the game world feel more authentic and immersive. GameMaker provides a built-in physics engine that allows you to simulate physics interactions, such as gravity, friction, and collisions.

Enabling Physics

To enable physics simulation in GameMaker, you need to perform the following steps:

1. Open the Game Options (Global Game Settings).
2. In the Physics section, check the "Enable Physics" option.
3. Configure the physics settings, including gravity and collision shapes.

Physics Objects and Fixtures

In physics simulation, objects are represented as physics objects, and their physical properties are defined using fixtures. A fixture defines the shape, density, friction, and restitution (bounciness) of an object.

You can create physics objects and fixtures in GameMaker by setting the "Physics Object" property in an object's properties window and then defining fixtures for that object.

Physics Actions

GameMaker provides a set of actions for applying forces, impulses, and torques to physics objects. You can use these actions to control the movement and behavior of objects in your game.

For example, to make an object jump when a button is pressed, you can use the "Apply Impulse" action:

```
if (keyboard_check_pressed(vk_space)) {
```

```
physics_apply_impulse(x, y, 0, -5);

}
```

2. Collision Detection

Collision detection is the process of determining when and where objects in your game intersect or collide with each other. GameMaker offers various collision detection techniques to handle different scenarios.

Bounding Boxes

Bounding boxes are the simplest form of collision detection, where objects are represented as rectangles. GameMaker provides functions like collision_rectangle() and collision_point() to check for collisions between bounding boxes and points.

```
if (collision_rectangle(x, y, x + width, y + height, obj_enemy, false, true)) {

// Collision with an enemy

// Perform actions like taking damage or scoring points

}
```

Precise Collision Detection

For more accurate collision detection, you can use precise collision functions like collision_line(), collision_circle(), or collision_ellipse(). These functions allow you to check for collisions based on specific shapes.

```
if (collision_circle(x, y, 16, obj_bullet, false, true)) {
```

```
// Collision with a bullet (circle-based)

// Take appropriate actions

}
```

Collision Events

In GameMaker, you can set up collision events that trigger when specific objects collide. These events allow you to define custom actions to take when collisions occur.

3. Physics and Collision Tips

- **Optimize Collisions:** Minimize the number of collision checks and optimize collision code for better performance, especially in complex scenes.

- **Collision Layers:** Use collision layers and masks to control which objects can collide with each other. This can help you manage interactions between different object types.

- **Sensor Fixtures:** Create sensor fixtures for objects that should detect collisions without physically interacting with other objects. Sensors can trigger events when collisions occur.

- **Callbacks:** Use collision callbacks and events to handle collisions gracefully. For example, when a player collides with a collectible item, you can trigger an event to increase the player's score.

- **Debugging:** Debugging collision issues can be challenging. Use debugging tools like show_debug_message() to print collision-related information to the console for analysis.

- **Friction and Restitution:** Experiment with different friction and restitution settings for physics objects to achieve the desired behavior. Adjust these properties to make objects slide, bounce, or stop realistically.

- **Continuous Collision Detection:** Enable continuous collision detection for fast-moving objects to prevent them from passing through other objects.

Physics simulation and collision detection are essential for creating dynamic and interactive game worlds. By mastering these concepts in GameMaker, you can achieve realistic gameplay mechanics and engaging player interactions in your games.

4.3 Implementing Player Movement and Actions

Implementing player movement and actions is a fundamental aspect of game development, as it directly affects how players interact with your game. In this section, we'll explore how to design and implement player controls, including character movement, actions, and user input responsiveness, using GameMaker.

1. Player Movement

Player movement is a core mechanic in many games, from platformers to top-down shooters. To implement player movement in GameMaker, follow these steps:

Character Object

1. Create a character object or sprite that represents the player character in your game.

User Input

1. Capture user input using input functions such as keyboard_check() or gamepad_button_check(). For example, to move the character left and right using the keyboard:

```
if (keyboard_check(vk_left)) {

x -= move_speed;

}

if (keyboard_check(vk_right)) {

x += move_speed;

}
```

Smooth Movement

1. Implement smooth movement by using variables like move_speed and direction. Adjust these variables based on player input and ensure that the character moves at a consistent speed.

Collision Detection

1. Implement collision detection to prevent the character

from passing through walls or obstacles. Use functions like place_meeting() to check for collisions with other objects:

```
if (!place_meeting(x + hspeed, y, obj_wall)) {

x += hspeed;

}
```

Gravity and Jumping

1. For platformer games, implement gravity and jumping mechanics. Apply gravity to the character's vertical speed (vspeed) and allow the character to jump when the jump button is pressed:

```
if (place_meeting(x, y + 1, obj_ground) && keyboard_check_pressed(vk_space)) {

vspeed = -jump_height;

}
```

2. Player Actions

Player actions encompass various interactions and abilities your character can perform in the game. These actions can include attacking, interacting with objects, using items, and more. To implement player actions:

Action States

1. Define action states or variables that represent the current state of the player character. For example, you might have

states like "idle," "walking," "attacking," or "interacting."

Input Handling

1. Use input functions to handle player actions based on the current state. For example, if the player is in the "attacking" state, pressing the attack button should trigger the character's attack animation and deal damage to enemies.

Animations

1. Create animations for each action state to provide visual feedback to the player. Use the sprite_index and image_speed properties to change the character's appearance and animate actions.

Action Timers

1. Implement action timers to control the timing of specific actions. For instance, if the character can perform a combo attack, use a timer to limit the player's input during the combo sequence.

Action Feedback

1. Provide feedback to the player to indicate the success or result of an action. This can include sound effects, visual effects, and UI elements.

3. User Input Responsiveness

User input responsiveness is crucial for creating a satisfying gaming experience. Here are some tips for enhancing input responsiveness:

- **Input Buffering:** Implement input buffering to ensure that player actions are registered even if the input is pressed slightly before it's needed.

- **Input Smoothing:** Apply input smoothing to prevent sudden, jerky movements. Use variables like lerp() to gradually adjust the character's speed.

- **Dead Zones:** For analog input devices like thumbsticks, use dead zones to filter out small, unintended movements.

- **Feedback:** Provide immediate feedback to the player when an input is recognized. This can be in the form of character animations, sound effects, or HUD elements.

- **Testing and Iteration:** Playtest your game extensively to fine-tune input responsiveness and ensure that it feels natural and enjoyable to play.

In GameMaker, the combination of user input handling, collision detection, and animation control allows you to create responsive and engaging player movement and actions. By carefully designing and implementing these mechanics, you can craft a gameplay experience that keeps players immersed in your game world.

4.4 Creating Interactive Game Objects

Interactive game objects are a cornerstone of engaging gameplay experiences. These objects respond to player actions, provide challenges, and contribute to the game's overall immersion. In this section, we'll explore how to design and create interactive game objects using GameMaker.

1. Object Interactivity

Object interactivity refers to the ability of in-game objects to respond to player actions, such as collisions, clicks, or input commands. Here's how to implement object interactivity:

Collision-Based Interactions

1. Use collision events in GameMaker to trigger specific actions when an object collides with another object. For example, when a player collides with a collectible item, you can increase the player's score and remove the collectible from the game world.

Mouse and Touch Interactions

1. Implement mouse or touch interactions for objects that players can click or tap. Use the mouse_check_button_pressed() or mouse_check_button_down() functions to detect mouse clicks or touch events. For example, a player might click on a button to open a door or activate a switch.

```
if (mouse_check_button_pressed(mb_left)) {

// Perform an action when the left mouse button is pressed

}
```

Keyboard or Gamepad Interactions

1. Create keyboard or gamepad interactions for objects that respond to specific key presses or button inputs. Use input

functions like keyboard_check_pressed() or gamepad_button_check_pressed() to detect player commands.

2. Object States and Properties

Interactive objects often have different states and properties that determine their behavior and appearance. To create interactive game objects with varying states:

State Machines

1. Implement a state machine for objects that can have multiple states. Each state represents a different behavior or interaction. For example, a door object might have states like "closed," "opening," and "open."

Property Variables

1. Use property variables to store information about objects. These variables can control aspects such as an object's health, damage, or inventory contents. For instance, a chest object might have a property variable that stores the items it contains.

3. Feedback and Visual Cues

Provide feedback and visual cues to players to communicate the interactivity of objects:

Highlighting

1. Highlight interactive objects when the player hovers the

mouse cursor over them or when they become actionable. This can be done by changing the object's sprite, color, or adding visual effects.

Tooltips

1. Display tooltips or information panels when players interact with objects. Tooltips can explain the object's function or provide context.

Sound Effects

1. Use sound effects to indicate successful interactions or provide auditory feedback when an object responds to player actions.

4. Puzzles and Challenges

Interactive objects can be integral to puzzle-solving and creating gameplay challenges. Here's how to design objects for puzzles and challenges:

Trigger-Based Puzzles

1. Create objects that act as triggers for puzzle elements. When a player interacts with these objects, they can activate or manipulate other parts of the puzzle.

Combining Objects

1. Design puzzles that require players to combine or interact with multiple objects in specific ways to progress. For example, players might need to find and combine key

objects to unlock a door.

Dynamic Obstacles

1. Use interactive objects as dynamic obstacles or hazards. These objects can pose challenges to players and require quick thinking and skill to overcome.

5. Testing and Balancing

Testing and balancing the interactivity of game objects are crucial steps in game development:

- **Playtesting:** Regularly playtest your game to ensure that interactive objects behave as expected and are enjoyable for players.

- **User Feedback:** Gather feedback from playtesters and players to identify any issues with object interactivity and make necessary adjustments.

- **Balancing:** Balance the difficulty and rewards associated with interactive objects to provide a satisfying gameplay experience. Ensure that challenges are neither too easy nor too frustrating.

Creating interactive game objects that respond to player actions and contribute to the game's narrative and challenges is a creative and rewarding aspect of game development. By carefully designing, implementing, and testing these objects, you can craft engaging and immersive gameplay experiences for your players.

4.5 Balancing Gameplay and Difficulty Levels

Balancing gameplay and difficulty levels is a critical aspect of game design that directly affects the player's experience. Achieving the right balance ensures that the game is challenging, engaging, and enjoyable for players of varying skill levels. In this section, we'll explore strategies for effectively balancing gameplay and difficulty in your GameMaker project.

1. Player Progression Curve

Balancing gameplay starts with understanding the player's progression curve. Consider how the difficulty should evolve throughout the game. Typically, games start with simpler challenges and gradually introduce more complex ones as players gain experience. Here are some key points to keep in mind:

- **Learning Phase:** Early levels or stages should serve as a learning phase, where players become familiar with the game's mechanics and controls. Keep challenges relatively straightforward to prevent overwhelming new players.

- **Difficulty Gradation:** Increase the difficulty gradually as players progress. Introduce new mechanics, enemy types, or obstacles over time to keep the gameplay fresh.

- **Pacing:** Pay attention to the pacing of your game. Offer moments of intensity and relaxation to create a balanced flow. Ensure that challenges are spaced evenly, with occasional peaks in difficulty.

2. Difficulty Levels and Accessibility

Allow players to choose their preferred difficulty level or provide accessibility options to accommodate a broader audience. Here's how to approach this:

- **Difficulty Settings:** Implement multiple difficulty settings, such as "easy," "normal," and "hard." Adjust factors like enemy health, damage, or the availability of resources based on the selected difficulty.

- **Accessibility Features:** Consider adding accessibility features like adjustable game speed, simplified controls, or an option to skip challenging segments for players who may have difficulty with certain gameplay elements.

3. Data-Driven Balancing

Use data-driven balancing techniques to fine-tune your game's difficulty. Collect and analyze player data to identify areas that may be too easy or too hard. Here's how to do it:

- **Telemetry Data:** Implement telemetry or analytics tools in your game to collect gameplay data, including player deaths, completion times, and level progress.

- **Player Feedback:** Encourage players to provide feedback on difficulty levels. Listen to their input and make adjustments accordingly.

- **Iterative Design:** Continuously iterate on your game's design based on collected data and player feedback. Balance gameplay elements like enemy health, damage output, and resource availability as needed.

4. Enemy and AI Design

Enemy and AI design plays a significant role in game difficulty. Here's how to balance these aspects effectively:

- **Enemy Variety:** Introduce a variety of enemy types with distinct behaviors and abilities. Each enemy should pose different challenges, requiring players to adapt their strategies.

- **AI Scaling:** Implement scalable AI behaviors that adjust to the player's skill level. For instance, if a player repeatedly struggles with a specific section, the AI can become slightly less aggressive or offer hints.

- **Boss Battles:** Boss battles should be challenging but fair. Design patterns and attack sequences that players can learn and counter effectively.

5. Resource Management

Resource management is another crucial aspect of balancing gameplay. Resources can include health items, ammunition, currency, or power-ups. Ensure that resource availability aligns with the game's difficulty:

- **Resource Scarcity:** In more challenging parts of the game, resources may be scarce, requiring careful resource management and decision-making by the player.

- **Resource Abundance:** During easier segments or after overcoming difficult challenges, reward players with ample resources to enhance their sense of accomplishment.

- **Economy Balance:** If your game features an in-game economy, carefully balance the cost of items and upgrades to prevent inflation or resource abundance.

6. Playtesting and Feedback

Playtesting is an invaluable tool for balancing gameplay. Here's how to make the most of it:

- **Diverse Playtesters:** Include a diverse group of playtesters with varying skill levels to gather feedback from different perspectives.

- **Iterative Testing:** Continuously test and adjust the game's balance throughout development. Focus on specific levels, challenges, or mechanics that require fine-tuning.

- **Feedback Channels:** Create channels for playtesters to provide feedback easily. This can include in-game feedback forms or dedicated playtesting sessions.

- **Objective Data:** Combine subjective feedback with objective data from telemetry and analytics to make informed balancing decisions.

7. Iterate and Refine

Balancing gameplay is an iterative process that continues even after the game's release. Monitor player feedback, collect post-launch data, and be prepared to release patches or updates to address any unforeseen balance issues.

Balancing gameplay and difficulty levels is an art that requires careful consideration, testing, and player feedback. By following these strategies and staying attentive to the player experience, you can create a game that provides a satisfying and enjoyable challenge for your audience.

Chapter 5: Sound and Music Integration

5.1 Basics of Sound Design in GameMaker

Sound and music are essential components of game development that greatly influence the player's immersion and overall experience. In this section, we'll explore the basics of sound design in GameMaker, including the importance of audio, creating and managing sound assets, and integrating them into your game.

Importance of Sound in Games

Sound in games serves multiple purposes, from enhancing immersion to conveying information. Here are some key roles of sound in game design:

- **Atmosphere:** Soundscapes, ambient noises, and music set the tone and atmosphere of your game. They can make a game world feel alive and believable.

- **Feedback:** Audio provides feedback to players, indicating successful actions, health status, or danger. For example, a satisfying "ping" sound when collecting an item communicates success.

- **Emotion:** Music can evoke emotions and enhance storytelling. It can make action sequences feel intense, sad moments more poignant, and victories more triumphant.

- **Localization:** Sound and voice acting are crucial for localizing games for different languages and cultures. They allow you to convey dialogue and context effectively.

Creating Sound Assets

Before integrating sound into your game, you need sound assets. Here's how to create and manage them:

- **Recording:** If you're creating your own sound effects or voiceovers, you'll need appropriate recording equipment and software.

- **Editing:** Use audio editing software to clean, trim, and enhance your recordings. Ensure that sound effects are clear and balanced.

- **Music Composition:** Compose or license music tracks that fit the mood and theme of your game. Music software can help with composition.

- **Asset Organization:** Organize your sound assets into a structured directory or folder system within your project to keep them easily accessible.

Sound Integration in GameMaker

GameMaker provides tools and functions to integrate sound into your game effectively:

- **Importing Sounds:** Use GameMaker's built-in sound editor to import and manage sound assets. You can import various sound formats, such as WAV or MP3.

- **Sound Effects:** To play sound effects, use the audio_play_sound() function. Specify the sound asset and adjust parameters like volume and pitch.

```
audio_play_sound(snd_collect_item, 1, false);
```

- **Background Music:** To play background music, use the audio_play_music() function. You can control the playback of music tracks, including looping and volume adjustments.

```
audio_play_music(mus_main_theme, true, 0.5);
```

- **Sound Groups:** GameMaker allows you to create sound groups to manage and control the playback of related sounds. This is useful for organizing sounds like footsteps or explosions.

```
audio_sound_group_gain(snd_group_explosions, 0.8);
```

Sound Optimization

Optimizing sound assets and their integration is crucial for efficient game development:

- **Compression:** Compress sound files to reduce their size without compromising quality. This helps minimize the game's storage requirements.

- **Streaming:** Consider streaming larger music tracks or audio files to reduce memory usage and improve performance.

- **Loading Sounds:** Preload essential sounds during game startup to reduce latency when playing them during gameplay.

- **Volume Balancing:** Ensure that all sound effects and music tracks have consistent volume levels. Inconsistent volumes can be jarring to players.

- **Testing:** Regularly test sound playback on different devices and platforms to ensure compatibility and quality.

Dynamic Audio and Soundscapes

For more immersive experiences, consider implementing dynamic audio and soundscapes:

- **Spatial Audio:** Implement 3D sound to make audio sources feel like they're coming from specific directions in the game world. This adds realism and can help players locate objects or threats.
- **Sound Layers:** Create layered soundscapes that change dynamically based on in-game events or player actions. For example, intensify background music during action sequences.
- **Sound Triggers:** Use sound triggers or zones to change the audio environment when players enter specific areas or trigger events.

Sound design is a powerful tool for enhancing gameplay, storytelling, and player immersion. By understanding the fundamentals of sound in games and effectively integrating sound assets into your GameMaker project, you can create a more engaging and memorable gaming experience for your players.

5.2 Importing and Managing Audio Assets

In GameMaker, importing and managing audio assets is a crucial part of sound and music integration. This section explores the process of importing and organizing audio assets in your

GameMaker project and provides insights into effectively managing them.

Audio File Formats

GameMaker supports various audio file formats, including WAV, MP3, OGG, and more. When choosing a format, consider factors like file size, audio quality, and platform compatibility. Here's a brief overview of common audio formats:

- **WAV:** Provides high-quality audio but often results in larger file sizes. Suitable for sound effects and music tracks.

- **MP3:** Offers a good balance between audio quality and compression. Ideal for background music tracks.

- **OGG:** A compressed format that maintains good audio quality while reducing file size. Suitable for both sound effects and music.

- **AAC:** Known for its high-quality compression, AAC is a good choice for mobile games.

Importing Audio Assets

To import audio assets into GameMaker, follow these steps:

1. **Open the Sound Editor:** In GameMaker, navigate to the "Resources" tab and double-click on "Sounds" to open the Sound Editor.
2. **Import Sound Files:** Click the "Import Sound" button or drag-and-drop your audio files directly into the Sound Editor. GameMaker will automatically convert some

formats to its preferred format (e.g., OGG).

3. **Asset Properties:** After importing, you can set properties for each sound, including its name, volume, pitch, and looping options. Ensure that you organize your sounds effectively by providing meaningful names.

Organizing Audio Assets

Effectively organizing your audio assets is essential, especially in larger projects. Consider the following organization strategies:

- **Folders and Subfolders:** Use folders and subfolders within the Sound Editor to categorize sounds. For instance, you can create folders for "Sound Effects" and "Music" to keep things tidy.

- **Naming Conventions:** Establish a consistent naming convention for your audio assets. This can help you quickly identify the purpose of each sound. For example, "sfx_jump" for a jumping sound effect.

- **Asset Groups:** Use asset groups to group related sounds together. For example, you can create a group called "Enemy Sounds" and add all enemy-related sound assets to it.

Sound Groups

GameMaker allows you to create and manage sound groups, which can help you control and adjust the volume of multiple sounds at once. Sound groups are particularly useful for managing categories of sounds like footsteps or environmental noises.

To create a sound group, follow these steps:

1. **Open the Sound Group Editor:** From the Sound Editor, click the "Open Sound Group Editor" button.
2. **Create a New Group:** Click the "New Group" button and give your group a name, such as "Ambient Sounds."
3. **Add Sounds to the Group:** Select the sounds you want to add to the group and click the "Add" button.
4. **Adjust Volume:** You can control the volume of all sounds within a group collectively using the group's volume slider.

Audio Management in Code

In your GameMaker project, you'll often need to manage audio assets dynamically through code. Here are some common audio-related functions in GameMaker:

- audio_play_sound(sound, priority, loop) plays a specified sound, allowing you to set priority and looping options.

- audio_play_music(music, loop, volume) plays background music with looping and volume control.

- audio_sound_gain(sound, volume) adjusts the volume of a specific sound.

- audio_sound_group_gain(group, volume) adjusts the volume of a sound group.

- audio_sound_gain(global.sound_volume) adjusts the global sound volume, affecting all sounds.

Optimizing Audio Assets

Optimizing audio assets is crucial for ensuring that your game runs smoothly and efficiently. Consider these optimization techniques:

- **Compression:** Compress audio files to reduce file size without significant loss in quality.
- **Streaming:** For large music tracks, consider streaming them to reduce memory usage.
- **Loading:** Load essential sounds during game startup to minimize delays when playing them during gameplay.
- **Volume Balancing:** Ensure that all sound assets have consistent volume levels to provide a seamless auditory experience.
- **Testing:** Regularly test audio playback on various devices and platforms to ensure compatibility and quality.

Effective management and organization of audio assets, along with optimization techniques, will help you create a polished and immersive audio experience in your GameMaker project.

5.3 Creating Immersive Soundscapes

Soundscapes play a pivotal role in creating immersive game environments and enhancing the player's overall experience. In this section, we'll delve into the art of crafting soundscapes that transport players into the world of your game.

What Are Soundscapes?

Soundscapes, in the context of game development, refer to the audio environment or atmosphere within the game world. They encompass ambient sounds, background noises, and environmental audio that contribute to the sense of place and time. Well-designed soundscapes can make the game world feel more alive, believable, and engaging.

Designing Soundscapes

Creating immersive soundscapes involves careful planning and design. Here are the key steps to consider:

1. Identify Environmental Elements

Start by identifying the environmental elements in your game world that should have corresponding audio. This could include natural sounds like wind, rain, or wildlife, as well as artificial sounds like machinery or traffic.

2. Gather Audio Resources

To craft authentic soundscapes, you'll need audio resources that match the game's setting. You can record real-world sounds, purchase royalty-free sound libraries, or hire a sound designer to create custom audio.

3. Layering and Variation

Layering is a fundamental technique in soundscape design. Rather than using a single audio loop, layer multiple audio tracks with varying sounds and intensities. For instance, a forest soundscape might include layers of birdsong, rustling leaves, and distant waterfalls.

4. Transition and Realism

Pay attention to how sounds transition as players move through the game world. Implement fade-ins and fade-outs to create smooth transitions between different sound layers. Realism is key, so consider how sound sources move relative to the player's position.

5. Interactive Elements

Incorporate sounds that respond to player actions or interactions with the environment. For example, when a character walks on different surfaces (e.g., grass, stone, or sand), the footstep sounds should change accordingly.

6. Emotional Impact

Soundscapes can evoke emotions and set the tone of a scene. Use music and sound effects strategically to enhance the emotional impact of key moments in your game, such as intense battles or dramatic reveals.

Implementing Soundscapes in GameMaker

GameMaker provides tools and functions to integrate soundscapes seamlessly into your game:

- **Background Sounds:** Use the audio_play_sound() function to play looping background sounds. Ensure that the soundscape sounds blend well with other game audio.

```
audio_play_sound(snd_forest_ambience, 1, true);
```

- **Spatial Audio:** Implement 3D audio to make sound sources feel like they're coming from specific directions in the game world. This adds realism and helps players locate objects or threats.

- **Dynamic Soundscapes:** Create dynamic soundscapes that change based on in-game events or locations. For instance, intensify background music during action sequences or add eerie sounds in dark, mysterious areas.

- **Layer Management:** Use sound groups to manage and control the playback of related sounds within a soundscape. Adjust the volume and properties of sound groups to achieve the desired effect.

Testing and Iteration

Testing is crucial to ensure that your soundscapes enhance the player's immersion rather than detract from it. Here are some testing and iteration tips:

- **Diverse Testing Environments:** Test soundscapes in various game environments to identify any issues with audio transitions or volume balancing.

- **Player Feedback:** Gather feedback from playtesters to assess the effectiveness of your soundscapes. Pay attention to whether the audio contributes to the overall gaming experience.

- **Balancing:** Continuously iterate on your soundscapes based on feedback and testing. Adjust volume levels, layering, and transitions as needed to achieve the desired atmosphere.

- **Optimization:** Optimize soundscapes for performance, especially in resource-intensive scenes. Consider using streaming or dynamic loading techniques.

Creating immersive soundscapes is a multi-faceted endeavor that combines artistry and technical implementation. When done effectively, soundscapes enrich your game world, making it more captivating and believable for players.

5.4 Synchronizing Music with Gameplay

Synchronizing music with gameplay is a crucial aspect of game development that can greatly impact the player's experience. In this section, we'll explore the techniques and strategies for effectively integrating music into your game using GameMaker.

The Role of Music in Gameplay

Music serves various functions in games, including setting the mood, enhancing storytelling, and providing feedback to players. Here are some key roles of music in gameplay:

- **Emotional Enhancement:** Music can evoke specific emotions, intensifying the player's connection with the game's narrative and atmosphere. For example, somber music can underscore a sad story moment, while upbeat music can accompany a victorious battle.

- **Immersion:** Well-composed music can transport players into the game world, making them feel like active participants in the story or action.

- **Feedback:** Music can provide feedback about the game's state or player actions. For instance, a change in music when nearing an enemy can create tension and indicate danger.

- **Pacing:** Music can influence the pacing of gameplay. Fast-paced music can heighten tension during action sequences, while slower music can offer respite during exploration.

Creating Game Music

Creating game music requires a balance between creativity and technical considerations. Here's a brief overview of the process:

1. Compose or License Music

You can either compose original music for your game or license pre-existing tracks from music libraries. When composing, consider the game's theme, mood, and gameplay situations.

2. Arrange and Loop

Arrange your music into suitable segments or loops. In GameMaker, you can use loop points within audio files to create seamless looping tracks for continuous gameplay.

3. Format and Compression

Optimize music files by choosing suitable formats (e.g., MP3 or OGG) and compression settings to balance audio quality and file size.

4. Interactive Music

For more dynamic experiences, create variations of music tracks that can be triggered based on in-game events or player actions. This allows music to adapt to the gameplay situation.

Integrating Music in GameMaker

GameMaker offers functionality to integrate music seamlessly into your game. Here are some key functions and strategies:

Playing Background Music

Use the audio_play_music() function to play background music. You can specify whether the music should loop and set the volume.

```
audio_play_music(mus_background, true, 0.7);
```

Dynamic Music

Implement dynamic music that changes based on game events. For instance, switch to intense music during a boss battle or shift to a calming melody during exploration.

```
if (player_in_boss_room) {

audio_play_music(mus_boss_battle, true, 0.8);

} else {

audio_play_music(mus_explore, true, 0.5);

}
```

Crossfading

Smoothly transition between different music tracks using crossfades. This avoids abrupt changes that can disrupt player immersion.

```
audio_sound_gain(mus_previous_track, 0.0);

audio_sound_gain(mus_new_track, 1.0);
```

Player Feedback

Use music to provide feedback to players. For example, change the music when they accomplish a significant task or when they enter a different game area.

```
if (player_collected_key) {

audio_play_music(mus_victory, false, 0.7);

}
```

Testing and Balancing

Testing is essential to ensure that music enhances rather than distracts from gameplay. Here's how to approach testing and balancing:

- **Consistency:** Ensure that music volume levels are consistent across different tracks. Abrupt volume changes can be jarring.

- **Testing Across Devices:** Test music playback on various devices and platforms to ensure compatibility and quality.

- **Player Feedback:** Gather feedback from playtesters to gauge the impact of music on their gaming experience. Make adjustments based on their input.

- **Balancing:** Strike a balance between music and other audio elements, such as sound effects and dialogue. They should complement each other without overpowering.

Effective synchronization of music with gameplay can elevate your game's quality and player engagement. By understanding the role of music, creating appropriate compositions, and integrating them thoughtfully into GameMaker, you can craft a memorable and immersive gaming experience.

5.5 Advanced Audio Techniques and Optimization

In this section, we will explore advanced audio techniques and optimization strategies for your GameMaker project. These techniques will help you create a more immersive audio experience for players while ensuring efficient use of system resources.

Advanced Audio Techniques

1. Realistic Spatial Audio

To enhance immersion, implement 3D spatial audio in your game. This technique makes sound sources appear to come from specific directions in the game world, providing players with audio cues about their surroundings. GameMaker allows you to control the position and direction of audio sources using the audio_emitter_x, audio_emitter_y, and audio_emitter_z functions.

```
// Set the position of a sound emitter

audio_emitter_x(snd_footstep, obj_player.x);

audio_emitter_y(snd_footstep, obj_player.y);
```

2. Adaptive Music Systems

Create adaptive music systems that respond to in-game events and player actions. This approach involves composing multiple music layers that can be dynamically combined to reflect the current game situation. You can use conditions in your code to trigger and blend these layers seamlessly.

```
if (player_in_combat) {

audio_play_sound(mus_combat_layer, false, 1.0);

audio_play_sound(mus_drums_layer, true, 0.5);

}
```

3. Dynamic Soundscapes

Extend your soundscapes by adding dynamic elements that react to gameplay. For example, you can include dynamic weather effects like rain that intensify or diminish based on the game's narrative or player location. These dynamic elements create a more responsive and engaging audio environment.

```
if (player_enters_forest) {

audio_play_sound(snd_rain, true, 0.3);

} else {
```

```
audio_stop_sound(snd_rain);

}
```

4. Voice Acting and Dialogues

If your game includes voice acting or dialogues, ensure that the audio recordings are clear and well-edited. Use appropriate voice actors for character roles and implement a system to trigger dialogues at the right moments in the game. GameMaker provides functions like audio_play_sound to manage voiceovers effectively.

```
if (player_approaches_npc) {

audio_play_sound(voiceover_npc_greeting, false, 1.0);

}
```

Audio Optimization Strategies

1. Audio Streaming

For large music tracks or long voiceovers, consider streaming audio data from storage rather than loading the entire file into memory. This reduces memory usage and allows for more extensive audio assets.

2. Audio Groups

Use audio groups to manage and control the playback of related sounds. Adjusting the volume and properties of sound groups collectively can simplify audio management, especially for sounds with similar characteristics.

3. Sound Prioritization

Assign priorities to different audio sources to ensure that critical sounds are heard even when multiple sounds are playing simultaneously. This can be essential for gameplay feedback or dramatic moments.

4. Audio Caching

Cache frequently used audio assets in memory to reduce load times and improve responsiveness during gameplay. Be mindful of memory limitations and balance caching with other resource requirements.

5. Code Profiling

Regularly profile your game's audio performance using GameMaker's built-in profiling tools or third-party profiling software. Identify any performance bottlenecks related to audio and optimize as needed.

6. Platform-Specific Optimization

Different platforms may have varying audio capabilities and requirements. Consider platform-specific audio optimization to ensure optimal performance on each target platform.

7. Quality vs. Compression

Strike a balance between audio quality and compression. While compression reduces file sizes, excessive compression can degrade audio quality. Adjust compression settings carefully.

Testing and Feedback

As with any aspect of game development, testing and player feedback are essential for refining your advanced audio techniques and optimizations. Conduct thorough testing across different devices and platforms to ensure that your audio enhancements work as intended. Collect feedback from playtesters to gauge the impact of your audio improvements on the overall gaming experience.

By incorporating these advanced audio techniques and optimization strategies into your GameMaker project, you can create a more immersive and efficient audio environment for your players. Balancing creativity with technical considerations will result in a memorable auditory experience that enhances your game's overall quality.

Chapter 6: Scripting with GML (GameMaker Language)

6.1 Introduction to GML

In this section, we will delve into the fundamentals of GameMaker Language (GML). GML is the scripting language used in GameMaker, and it provides the flexibility and power to create complex game behaviors and interactions. Whether you're a beginner or an experienced programmer, understanding GML is crucial for harnessing the full potential of GameMaker.

What is GML?

GameMaker Language, often referred to as GML, is a scripting language designed specifically for game development within the GameMaker environment. It is a high-level language that simplifies many common programming tasks and allows game developers to focus on creating gameplay mechanics, interactions, and logic without dealing with low-level details.

GML is based on C-like syntax, which makes it relatively easy to learn for those familiar with programming concepts. However, even if you're new to programming, GML's simplicity and GameMaker's user-friendly interface make it accessible for beginners.

Variables and Data Types in GML

Let's start by exploring variables and data types in GML. Like most programming languages, GML allows you to store and manipulate data using variables. Here are some common data types in GML:

1. **Number**: Used to store numerical values, both integers and

floating-point numbers.

var playerScore = 100;

var gravity = 9.8;

1. **String**: Used to store text or sequences of characters.

var playerName = "John";

var welcomeMessage = "Welcome to the game!";

1. **Boolean**: Represents true or false values.

var isGameOver = false;

var isJumping = true;

1. **Array**: An ordered collection of values that can be of any data type.

var highScores = [120, 85, 160, 200, 75];

1. **Object**: GML allows you to work with instances of objects in your game. Objects have properties and can execute code.

var playerObj = obj_player;

playerObj.x += 5; // Move the player object 5 pixels to the right.

Variables and Assignment

To create a variable in GML, you use the var keyword, followed by the variable name and an optional assignment of a value. Variables can be assigned values using the equal sign (=) operator.

var playerHealth;

playerHealth = 100; // Assign the value 100 to the playerHealth variable.

You can also declare and assign a value to a variable in a single line:

var playerScore = 0; // Declare and initialize playerScore with the value 0.

Comments in GML

Comments are essential for documenting your code and making it more readable. In GML, you can add comments using double slashes (//) for single-line comments or enclose multi-line comments within /* and */.

// This is a single-line comment.

/*

This is a

multi-line comment.

*/

Basic Operators

GML supports various operators for performing operations on variables and values. Here are some common operators:

- **Arithmetic Operators**: Used for mathematical calculations.

```
var a = 5;

var b = 3;

var sum = a + b; // Addition

var difference = a - b; // Subtraction

var product = a * b; // Multiplication

var quotient = a / b; // Division
```

- **Comparison Operators**: Used for comparing values and producing Boolean results.

```
var x = 10;

var y = 20;

var isEqual = (x == y); // Check if x is equal to y

var isNotEqual = (x != y); // Check if x is not equal to y
```

- **Logical Operators**: Used for combining or negating Boolean values.

```
var isTrue = true;

var isFalse = false;

var logicalAnd = isTrue && isFalse; // Logical AND

var logicalOr = isTrue || isFalse; // Logical OR
```

```
var logicalNot = !isTrue; // Logical NOT
```

Control Structures in GML

Control structures in GML allow you to control the flow of your game's logic. Common control structures include:

- **Conditional Statements (if, else, switch)**: Used to make decisions based on conditions.

```
var playerHealth = 75;

if (playerHealth > 50) {

// Player is healthy.

// Execute code here.

} else {

// Player is injured.

// Execute different code here.

}
```

- **Loops (for, while, repeat)**: Used for repetitive tasks and iterating through data.

```
for (var i = 0; i < 5; i++) {

// Execute code 5 times.

}

var counter = 0;
```

```
while (counter < 10) {

// Execute code while the condition is true.

counter++;

}
```

- **Functions**: Allow you to encapsulate and reuse code.

```
// Define a custom function.

function CalculateDamage(damage, defense) {

return damage - defense;

}

// Call the function.

var actualDamage = CalculateDamage(50, 10);
```

These are the fundamental concepts of GML that you need to grasp before diving deeper into scripting with GameMaker. In the following sections, we'll explore variables, operators, functions, and advanced scripting techniques in more detail to empower you with the skills to create complex game logic.

6.2 Variables, Operators, and Control Structures in GML

In this section, we'll delve deeper into GML by exploring variables, operators, and control structures, which are fundamental to programming and game development. Understanding these concepts is crucial for creating interactive and dynamic gameplay in GameMaker.

Variables and Data Types

Variables are used to store and manage data in GML. We've already seen some common data types in GML, but let's expand on this:

- **Numbers**: As mentioned earlier, numbers can be integers or floating-point values. They are used for various purposes, such as tracking scores, health, or positions.

```
var playerScore = 100;

var gravity = 9.8;
```

- **Strings**: Strings store text or sequences of characters. They are handy for displaying messages, names, or dialogue in your game.

```
var playerName = "Alice";

var welcomeMessage = "Welcome to the adventure!";
```

- **Booleans**: Booleans represent true or false values and are used for making decisions in your game logic.

```
var isGameOver = false;

var isJumping = true;
```

- **Arrays**: Arrays are collections of values. They can store multiple values of the same or different data types, making them useful for managing lists of items or character attributes.

```
var inventory = ["sword", "shield", "potion"];

var playerStats = [100, 75, 50, 10];
```

Variable Scope

In GML, variables can have different scopes, which determine where they can be accessed and modified. There are two primary scopes:

- **Local Variables**: Local variables are defined and accessible only within the current code block or function. They are temporary and cease to exist once the block or function completes execution.

```
// Local variable inside a function.

function CalculateDamage(damage, defense) {

var adjustedDamage = damage - defense;

return adjustedDamage;

}

var result = CalculateDamage(50, 10);

// The 'adjustedDamage' variable is not accessible here.
```

- **Instance Variables**: Instance variables belong to an object instance and can be accessed and modified within that instance's code. They are useful for storing object-specific data.

```
// Instance variable of an object.

obj_player.health = 100;
```

```
obj_enemy.health = 50;

// Accessing instance variables in the object's code.

var playerHealth = obj_player.health;

var enemyHealth = obj_enemy.health;
```

Operators in GML

Operators are symbols or keywords used to perform operations on variables and values. GML supports various types of operators:

- **Arithmetic Operators**: Used for mathematical calculations.

```
var a = 5;

var b = 3;

var sum = a + b; // Addition

var difference = a - b; // Subtraction

var product = a * b; // Multiplication

var quotient = a / b; // Division
```

- **Comparison Operators**: Used for comparing values.

```
var x = 10;

var y = 20;

var isEqual = (x == y); // Check if x is equal to y
```

```
var isNotEqual = (x != y); // Check if x is not equal to y
```

- **Logical Operators**: Used for combining or negating Boolean values.

```
var isTrue = true;

var isFalse = false;

var logicalAnd = isTrue && isFalse; // Logical AND

var logicalOr = isTrue || isFalse; // Logical OR

var logicalNot = !isTrue; // Logical NOT
```

- **Assignment Operators**: Used to assign values to variables while performing an operation.

```
var count = 5;

count += 3; // Equivalent to count = count + 3;
```

Control Structures

Control structures allow you to control the flow of your game's logic. Let's explore some common control structures in GML:

- **Conditional Statements (if, else, switch)**: These statements allow you to make decisions based on conditions.

```
var playerHealth = 75;

if (playerHealth > 50) {

// Player is healthy.
```

```
// Execute code here.

} else {

// Player is injured.

// Execute different code here.

}
```

• **Loops (for, while, repeat)**: Loops are used for repetitive tasks and iterating through data.

```
for (var i = 0; i < 5; i++) {

// Execute code 5 times.

}

var counter = 0;

while (counter < 10) {

// Execute code while the condition is true.

counter++;

}
```

• **Functions**: Functions allow you to encapsulate and reuse code.

```
// Define a custom function.

function CalculateDamage(damage, defense) {
```

```
return damage - defense;

}

// Call the function.

var actualDamage = CalculateDamage(50, 10);
```

These concepts are the building blocks of GML programming. By mastering variables, operators, and control structures, you'll have the tools needed to create complex game mechanics and interactive gameplay experiences in GameMaker.

6.3 Functions and Events in GML

In this section, we'll explore the concept of functions and events in GameMaker Language (GML). Functions and events are essential components of GML programming, allowing you to organize your code, handle game events, and create modular and reusable code structures.

Functions in GML

Functions in GML are blocks of code that can be defined and called to perform specific tasks. They enable you to encapsulate logic into reusable modules, making your code more organized and maintainable. Here's how you define and use functions in GML:

```
// Define a custom function.

function CalculateDamage(damage, defense) {

return damage - defense;

}
```

```
// Call the function.

var actualDamage = CalculateDamage(50, 10);
```

In the example above, we've defined a function called CalculateDamage that takes two parameters (damage and defense) and returns the result of subtracting defense from damage. This function can be called with different values to calculate damage in various situations.

Functions can also have no parameters or return values if needed. They allow you to modularize your code, making it easier to understand and maintain. Additionally, you can use functions to avoid duplicating code by centralizing common operations.

Events in GML

Events are special functions in GML that are automatically called by GameMaker in response to specific game events or conditions. They are a fundamental part of object-oriented programming in GameMaker, as objects respond to events to define their behavior.

Here's an example of an event in GML:

```
// Create Event

// This event is automatically called when an instance of this object is created.

var playerHealth = 100;
```

In this case, the code within the "Create Event" is executed when an instance of the object associated with this code is created. Events like the "Create Event," "Step Event," and "Collision Event" are crucial for defining the behavior of game objects.

User-Defined Events

In addition to built-in events, you can also define custom events in GML. These events are useful for creating complex interactions and behaviors within your game. To define a custom event, you can use the event_user function:

```
// Define a custom event

event_user(0) {

// Custom event code goes here.

}
```

You can then trigger this custom event in your code using the event_perform function:

```
// Trigger the custom event

event_perform(ev_user0, 0);
```

Custom events are powerful because they allow you to create your own game-specific events that are not covered by the built-in events.

Event Order and Execution

Understanding the order in which events are executed is crucial in GameMaker. Events are processed in a specific order, and this order can influence the behavior of your game objects. Here are some important event-related concepts:

- **Create Event**: Occurs when an instance of an object is created.
- **Step Event**: Occurs in every game step and is used for continuous behavior.

- **Collision Event**: Occurs when an object collides with another object.
- **Draw Event**: Occurs when an instance is drawn on the screen.
- **Alarm Event**: Used to set alarms that trigger events after a specified time.
- **Keyboard and Mouse Events**: Respond to keyboard and mouse input.
- **User-Defined Events**: Custom events created by the developer.

Understanding event order and using the appropriate events for specific behaviors is essential for creating responsive and dynamic gameplay.

In conclusion, functions and events are fundamental aspects of GML programming in GameMaker. Functions allow you to create reusable code modules, while events define the behavior of game objects and handle various game events. By mastering these concepts, you can create organized, modular, and interactive game logic in GameMaker.

6.4 Advanced Scripting Techniques

In this section, we will explore advanced scripting techniques in GameMaker Language (GML) that go beyond the basics. These techniques are essential for creating complex and feature-rich games in GameMaker.

Object-Oriented Programming (OOP)

Object-Oriented Programming is a powerful paradigm that GameMaker fully supports. In OOP, you create objects that encapsulate both data (variables) and functions (methods). This approach helps organize your code and allows for better code reuse.

Here's a simplified example of an object-oriented approach in GML:

```
// Define an object with variables and methods.

obj_enemy = {

health: 100,

// Method to damage the enemy.

takeDamage: function(damage) {

this.health -= damage;

if (this.health <= 0) {

// Enemy is defeated.

instance_destroy();

}

}

};

// Create an instance of the object.

var enemy_instance = instance_create(x, y, obj_enemy);

// Call a method on the instance.
```

```
enemy_instance.takeDamage(20);
```

In this example, obj_enemy is an object that has both a health variable and a takeDamage method. We create an instance of this object and call its takeDamage method to reduce its health.

OOP makes it easier to manage complex game entities and behaviors. You can create inheritance hierarchies, reuse code, and create robust game systems with this approach.

Data Structures

GameMaker provides various data structures to store and manage data efficiently. These include arrays, grids, and data structures like lists, queues, and stacks. Leveraging these data structures can significantly improve the organization and performance of your game.

For example, you can use arrays to manage inventory items:

```
// Create an inventory array.

var inventory = ds_list_create();

// Add items to the inventory.

ds_list_add(inventory, "Sword");

ds_list_add(inventory, "Potion");

ds_list_add(inventory, "Shield");

// Access items in the inventory.

var item = ds_list_find_value(inventory, 0); // Get the first item.
```

Data structures offer flexibility and efficiency, especially when dealing with large amounts of data. They can be used for everything from managing lists of items to creating custom data-driven systems.

Asynchronous Programming

Asynchronous programming allows you to perform tasks concurrently, which is crucial for handling complex gameplay logic and resource loading. GML provides mechanisms for working with asynchronous operations, such as using alarms, timelines, and asynchronous events.

Here's an example of using an alarm for an asynchronous operation:

```
// Set an alarm to perform an action after a delay.

alarm[0] = 60; // Alarm 0 will trigger after 60 steps (1 second at 60 FPS).

// Alarm event to execute code when the alarm triggers.

alarm[0] event:

// Code to execute after the delay.

show_message("Alarm triggered!");
```

In this example, we set an alarm to trigger after a delay, and when it triggers, it executes a specific code block. This is just one way to handle asynchronous tasks in GameMaker.

Advanced Debugging and Profiling

Debugging and profiling are crucial for identifying and fixing issues in your game. GameMaker offers advanced debugging and profiling tools to help you optimize your game's performance and squash bugs efficiently.

You can use the built-in debugger to step through your code, inspect variables, and analyze the flow of your game logic. Profiling tools can help you identify performance bottlenecks and optimize critical sections of your code.

Third-Party Integrations

GameMaker allows you to integrate third-party libraries and tools to extend its capabilities. You can leverage external libraries for features like physics simulations, networking, and more. This can be especially useful when you need advanced functionality not available out-of-the-box.

To integrate a third-party library, you typically import or link the library's resources and write GML code to interact with it. Always refer to the documentation of the specific library you're using for detailed integration instructions.

In conclusion, mastering advanced scripting techniques in GameMaker Language can elevate your game development skills to the next level. Object-oriented programming, data structures, asynchronous programming, debugging, profiling, and third-party integrations are all valuable tools for creating sophisticated and polished games. By combining these techniques, you can bring your game development projects to new heights.

6.5 Debugging and Optimizing GML Code

Debugging and optimizing GameMaker Language (GML) code are essential steps in the game development process. Debugging helps you find and fix issues in your code, while optimization ensures your game runs smoothly and efficiently. In this section, we will explore techniques and tools for debugging and optimizing your GML code.

Debugging Techniques

1. Using Debug Messages: Debug messages are a simple yet effective way to inspect the values of variables and check the flow of your code. You can use the show_debug_message() function to print messages to the output window.

```
var playerHealth = 100;

show_debug_message("Player health: " + string(playerHealth));
```

2. Debugging Draw Events: In GameMaker, you can use the Draw Event of objects to visualize variables and conditions. For example, you can draw the collision mask of an object to check for collision issues.

```
// In the Draw Event of an object:

draw_self(); // Draw the object sprite.

draw_collision_rectangle(collision_xmin, collision_ymin, collision_xmax, collision_ymax, false);
```

3. Breakpoints: GameMaker's built-in debugger allows you to set breakpoints in your code. When the game reaches a breakpoint, it pauses execution, allowing you to inspect variables and step through code.

4. Variable Watcher: GameMaker's Variable Watcher tool lets you monitor the values of specific variables during runtime. You can

add variables to the Variable Watcher and observe how their values change.

Profiling and Optimization

1. Profiling Tools: GameMaker provides profiling tools to analyze the performance of your game. You can access these tools by running your game in debug mode. Profiling helps identify performance bottlenecks and areas that need optimization.

2. Efficient Collision Checking: Optimizing collision checking is crucial for performance. Use efficient collision functions like collision_line, collision_point, and collision_rectangle when checking for collisions. Avoid complex collision masks when simpler shapes will suffice.

3. Sprite and Image Optimization: Use appropriately sized sprites and images to reduce memory usage. GameMaker has functions for resizing sprites during runtime (sprite_resize), which can help optimize your game.

4. Object Pooling: Object pooling is a technique where you reuse objects instead of creating and destroying them frequently. This can reduce memory allocation and improve performance, especially for bullets, particles, or other frequently spawned objects.

5. Delta Time: Use delta time to make your game frame rate-independent. Delta time is the time elapsed since the last frame, and it ensures that your game runs consistently regardless of the frame rate.

```
// In the Step Event:

var moveSpeed = 5; // Pixels per second

var deltaTime = 1 / room_speed; // Calculate delta time

x += moveSpeed * deltaTime;
```

6. Sprite Atlas and Texture Groups: Combine multiple sprites into a single sprite atlas or use texture groups to reduce the number of texture swaps. This can improve rendering performance, especially on mobile devices.

7. Script Optimizations: Review your scripts for optimizations. Avoid unnecessary loops, and prefer built-in GML functions over custom code where possible. Profiling tools can help identify which scripts are consuming the most time.

8. Memory Management: Be mindful of memory management. Avoid memory leaks by properly destroying instances and freeing resources when they are no longer needed. Use GameMaker's resource management functions to release memory.

9. Disable Unnecessary Features: In the debugging and testing phase, you may have various debugging features and verbose logging enabled. Ensure that these are disabled in the final release to improve performance.

10. Testing on Target Platforms: Test your game on your target platforms to identify platform-specific performance issues. Different platforms may have varying hardware capabilities, so optimization may be required for each.

In conclusion, debugging and optimizing GML code are critical aspects of game development. Effective debugging techniques help you identify and resolve issues in your code, while optimization ensures that your game runs smoothly and efficiently on various platforms. By following these best practices and utilizing GameMaker's debugging and profiling tools, you can create high-quality, optimized games.

Chapter 7: Level Design and World Building

7.1 Concepts of Level Design in Game Development

Level design plays a crucial role in shaping the player's experience and engagement in a game. It involves creating the environments, challenges, and pacing that players will encounter as they progress through a game. In this section, we will delve into the key concepts of level design in the context of game development.

The Role of Level Design

Level design is more than just creating visually appealing game worlds; it's about crafting interactive spaces that facilitate gameplay and storytelling. Here are some essential aspects of level design:

1. **Flow and Pacing**: Level designers are responsible for controlling the flow of a game. They determine when players face challenges, encounter puzzles, or experience moments of calm. Pacing keeps players engaged and prevents them from becoming overwhelmed or bored.
2. **Narrative Integration**: Levels should integrate with the game's narrative. Whether it's a platformer, RPG, or puzzle game, the level design should align with the story's context and provide opportunities for narrative progression.
3. **Gameplay Mechanics**: Level designers need to consider the game's mechanics. They create situations where players can use their abilities, solving puzzles or overcoming obstacles that make the most of the game's unique features.
4. **Balance**: Balancing difficulty is crucial. Levels should

become progressively more challenging, but not to the point of frustration. Well-designed levels provide players with a sense of accomplishment as they overcome obstacles.

5. **Exploration and Reward**: Levels should encourage exploration. Hidden secrets, collectibles, and rewards make exploration rewarding and provide additional goals for players.
6. **Consistency**: Maintaining a consistent visual and thematic style throughout a level or game is vital for immersion. Players should feel like they are part of a cohesive world.
7. **Accessibility**: Level designers should consider player accessibility. A well-designed level accommodates players of different skill levels and abilities, ensuring that everyone can enjoy the game.

Principles of Level Design

Successful level design often adheres to certain principles that enhance the player's experience. These principles include:

- **Clear Goals**: Levels should communicate clear objectives to the player. Whether it's reaching a goal, defeating a boss, or solving a puzzle, players should know what they need to do.

- **Player Guidance**: Level designers use level geometry, lighting, and visual cues to guide players. This helps players navigate the environment and understand where to go next.

- **Variety**: Introducing variety in gameplay, environments, and challenges keeps the experience fresh. Repeating the same gameplay elements can lead to monotony.

- **Rhythm**: Level designers establish a rhythm of gameplay, alternating between moments of tension and relaxation. This rhythm keeps players engaged and adds emotional depth to the experience.

- **Storytelling through Environment**: Environments can tell stories. Level designers often embed storytelling elements in the scenery, allowing players to piece together the narrative through exploration.

- **Satisfying Endings**: Levels should culminate in satisfying conclusions, such as boss battles or dramatic events, rewarding players for their efforts.

Iteration and Playtesting

Level design is an iterative process. Designers create, playtest, and refine levels multiple times to ensure they are enjoyable and well-balanced. Playtesting involves observing how players interact with the level, gathering feedback, and making adjustments based on the data collected. This iterative approach is essential for creating polished and engaging levels.

In summary, level design in game development involves crafting interactive spaces that enhance gameplay, storytelling, and player engagement. It requires careful consideration of flow, pacing, narrative integration, mechanics, balance, and accessibility. Successful level design adheres to principles that guide players, provide variety, establish rhythm, and offer satisfying conclusions.

Through iteration and playtesting, level designers refine their creations to create memorable and immersive gaming experiences.

7.2 Building and Structuring Game Levels

Building and structuring game levels is a fundamental aspect of level design in game development. In this section, we will explore the key considerations and techniques involved in creating well-designed game levels.

Planning and Conceptualization

Before diving into level creation, it's essential to have a clear plan and concept for your game's levels. Here are some steps in the planning phase:

1. **Game Design Document**: Refer to your game design document, which outlines the overall vision for your game. It should contain information on the game's mechanics, objectives, story, and the role of each level in advancing the narrative.
2. **Level Themes**: Define the themes, settings, and aesthetics for each level. Consider how they tie into the game's narrative and overall style.
3. **Level Goals**: Determine the primary objectives of each level. What do players need to achieve or overcome to progress? These goals can be defeating a boss, solving a puzzle, or reaching a specific destination.
4. **Progression**: Plan the progression curve of your levels. Start with simpler challenges and gradually increase the difficulty to maintain player engagement.

Layout and Flow

The layout and flow of a level are critical to the player's experience. Here are some key considerations:

1. **Layout Design**: Create a blueprint for the level's layout. This includes the placement of platforms, obstacles, enemies, and interactive elements. The layout should support gameplay mechanics and objectives.
2. **Pacing**: Control the pacing of the level by strategically placing moments of action, exploration, and rest. Pacing can be achieved through level design, enemy encounters, and the arrangement of challenges.
3. **Player Guidance**: Use level design elements such as visual cues, lighting, and path markers to guide players through the level. Players should have a clear sense of direction without feeling lost.
4. **Backtracking and Exploration**: Consider opportunities for backtracking and exploration. Hidden areas with rewards or secrets can add depth to the level and encourage players to explore.

Challenges and Gameplay

Levels should provide engaging challenges that align with the game's mechanics. Here's how to design challenges effectively:

1. **Balanced Difficulty**: Maintain a balance between difficulty and fairness. Avoid overly frustrating sections that may discourage players.
2. **Variety of Challenges**: Introduce a variety of challenges, such as platforming, combat encounters, puzzles, and environmental hazards. Variety keeps gameplay interesting.
3. **Teaching Through Level Design**: Use early levels to teach

players how to use game mechanics and gradually introduce more complex challenges as they progress.

4. **Checkpoints**: Implement checkpoints or save points strategically to provide a sense of progress and prevent players from having to repeat long sections.

Visuals and Atmosphere

The visual design of a level greatly influences the player's immersion and emotional engagement. Consider these factors:

1. **Visual Cohesion**: Ensure that the visual elements of the level align with the overall theme and style of the game. Cohesiveness enhances immersion.
2. **Atmosphere and Mood**: Use lighting, color schemes, and environmental details to create a specific atmosphere or mood for each level. This can greatly enhance storytelling.
3. **Background and Foreground**: Incorporate background and foreground elements to add depth and dimension to the level. Parallax scrolling can be used to create an illusion of depth.

Testing and Iteration

Playtesting is an essential part of level design. It involves thoroughly testing the level, gathering feedback, and making improvements. Here's how to approach playtesting:

1. **Internal Playtesting**: Initially, have your development team playtest the level. Look for any technical issues, bugs, or design flaws.
2. **External Playtesting**: After addressing internal feedback, conduct external playtesting with a group of players who are unfamiliar with the level. Collect their feedback on the

level's difficulty, fun factor, and any areas that need improvement.

3. **Iteration**: Based on feedback, iterate on the level design. Make necessary adjustments to improve gameplay, flow, and visuals.

In conclusion, building and structuring game levels require careful planning, layout design, and consideration of challenges, gameplay, visuals, and atmosphere. A well-designed level enhances player engagement and contributes to the overall enjoyment of the game. Playtesting and iteration are crucial steps in refining level design to create memorable and immersive gaming experiences.

7.3 Creating Engaging and Challenging Levels

Creating engaging and challenging levels is a core aspect of level design in game development. In this section, we will delve into the techniques and principles that level designers use to craft levels that captivate players and provide rewarding experiences.

Understanding Player Engagement

Before designing levels, it's crucial to understand what engages players. Engagement can be achieved through various means:

1. **Clear Objectives**: Levels should have clear objectives or goals that players understand. Knowing what they need to achieve keeps players motivated.
2. **Progression**: Gradual progression in difficulty or complexity maintains player engagement. Levels should start with simpler challenges and gradually introduce more demanding ones.

3. **Variety**: Offering a variety of gameplay elements, challenges, and environments prevents monotony. Players appreciate new experiences within the same level.
4. **Story Integration**: Levels should integrate with the game's narrative and provide players with a sense of purpose and context for their actions.
5. **Feedback and Rewards**: Frequent feedback on the player's performance, such as visual or auditory cues, reinforces engagement. Rewards for completing challenges or finding secrets add satisfaction.

Balancing Challenge

Balancing challenge is a delicate task in level design. Levels should be challenging enough to be engaging but not so difficult that players become frustrated. Here are some strategies for achieving the right balance:

1. **Ramp-Up Difficulty**: Start levels with easier challenges to allow players to become familiar with the mechanics. Gradually increase difficulty as they progress.
2. **Player Skill vs. Game Skill**: Consider the skill level of your target audience. Levels should be designed to cater to the intended player skill level, whether they are newcomers or experienced gamers.
3. **Optional Challenges**: Include optional challenges or secrets that provide an extra layer of difficulty for players seeking it. This allows for broader appeal.
4. **Feedback**: Pay attention to player feedback, both from internal playtesting and external sources. Adjust level difficulty based on player reactions.

Exploration and Secrets

Encouraging exploration is a great way to engage players and add depth to levels. Here's how to incorporate exploration and secrets:

1. **Hidden Paths**: Include hidden paths or alternative routes that players can discover. These paths can lead to rewards or shortcuts.
2. **Collectibles**: Scatter collectibles throughout the level. Collectibles can serve as secondary objectives and motivate players to explore thoroughly.
3. **Environmental Storytelling**: Use level design to tell a story without words. Environmental details, such as ruins, graffiti, or abandoned items, can provide narrative context.

Pacing and Flow

Pacing and flow are critical to maintaining player engagement. Here's how to manage these aspects:

1. **Rhythm**: Create a rhythm in the level design by alternating between moments of tension and moments of relaxation. Tension could be combat encounters, while relaxation might involve exploration or puzzle-solving.
2. **Set Pieces**: Include set pieces or scripted events that provide memorable moments. These can include epic battles, dramatic escapes, or cinematic sequences.
3. **Visual Guidance**: Use visual cues to guide players through the level. Lighting, landmarks, and level geometry can direct players without the need for excessive hand-holding.

Player Choice and Consequence

Levels can offer players choices that impact the outcome or progression. These choices can add depth to the gameplay:

1. **Branching Paths**: Create branching paths or decisions that lead to different outcomes. These choices can affect the story, level progression, or access to resources.
2. **Consequences**: Ensure that player choices have meaningful consequences, whether in terms of narrative impact, gameplay changes, or character interactions.

Iterative Design and Playtesting

Like all aspects of game development, level design benefits from iteration and playtesting:

1. **Iterative Design**: Create multiple iterations of a level, refining it based on feedback and observations. Levels improve with each iteration.
2. **Playtesting**: Conduct extensive playtesting with different player profiles to gather feedback. Listen to player comments and use this feedback to enhance the level.
3. **Objective Feedback**: Objective feedback from playtesters can help identify areas of the level that may need adjustment. Metrics such as completion time and death count can be valuable.

In conclusion, creating engaging and challenging levels requires a deep understanding of player engagement, balance, exploration, pacing, and player choice. Level designers must craft experiences that captivate players, offer rewards for exploration, and strike the right balance between challenge and enjoyment. Iteration and playtesting are integral to refining levels and ensuring they provide rewarding experiences for players.

7.4 Environmental Storytelling and Atmosphere

Environmental storytelling and atmosphere are powerful tools in level design that immerse players in the game world and enhance the narrative experience. In this section, we will explore the concepts of environmental storytelling and atmosphere and how they contribute to creating memorable game levels.

What is Environmental Storytelling?

Environmental storytelling is a narrative technique where the game world and its elements convey a story or information without the need for explicit dialogue or exposition. It allows players to piece together the narrative through their observations and interactions with the environment. Here's how it works:

1. **Details and Clues**: Level designers place details, objects, and visual cues within the game world. These can be subtle hints, notes, graffiti, or even the arrangement of objects that provide context or backstory.
2. **Player Exploration**: Players are encouraged to explore the environment to uncover these details. This exploration can be driven by curiosity or the need to progress in the game.
3. **Narrative Context**: As players discover these elements, they begin to form a narrative context or backstory in their minds. This engagement makes the game world feel richer and more immersive.

Creating Atmosphere

Atmosphere in a game level refers to the emotional and sensory experience that the environment evokes in players. It sets the tone, mood, and overall feel of the level. Here's how to create atmosphere:

1. **Visual Elements**: The visual design of the level, including lighting, colors, and textures, plays a significant role in creating atmosphere. For example, dark and desaturated colors can evoke a sense of foreboding, while bright and vibrant colors may convey a cheerful atmosphere.
2. **Audio Design**: Sound effects, music, and ambient sounds are crucial in establishing atmosphere. The right audio cues can make players feel tense, relaxed, excited, or fearful.
3. **Environmental Details**: Pay attention to environmental details such as weather effects, particle systems, and weathered textures. These details can add depth and realism to the environment.
4. **Level Geometry**: The layout and structure of the level can influence atmosphere. Narrow corridors may create a sense of claustrophobia, while open spaces can make players feel free and unburdened.
5. **Narrative Integration**: Ensure that the atmosphere aligns with the narrative and theme of the level. The atmosphere should complement the story being told.

Examples of Environmental Storytelling

Let's look at some examples of environmental storytelling:

1. **Abandoned Laboratory**: In a post-apocalyptic game, players explore an abandoned laboratory. Broken test tubes, spilled chemicals, and flickering lights tell the story of a scientific experiment gone wrong without any explicit

exposition.

2. **Graffiti Messages**: In a cyberpunk cityscape, graffiti on walls can provide clues about the resistance movement, secret codes, or warnings about dangerous areas.
3. **Deserted Town**: A deserted town in a horror game may have eerie music, flickering streetlights, and scattered journals that reveal the town's history and the mysterious events that unfolded.

Balancing Environmental Storytelling and Gameplay

While environmental storytelling is a powerful technique, it must be balanced with gameplay considerations:

1. **Clarity**: Ensure that the environmental clues are clear enough for players to understand the narrative context without becoming frustrated or lost.
2. **Progression**: Integrate environmental storytelling seamlessly with gameplay progression. Players should not feel forced to explore but should be rewarded for doing so.
3. **Variety**: Mix environmental storytelling with other gameplay elements to maintain variety and engagement. A level entirely focused on storytelling may become monotonous.

Iterative Design and Player Feedback

As with other aspects of level design, environmental storytelling and atmosphere benefit from iterative design and playtesting:

1. **Testing**: Playtesters can provide valuable feedback on the effectiveness of environmental storytelling and the atmosphere. Listen to their impressions and adjust the level accordingly.

2. **Refinement**: Iteratively refine the level's environmental storytelling based on playtester feedback and observations. Small changes can significantly impact the player's experience.

In conclusion, environmental storytelling and atmosphere are essential tools in level design, enriching the player's narrative experience and immersion. By carefully crafting the details, visuals, audio, and layout of a level, designers can create environments that convey stories and evoke emotional responses. Balancing these elements with gameplay considerations and incorporating player feedback leads to well-crafted, atmospheric game levels that leave a lasting impact on players.

7.5 Level Testing and Player Feedback

Level testing and gathering player feedback are essential steps in the level design process. These processes help identify issues, fine-tune gameplay, and ensure that the level provides an enjoyable experience for players. In this section, we will explore the significance of level testing and how to effectively gather and utilize player feedback.

The Importance of Level Testing

Level testing is a crucial quality assurance step in game development. It serves several essential purposes:

1. **Bug Detection**: Testing helps uncover technical issues, glitches, or unexpected behaviors in the level. Identifying and resolving these problems is essential for a polished gaming experience.
2. **Balancing**: Testing allows designers to assess the level's difficulty, pacing, and balance. It ensures that the level

offers an appropriate challenge without being too easy or frustrating.

3. **Flow and Progression**: Playtesting helps evaluate the flow of the level, ensuring that players can navigate and progress through it logically and without confusion.
4. **Accessibility**: Testing helps identify accessibility issues, such as parts of the level that may be too difficult for certain players. This information can inform adjustments to improve accessibility.
5. **Player Experience**: Ultimately, level testing aims to enhance the overall player experience. A well-tested level is more likely to be engaging, enjoyable, and memorable.

Effective Playtesting

Effective playtesting involves a structured approach to ensure that valuable insights are gathered. Here are some key considerations for successful playtesting:

1. **Diverse Testers**: Enlist a diverse group of playtesters with varying levels of gaming experience. This diversity provides a range of perspectives and identifies issues that may affect different player types.
2. **Clear Objectives**: Define specific testing objectives. Are you testing a particular gameplay mechanic, a specific challenge, or the overall flow of the level? Clear objectives help focus testing efforts.
3. **Testing Phases**: Conduct testing in different phases of level development. Early testing can catch major issues, while later testing focuses on fine-tuning and polish.
4. **Feedback Collection**: Establish a systematic method for collecting feedback. This can include surveys, feedback forms, or in-person interviews with playtesters.

5. **Observation**: Observe playtesters as they navigate the level. Pay attention to their reactions, frustrations, and moments of enjoyment. These observations can provide valuable insights.
6. **Iteration**: Use the feedback gathered during playtesting to make iterative improvements to the level. Address identified issues and refine the design based on player input.

Tools and Resources for Playtesting

Several tools and resources can aid in the playtesting process:

1. **Playtesting Sessions**: Organize playtesting sessions with designated playtesters. These sessions can be in-person or remote, depending on the circumstances.
2. **Feedback Forms**: Create feedback forms or surveys that ask specific questions about the level. Questions can address difficulty, enjoyment, and any issues encountered.
3. **Recording Software**: Use recording software to capture gameplay sessions. This can be valuable for reviewing player actions, reactions, and identifying pain points.
4. **Analytics Tools**: Some game engines and platforms offer analytics tools that provide data on player behavior, such as where players struggle or quit. Utilize these tools to inform level adjustments.
5. **Beta Testing**: If possible, release a beta version of the game to a larger audience. This can uncover issues that may not surface in smaller-scale playtesting.

Handling Feedback

Handling player feedback effectively is crucial to improving the level. Here are some guidelines for managing feedback:

1. **Prioritization**: Prioritize feedback based on severity and impact. Address critical issues first, and then move on to smaller, less impactful improvements.
2. **Constructive Communication**: When providing feedback to playtesters, use a constructive and non-confrontational approach. Focus on solutions rather than criticism.
3. **Version Control**: Keep track of different versions of the level to compare changes and assess the impact of adjustments made based on feedback.
4. **Iterative Improvement**: Continue to iterate and test the level as changes are implemented. Ensure that adjustments have the desired effect on gameplay and player experience.

Conclusion

Level testing and player feedback are indispensable processes in level design. Effective testing helps identify issues, refine gameplay, and ensure that the level provides an enjoyable and engaging experience for players. By enlisting diverse playtesters, defining clear objectives, and utilizing various tools and resources, designers can gather valuable insights and make informed improvements to their levels. The iterative process of testing and adjustment ultimately leads to the creation of polished and memorable game levels.

Chapter 8: AI and Enemy Design

8.1 Basics of AI in Games

Artificial Intelligence (AI) in games is a dynamic field that empowers non-player characters (NPCs) and entities to behave intelligently and realistically within the game world. In this section, we will explore the fundamentals of AI in games, including its significance, common AI techniques, and the role it plays in creating engaging gameplay experiences.

The Significance of AI in Games

AI is a critical component of modern video games. It enhances the gameplay experience in various ways:

1. **Challenging Opponents**: AI-controlled enemies and opponents provide challenges for players. These enemies adapt, strategize, and make decisions to test the player's skills.
2. **NPC Behaviors**: NPCs in open-world games exhibit lifelike behaviors, such as wandering, social interactions, and realistic responses to the game world. This creates a more immersive environment.
3. **Storytelling**: AI can drive the game's narrative by controlling character interactions, dialogues, and story progression. AI-driven storytelling adds depth to the game's narrative.
4. **Dynamic Environments**: AI can control dynamic elements in the game world, such as weather patterns, traffic, and ecosystem simulations, making the world feel more alive.

5. **Player Assistance**: AI can assist players through tutorials, hints, and adaptive difficulty adjustments to ensure that players of varying skill levels can enjoy the game.

Common AI Techniques in Games

Game developers employ a range of AI techniques to achieve the desired behavior and challenge in games:

1. **Finite State Machines (FSM)**: FSMs are widely used for character behavior. An NPC can transition between predefined states (e.g., idle, patrolling, attacking) based on specific conditions.
2. **Pathfinding**: Pathfinding algorithms, like A* or Dijkstra's, enable NPCs to find the optimal path to reach a destination, avoiding obstacles and obstacles dynamically.
3. **Behavior Trees**: Behavior trees provide a hierarchical way to define complex NPC behaviors. Nodes in the tree represent actions or conditions, allowing for flexible and understandable AI design.
4. **Utility Theory**: Utility theory assesses the desirability of different actions based on their utility or benefit. It is used to make decisions in AI, considering factors like player proximity, health, and objectives.
5. **Machine Learning**: Machine learning techniques, such as neural networks and reinforcement learning, are increasingly used for adaptive AI that learns from player behavior and adjusts over time.

Enemy AI in Action

Enemy AI is a common application of AI in games. Let's consider a few examples of how enemy AI enhances gameplay:

1. **Combat Behavior**: Enemies in action games use AI to determine their combat tactics, such as taking cover, flanking, or retreating when injured.
2. **Stealth Games**: In stealth games, enemy AI is crucial. Enemies have routines, field of vision, and alertness levels that challenge players to remain undetected.
3. **Horror Games**: In horror games, AI controls the behavior of terrifying creatures, enhancing the tension and unpredictability of encounters.
4. **Strategy Games**: In strategy games, AI governs the decisions of computer-controlled factions, determining their resource management, troop movements, and strategies.

Designing Engaging AI

Creating engaging AI is an art that involves finding the right balance between challenge and fairness. Here are some tips for designing AI that enhances gameplay:

1. **Balanced Difficulty**: Ensure that the AI's skill level aligns with the player's progression in the game. Ramp up the AI's complexity as players become more skilled.
2. **Predictability vs. Surprise**: Strike a balance between making AI behaviors predictable enough for players to strategize and adding elements of surprise to keep gameplay fresh.
3. **Feedback**: Use feedback from playtesting to refine AI behavior. Playtesters can identify areas where AI may be too challenging or too predictable.
4. **Adaptation**: Consider implementing adaptive AI that learns from player actions. This can make the game more challenging for experienced players while accommodating

newcomers.

5. **Player Empowerment**: Ensure that AI challenges empower players to use their skills and creativity to overcome obstacles. Avoid situations where AI feels unfair or insurmountable.

Conclusion

AI is a fundamental component of modern video games that enhances gameplay, storytelling, and immersion. Understanding the basics of AI in games, including its significance, common techniques, and its role in enemy design, is crucial for game developers. Designing engaging AI involves striking a balance between challenge and fairness, adapting to player skills, and providing opportunities for player empowerment. Effective AI design contributes to the overall enjoyment and replayability of games.

8.2 Creating Simple Enemy Behaviors

Creating simple enemy behaviors is a foundational step in enemy design within game development. Simple enemy behaviors serve as building blocks for more complex AI systems and can enhance gameplay by providing challenges for players. In this section, we will explore how to design and implement basic enemy behaviors in games.

Behavior States and Transitions

A common approach to designing enemy behaviors is to use a finite state machine (FSM). In an FSM, an enemy has various states that represent its behavior, and transitions between these states occur based on certain conditions. Here are some typical states for enemies:

1. **Idle**: The enemy is not actively engaged in any action and may be patrolling or waiting for the player's presence.
2. **Chase**: When the player enters the enemy's detection radius, it transitions to the chase state. In this state, the enemy pursues the player.
3. **Attack**: Once in close proximity to the player, the enemy transitions to the attack state. It performs actions such as melee attacks or shooting in this state.
4. **Patrol**: Enemies can patrol predefined routes, and the patrol state dictates their behavior during this phase.
5. **Flee**: In certain situations, enemies may flee from the player or other threats. The flee state governs this behavior.
6. **Alert**: After spotting the player but not being in direct pursuit, enemies may enter an alert state. They may search the area for the player in this state.

Creating transitions between these states involves defining conditions. For instance, an enemy might transition from the idle state to the chase state when it detects the player within a certain radius.

Sensing and Perception

For enemies to respond to the player's presence, they must have a means of detecting the player. Sensing and perception systems play a vital role in this regard. Common elements include:

1. **Line of Sight**: Enemies may have a cone of vision, and if the player enters this cone, they become aware of the player's presence.
2. **Hearing**: Sound generated by the player, such as footsteps or gunfire, can attract enemies, even if the player is not within their line of sight.

3. **Proximity Sensors**: Enemies can use proximity sensors to detect the player's presence when they come within a certain range.
4. **Alarms and Communication**: Some enemies may alert others when they detect the player, leading to coordinated responses.

Implementing these sensing and perception systems often involves raycasting, trigger zones, or other techniques to determine when the player is within the enemy's awareness.

Decision-Making and Actions

Once an enemy detects the player and enters an active state like "chase" or "attack," it needs decision-making logic to determine its actions. Common decisions include:

1. **Navigation**: Enemies need to navigate the game world to reach the player. Pathfinding algorithms, like A* or Dijkstra's, help determine the best path.
2. **Attack Selection**: Based on the enemy's capabilities, it may choose different attacks or behaviors when engaging the player. For instance, a melee enemy might approach and strike, while a ranged enemy may maintain distance and shoot.
3. **Cover and Evasion**: Some enemies may use cover or attempt to evade the player's attacks to increase their chances of survival.
4. **Health and Damage**: Implement logic for tracking the enemy's health and applying damage when the player attacks. Determine the conditions for an enemy's defeat.

Testing and Balancing

Testing enemy behaviors is crucial to ensure they provide a balanced and enjoyable challenge for players. Consider the following aspects:

1. **Difficulty Levels**: Implement different difficulty levels that adjust enemy behaviors, such as reaction times, accuracy, and damage output.
2. **Playtesting**: Continuously playtest the game to gather feedback on enemy behaviors. This feedback can help identify issues and areas for improvement.
3. **Iterative Design**: Be prepared to iterate on enemy behaviors based on playtester feedback and observations. Small adjustments can have a significant impact on gameplay.
4. **AI Behavior Tweaking**: Fine-tune AI behavior parameters, such as detection ranges, attack cooldowns, or patrol routes, to achieve the desired level of challenge.

Conclusion

Creating simple enemy behaviors is a fundamental step in enemy design for games. It involves defining behavior states, transitions, and decision-making logic for enemies based on player interactions. Implementing sensing and perception systems, as well as testing and balancing, are critical aspects of ensuring that enemy behaviors enhance the gameplay experience and provide engaging challenges for players.

8.3 Advanced AI Techniques and Pathfinding

Advanced AI techniques and pathfinding play a crucial role in creating engaging and challenging gameplay experiences in video games. In this section, we will delve into more advanced AI concepts and explore the intricacies of pathfinding algorithms used by game characters and enemies.

Advanced AI Concepts

As games become more complex, so do the AI systems within them. Here are some advanced AI concepts commonly used in modern video games:

1. **Decision Trees**: Decision trees are hierarchical structures used to make complex decisions. Each node in the tree represents a decision point, and the branches represent possible choices. Decision trees allow for intricate decision-making in AI, such as determining enemy tactics or character behaviors.
2. **Behavior Trees**: Behavior trees are a more versatile extension of decision trees. They are used to create complex, state-driven AI behaviors. Behavior trees are especially useful for defining character behaviors in open-world or sandbox games.
3. **Goal-Oriented Action Planning (GOAP)**: GOAP is an AI technique that focuses on goal-driven behavior. Characters or NPCs using GOAP consider their current state, desired goals, and available actions to formulate a plan and execute it. This approach leads to dynamic and adaptive behaviors.
4. **Machine Learning**: Machine learning techniques, including neural networks and reinforcement learning, are increasingly used to create adaptive and learning AI. These AI systems can improve their performance over time by learning from player interactions.

Pathfinding Algorithms

Pathfinding is a core component of AI in games, enabling characters and enemies to navigate the game world intelligently. Several pathfinding algorithms are commonly used:

1. __A_ Algorithm_: *A* (pronounced “A-star”) is one of the most popular pathfinding algorithms. It uses a heuristic to estimate the cost of reaching a goal from a given point. A* is efficient and widely used in games for its accuracy and adaptability.
2. **Dijkstra’s Algorithm**: Dijkstra’s algorithm finds the shortest path between two points in a graph. While it is less efficient than A* in some cases, it guarantees the shortest path and is suitable for games where accuracy is essential.
3. **Breadth-First Search (BFS)**: BFS explores all possible paths outward from the starting point until it reaches the goal. It ensures that the shortest path is found in unweighted graphs but may be less efficient in complex environments.
4. **Depth-First Search (DFS)**: DFS explores paths as deeply as possible before backtracking. While not suitable for finding the shortest path, it can be useful for certain game scenarios.
5. **Navigation Mesh**: In complex 3D environments, navigation meshes or navmeshes are often used. These are precomputed representations of walkable areas in the game world, allowing characters to navigate efficiently.

Dynamic Pathfinding

In dynamic game worlds, where obstacles or conditions change over time, dynamic pathfinding is crucial. Here are some techniques for handling dynamic environments:

1. **Recast and Detour**: Recast and Detour is a popular library for dynamic pathfinding in 3D environments. It allows for real-time updates of navigation meshes to adapt to changing terrain.
2. **Local Avoidance**: Local avoidance algorithms, such as the Velocity Obstacle (VO) method or Reciprocal Velocity Obstacles (RVO), enable characters to avoid collisions with other moving entities dynamically.
3. **Grid-Based Approaches**: In grid-based games, dynamic obstacles can be represented as impassable grid cells. Algorithms like Jump Point Search (JPS) and Adaptive A* can efficiently handle dynamic grids.

Integration with Gameplay

To create compelling gameplay experiences, AI and pathfinding must seamlessly integrate with game mechanics. Here are some considerations for integration:

1. **Player Interaction**: AI should react to player actions and provide meaningful challenges. For example, enemies may adapt their tactics based on the player's behavior.
2. **Level Design**: AI and pathfinding should consider the layout and design of game levels. They should interact with environmental elements like cover, obstacles, and traps.
3. **Storytelling**: AI characters can play a significant role in advancing the game's narrative. Their behaviors and decisions can influence the story's progression.

4. **Balancing**: Balancing AI difficulty is essential to ensure that encounters remain challenging but not frustrating. Adjust AI behaviors and pathfinding to match the player's skill level.

Conclusion

Advanced AI techniques and pathfinding algorithms are integral to creating immersive and engaging gameplay experiences in modern video games. Game developers leverage decision trees, behavior trees, GOAP, and machine learning to create intelligent and adaptive AI. Pathfinding algorithms like A*, Dijkstra's, and navmeshes facilitate character navigation in complex game worlds. Dynamic pathfinding and integration with gameplay mechanics enhance the overall player experience, making AI and pathfinding vital components of game development.

8.4 Balancing AI Difficulty and Fairness

Balancing the difficulty of AI in video games is a critical aspect of game design. Players expect a challenging and enjoyable experience, but the AI should also be fair and not feel insurmountable. Achieving the right balance can greatly impact the overall player experience. In this section, we will explore how to balance AI difficulty effectively.

The Challenge of Balancing AI

Balancing AI difficulty can be a complex task because it depends on various factors, including the player's skill level, the game's genre, and the overall design. Here are some considerations:

1. **Player Skill**: Players of varying skill levels will play the game. Balancing should accommodate both newcomers

and experienced players.

2. **Genre**: The genre of the game plays a significant role. An action game may require different AI balancing than a puzzle or strategy game.
3. **Progression**: AI difficulty may need to ramp up gradually as players progress through the game. Early levels should be accessible, while later levels can challenge even skilled players.
4. **Fairness**: It's essential that AI does not feel unfair. Frustration can lead to a negative player experience. AI should provide opportunities for players to strategize and succeed.

Adjustable Difficulty Levels

One common approach to balancing AI difficulty is to implement adjustable difficulty levels. These levels can cater to different player preferences and skill levels. Common difficulty levels include:

1. **Easy**: In easy mode, AI opponents may have reduced accuracy, slower reaction times, or fewer hit points. This allows players to progress with minimal challenges.
2. **Normal**: Normal mode provides a balanced experience, where AI behaves according to the game's intended challenge level. It serves as a baseline for most players.
3. **Hard**: Hard mode increases the challenge by enhancing AI behaviors. Enemies may be more aggressive, accurate, or employ advanced tactics.
4. **Expert**: Expert mode is for highly skilled players seeking a significant challenge. AI in this mode can be extremely aggressive, precise, and strategic.
5. **Custom**: Some games offer a custom difficulty setting that allows players to tweak specific AI parameters, providing a

tailored experience.

Adaptive AI

Another approach to balancing AI difficulty is to make it adaptive. Adaptive AI can learn from the player's actions and adjust its behavior accordingly. Here are some techniques:

1. **Reinforcement Learning**: Implement reinforcement learning algorithms that reward the AI for making challenging decisions. Over time, the AI becomes better at responding to player strategies.
2. **Player Profiling**: Create player profiles based on behavior patterns. The AI can then adjust its tactics to match the player's preferred playstyle and skill level.
3. **Dynamic Scaling**: Use dynamic scaling to change AI parameters during gameplay. For example, if a player is struggling, the AI's accuracy or reaction times could be temporarily reduced.

Player Feedback and Iteration

Gathering player feedback through playtesting is crucial for balancing AI effectively. Playtesters can identify issues with AI difficulty and provide valuable insights. Here's how to approach player feedback:

1. **Surveys and Questionnaires**: Create surveys or questionnaires to collect feedback from playtesters. Ask about their perception of AI difficulty and any frustrating experiences.
2. **Observations**: Observe playtesters as they interact with the AI. Pay attention to moments of frustration or satisfaction.

3. **Iterative Design**: Be prepared to make iterative adjustments to AI difficulty based on player feedback. Small changes can have a significant impact on the player's experience.
4. **Beta Testing**: Conduct beta testing with a larger player base to gather feedback from a diverse range of players. This can help identify issues that playtesting may have missed.

Balancing AI Cheating

It's important to note that AI difficulty should not rely solely on giving AI opponents unfair advantages, also known as "cheating AI." While a minor degree of AI advantage can create challenge, it should not feel like the AI is breaking the rules of the game. Players generally prefer AI that operates within the same constraints as they do.

Conclusion

Balancing AI difficulty and fairness is a critical aspect of game design that greatly influences the player's experience. Adjustable difficulty levels cater to different player preferences, while adaptive AI can provide a personalized challenge. Player feedback and iteration are key to achieving the right balance, ensuring that the game remains engaging and enjoyable for a wide range of players. Balancing AI without resorting to unfair advantages is essential for maintaining player trust and satisfaction.

8.5 Integrating AI into Gameplay

Integrating AI into gameplay is a crucial aspect of game development, as it directly impacts the player's experience. Well-integrated AI can make a game more immersive, challenging, and enjoyable. In this section, we will explore various ways to seamlessly incorporate AI into different aspects of gameplay.

Enemy Behavior and Challenges

One of the most common uses of AI in gameplay is for controlling enemy behavior. Enemies can be more than mere obstacles; they can serve as dynamic challenges that adapt to the player's actions. Here are some considerations for integrating AI-driven enemy behavior:

1. **Adaptive Tactics**: Enemies can change their tactics based on the player's actions. For example, if the player relies on a particular strategy, enemies can adapt to counter it.
2. **Group Coordination**: AI-controlled enemies can coordinate their actions, making battles more dynamic and challenging. They can use flanking maneuvers, cover, and teamwork to engage the player.
3. **Boss Fights**: Boss characters often use advanced AI behaviors and have multiple phases. These fights can be memorable and engaging if AI-driven patterns change as the battle progresses.
4. **Stealth and Detection**: In stealth games, AI-controlled guards should have realistic detection behaviors. Their responses to sound, sight, and player actions should be consistent with the game's mechanics.

Non-Player Characters (NPCs)

NPCs play various roles in games, from quest givers to merchants. AI-driven NPCs can enhance immersion and provide depth to the game world:

1. **Conversations**: Implement AI for NPCs to engage in meaningful conversations with the player. They can

provide information, clues, or story progression.

2. **Schedules and Routines**: NPCs can follow schedules and routines, making the game world feel alive. They can go about their daily tasks, visit locations, or react to in-game events.
3. **Dynamic Quests**: NPCs can offer dynamic quests based on the player's actions or the state of the game world. AI can help generate quest objectives and determine rewards.
4. **Emotional States**: NPCs can have emotional states influenced by the game's events or the player's choices. AI can drive their reactions and interactions accordingly.

Companion AI

In games where players have companions or allies, companion AI is crucial for creating a sense of teamwork and camaraderie:

1. **Tactical Coordination**: Companion AI can follow the player's orders or adapt to the player's playstyle. They can provide support in combat, healing, or other roles.
2. **Relationship Systems**: Implement relationship systems that track the player's interactions with companions. AI can react to the player's choices and build trust or conflict.
3. **Story Integration**: Companions can be integral to the game's narrative. AI-driven character arcs and development can enrich the story.

Puzzles and Challenges

AI can be used to create dynamic puzzles and challenges that respond to the player's actions:

1. **Dynamic Puzzle Elements:** In puzzle games, AI can control puzzle elements that adapt to the player's progress.

Puzzles can become more complex as the player advances.

2. **Environmental Challenges**: In platformers or action-adventure games, AI can control environmental hazards that move or change based on the player's location.
3. **Randomization**: AI-driven randomization can add replay value by creating unique challenges each time a player attempts a level or quest.

AI Directors and Procedural Content

AI directors are responsible for controlling the pacing and difficulty of the game. They can dynamically adjust challenges and events:

1. **Difficulty Scaling**: AI directors can scale difficulty based on the player's performance, ensuring that the game remains challenging but not frustrating.
2. **Dynamic Events**: AI directors can trigger dynamic events or encounters based on the player's progress. This keeps the gameplay fresh and unexpected.
3. **Procedural Content Generation**: AI can generate procedural content, such as levels, maps, or quests. This approach adds replayability and diversity to the game.

User Experience and Accessibility

Consider AI's impact on the overall user experience and accessibility:

1. **Assistive AI**: Implement AI systems that assist players with disabilities, such as providing auditory cues for visually impaired players.
2. **Difficulty Options**: Provide various difficulty options to accommodate players of different skill levels.
3. **Tutorials and Hints**: Use AI-driven tutorials and hints to

help newcomers grasp the game's mechanics.

Conclusion

Integrating AI into gameplay is a multifaceted process that involves enhancing enemy behavior, creating dynamic NPCs, managing companion AI, designing puzzles and challenges, and controlling the game's pacing through AI directors. Effective AI integration can significantly impact a game's immersion, challenge, and overall player experience. It requires careful consideration of game design, mechanics, and player feedback to achieve a seamless and engaging gameplay experience.

9.1 Principles of UI Design in Games

User interface (UI) design in games plays a pivotal role in shaping the player's experience and interaction with the game world. Effective UI design not only ensures clarity and usability but also enhances immersion and engagement. In this section, we will delve into the principles of UI design specific to games.

Purpose of Game UI

Game UI serves several essential functions:

1. **Information Conveyance**: UI elements communicate vital information to the player, such as health, ammo, objectives, and character status. Clarity and readability are paramount.
2. **Interaction**: UI provides a means for players to interact with the game world, whether through menus, buttons, or in-game controls.
3. **Immersion**: Well-designed UI can enhance the player's immersion by seamlessly integrating with the game's theme

and aesthetics.

4. **Feedback**: UI elements give feedback on player actions, indicating the consequences of their choices and progress.
5. **Accessibility**: Game UI should be accessible to players of all abilities. It should consider color blindness, readability, and controller support.

Consistency and Theme

Consistency in UI design is crucial for creating a cohesive and polished game experience:

1. **Visual Consistency**: Maintain a consistent visual style throughout the UI. Use a unified color palette, typography, and iconography to create a cohesive look.
2. **Theme Integration**: The UI design should align with the game's theme and setting. For example, a fantasy game might use ornate, medieval-style UI elements, while a sci-fi game could feature futuristic designs.
3. **User Expectations**: Consider established UI conventions and standards in the gaming industry. Deviating too far from these norms can confuse players.

Clarity and Readability

UI elements should be clear and easily readable to avoid player frustration:

1. **Hierarchy**: Prioritize information based on importance. Essential elements like health bars or objective markers should be more prominent than secondary information.
2. **Font Choice**: Select fonts that are legible and fit the game's aesthetic. Avoid overly decorative or hard-to-read fonts.
3. **Contrast**: Ensure adequate contrast between text and

background to make text readable. Avoid using color combinations that may be difficult for color-blind players.

4. **Iconography**: Use intuitive icons and symbols to represent actions or information. Test them with players to ensure they are universally understood.

Usability and Player Interaction

User-friendly UI design is essential for a smooth gaming experience:

1. **Responsive Controls**: UI elements should respond promptly to player input. Buttons, menus, and navigation should feel intuitive and smooth.
2. **Minimize Clutter**: Avoid cluttering the screen with excessive UI elements. Keep it minimal and only display what is necessary at any given moment.
3. **Customization**: Offer UI customization options when possible. Allow players to adjust the HUD layout, opacity, and other preferences.
4. **Tooltips and Tutorials**: Use tooltips and tutorials to introduce players to UI elements and game mechanics gradually. Avoid overwhelming newcomers with complex UI elements early in the game.

Feedback and Animation

Effective UI provides feedback and enhances the player's sense of agency:

1. **Animations**: Use subtle animations to draw attention to important UI elements or to indicate transitions between game states. Avoid excessive or distracting animations.
2. **Audio Feedback**: Incorporate sound effects or audio cues that complement UI interactions. Sound can provide

valuable feedback, especially in situations like button presses or menu selections.

3. **Progress Indicators**: Display progress bars or visual cues when performing tasks, such as loading screens or character upgrades. This keeps players informed and engaged during wait times.

Accessibility and Inclusivity

Consider the needs of all players when designing game UI:

1. **Color Blindness**: Ensure that UI elements are distinguishable for players with color blindness. Use patterns, textures, or alternative color schemes to convey information.
2. **Text Size and Font**: Allow players to adjust text size and font options to accommodate those with visual impairments.
3. **Controller Support**: Ensure that the game's UI is accessible for players using different input devices, including controllers and keyboard/mouse setups.
4. **Subtitles and Localization**: Provide subtitles and localization options to cater to players who may have hearing impairments or speak different languages.

Conclusion

UI design in games is a multidimensional task that combines aesthetics, functionality, and accessibility. By following principles of consistency, clarity, usability, and inclusivity, game developers can create UIs that enhance player experiences, facilitate engagement, and contribute to the overall success of their games. Thoughtful UI design ensures that players can interact with the game world seamlessly, understand the game's mechanics, and stay immersed in the gaming experience.

9.2 Creating Menus, Buttons, and Panels

Menus, buttons, and panels are fundamental UI components in games, providing players with a means to navigate, make choices, and access various game features. In this section, we will explore how to design and implement these essential UI elements effectively.

Menus

Menus serve as the primary navigation interface in games, allowing players to access different game sections, configure settings, and manage their progress. Here are some considerations when designing and implementing menus:

1. **Main Menu**: The main menu is the first screen players see when starting the game. It should provide options for starting a new game, loading a saved game, adjusting settings, and exiting the game.
2. **Pause Menu**: In-game pause menus allow players to access settings, save their progress, or quit the game temporarily. Ensure that pausing the game feels seamless and responsive.
3. **Navigation**: Use clear and intuitive navigation mechanisms, such as arrow keys, WASD, or controller inputs, to navigate through menus. Consider adding visual cues like highlighting or animated transitions to guide the player's focus.
4. **Visual Feedback**: Highlight the selected menu item to provide visual feedback to the player. This can be done through color changes, outlines, or animations.
5. **Settings Menu**: Offer a settings menu that allows players

to customize audio, video, control, and gameplay options. Provide options for adjusting sound volume, screen resolution, and input preferences.

6. **Confirmation Prompts**: When players make significant choices, like quitting the game or starting a new game, use confirmation prompts to prevent accidental actions. Allow players to confirm or cancel their choices.

Buttons

Buttons are interactive UI elements used for making selections or triggering actions. Proper button design ensures usability and player engagement:

1. **Visual Design**: Buttons should stand out from the background and convey their function through visual cues. Use contrasting colors, shapes, and icons to make buttons recognizable.
2. **Text Labels**: Include descriptive text labels on buttons to indicate their purpose. Use clear and concise language to avoid ambiguity.
3. **Button States**: Buttons can have different states, such as normal, hover, and pressed. Provide distinct visual feedback for each state to enhance interactivity.
4. **Button Placement**: Position buttons consistently across menus to establish a predictable layout. Common button placements include the bottom right for confirmation and the bottom left for cancellation.
5. **Button Sounds**: Add sound effects to button interactions to provide auditory feedback to players. Sound can enhance the tactile feel of button presses.
6. **Button Interactivity**: Buttons should respond to player interactions promptly. Implement click or tap animations

to give players the feeling of physically interacting with the UI.

Panels

Panels are containers for grouping related UI elements, displaying information, and organizing content. They are used for various purposes, such as displaying character inventories, quest logs, or in-game maps:

1. **Layout and Organization**: Plan the layout of panels to ensure efficient use of screen space. Use grids, columns, or tabs to organize content logically.
2. **Transparency and Opacity**: Panels can be semi-transparent to maintain visibility of the game world while displaying information. Implement opacity settings to allow players to adjust panel visibility.
3. **Dynamic Panels**: Create panels that can be toggled on and off, allowing players to control when they access specific information or features. This keeps the screen uncluttered when the information is not needed.
4. **Resizable Panels**: In some cases, resizable panels can be beneficial. For instance, an inventory panel that can be expanded or collapsed based on the player's preference.
5. **Interactivity**: Panels may contain interactive elements, such as buttons, sliders, or checkboxes, for performing actions or adjusting settings within the panel.

Localization and Accessibility

Consider localization and accessibility when designing menus, buttons, and panels:

1. **Localization**: Ensure that all UI text and content can be

easily translated to different languages. Design UI elements with flexibility in mind to accommodate varying text lengths.

2. **Accessibility**: Make UI elements accessible to players with disabilities. Provide options for larger text, high contrast, and keyboard navigation. Use accessible color palettes and ensure that screen readers can interpret UI elements.

Conclusion

Creating menus, buttons, and panels in games requires careful consideration of usability, aesthetics, and accessibility. Well-designed UI elements enhance the player's experience by providing clear navigation, interactivity, and customization options. Whether it's the main menu, in-game buttons, or content panels, effective UI design is essential for creating a user-friendly and immersive gaming experience.

9.3 Designing an Effective HUD

The Heads-Up Display (HUD) is a crucial aspect of game UI design, providing players with real-time information about their character, surroundings, and game progress. An effective HUD enhances player immersion while conveying essential information. In this section, we will explore the principles and considerations for designing a successful HUD.

HUD Elements

HUD elements are typically displayed on the screen throughout gameplay. They include:

1. **Health and Vitality**: Display the player character's health or vitality, often using a visual representation like a health

bar or hearts. This element informs players of their character's well-being.

2. **Ammo and Resources**: If the game involves shooting or resource management, show the player's ammo count, inventory, or resource levels. This helps players make decisions during combat or exploration.
3. **Mini-Map**: Provide a mini-map to help players navigate the game world, locate objectives, and avoid getting lost. Mini-maps can include markers for points of interest and enemies.
4. **Objective Tracker**: Display the current objectives or quests, along with waypoints or markers pointing to the next goal. This keeps players on track and engaged with the game's narrative.
5. **Score and Progress**: Show the player's score, progress towards achievements, or completion percentage. This element provides feedback on the player's overall performance.
6. **Status Effects**: If the game includes status effects, buffs, or debuffs, indicate their presence and duration on the HUD. Players need to know their character's current condition.
7. **Character Information**: Display the player character's name, level, and other relevant information. This element can enhance player attachment to the character.

Design Principles

When designing a HUD, adhere to the following principles:

1. **Clarity**: Ensure that HUD elements are clear and easily readable. Use legible fonts, appropriate iconography, and color-coding to convey information. Prioritize important elements.

2. **Minimalism**: Avoid cluttering the screen with excessive HUD elements. Show only what is necessary to prevent distractions and maintain immersion.
3. **Opacity and Translucency**: Use opacity or translucency to make HUD elements semi-transparent. This allows players to see the game world behind the HUD, reducing obstruction.
4. **Customization**: Offer HUD customization options, allowing players to adjust its size, position, or opacity to suit their preferences.
5. **Dynamic Visibility**: Implement dynamic HUD elements that appear or disappear contextually. For example, display the health bar only during combat or the mini-map when exploring.
6. **Feedback Animation**: Use animations to provide feedback, such as health bar animations for damage or reload indicators for ammunition.

HUD Placement

Consider the placement of HUD elements to avoid obscuring critical gameplay elements:

1. **Health Bar**: Place the health bar near the character's avatar or close to the center of the screen, making it easy to monitor without shifting focus away from the action.
2. **Mini-Map**: Position the mini-map in a corner of the screen, often in the top right or left, so players can glance at it for navigation without blocking their view.
3. **Objective Tracker**: Keep the objective tracker at the top or bottom of the screen, displaying current objectives and waypoints without interfering with gameplay.
4. **Ammo and Resources**: Place the ammo/resource counter

near the weapon or inventory slot for quick reference.

5. **Status Effects**: Display status effects near the character's portrait or in a corner of the screen, ensuring they are visible but not distracting.

Consistency and Theming

Maintain visual consistency in the HUD design to ensure it aligns with the game's theme and aesthetics:

1. **Color Palette**: Use a color palette that complements the game's overall visuals. Consistent use of colors can reinforce the game's mood and style.
2. **Visual Style**: Ensure that HUD elements match the game's art style. For example, a futuristic game may have a high-tech, holographic HUD, while a fantasy game might feature ornate, medieval designs.
3. **Font and Typography**: Use fonts and typography that are in harmony with the game's theme. Avoid fonts that clash with the game's aesthetics.

HUD for Different Game Genres

The design of the HUD should align with the game's genre:

1. **First-Person Shooters (FPS)**: FPS games often feature minimalistic HUDs with weapon information, ammo counters, and health indicators. Immersion is a priority, so HUD elements are typically integrated into the game world or kept unobtrusive.
2. **Role-Playing Games (RPGs)**: RPGs may have more elaborate HUDs, including character statistics, inventory management, and quest tracking. The HUD should support the depth of gameplay and character development.

3. **Platformers**: Platformer games tend to have straightforward HUDs, displaying only essential information like character health and lives remaining. The focus is on gameplay and level exploration.

Conclusion

Designing an effective HUD is essential for delivering a seamless and immersive gaming experience. By following principles of clarity, minimalism, customization, and theming, game developers can create HUDs that enhance player immersion while providing vital information. The HUD should be consistent with the game's theme and genre, ensuring that it complements the overall visual and narrative style. Ultimately, a well-designed HUD enhances the player's connection to the game world and contributes to their enjoyment of the gameplay.

9.4 Scripting UI Elements and Interactions

Scripting UI elements and interactions is a fundamental aspect of game development that empowers developers to create dynamic and responsive user interfaces. In this section, we will explore the process of scripting UI elements and interactions, providing insights into how to make UI elements come to life.

UI Elements in Game Development

UI elements in games are often created using a combination of scripting languages and design tools. Some commonly used game engines, like Unity or Unreal Engine, provide visual UI editors that allow designers to create and arrange UI elements easily. However, these elements require scripting to make them functional.

Scripting Languages for UI

Different game engines use various scripting languages for UI scripting. Here are a few examples:

1. **Unity**: Unity uses C# for scripting UI elements. Developers can access and manipulate UI elements by attaching scripts to GameObjects representing UI elements.
2. **Unreal Engine**: Unreal Engine primarily uses Blueprints for visual scripting, including UI interactions. Designers can create UI functionality by connecting nodes in a visual scripting interface.
3. **GameMaker**: GameMaker uses its scripting language, GML (GameMaker Language), for UI scripting. Developers can create and manipulate UI elements using GML functions.

Creating UI Interactions

Creating interactions for UI elements involves defining how they respond to player input or other events. Here are the steps involved in scripting UI interactions:

1. **Accessing UI Elements**: In most game engines, UI elements are represented as objects or components. Developers need to access these objects to interact with them. This is typically done by referencing them in code using their unique identifiers or by finding them in the scene hierarchy.
2. **Event Handling**: UI interactions are often event-driven. This means that developers define how UI elements respond to specific events, such as button clicks, mouse hover, or key presses. Event handlers are functions or

methods that get executed when these events occur.

3. **Defining Behavior**: Developers need to script the behavior they want for the UI element in response to events. For example, clicking a button might trigger a function that opens a menu, changes the game state, or performs some other action.
4. **Conditional Logic**: UI interactions often involve conditional logic. Developers use if statements, switches, or other conditional constructs to determine how UI elements should behave under different circumstances. For example, a button might behave differently if the player has enough resources to purchase an item.

Example: Unity UI Button Click

Here's a simplified example in Unity using C# to script a UI button click interaction:

```
using UnityEngine;

using UnityEngine.UI;

public class ButtonController : MonoBehaviour

{

// Reference to the button UI element

public Button myButton;

void Start()

{

// Attach a function to the button's click event

myButton.onClick.AddListener(ButtonClick);
```

```
}

void ButtonClick()

{

// Define the behavior when the button is clicked

Debug.Log("Button clicked! Implement your action here.");

}

}
```

In this example, a reference to the button UI element is established, and a function (ButtonClick) is attached to the button's click event. When the button is clicked, the function is executed, logging a message to the console.

Debugging UI Scripts

Debugging UI scripts is a crucial part of the development process. Developers use debugging tools provided by the game engine to identify and fix issues in UI interactions. Debugging can involve checking variable values, inspecting the call stack, and testing UI elements in different scenarios to ensure they behave as expected.

Conclusion

Scripting UI elements and interactions is a fundamental skill for game developers. It allows for the creation of dynamic and engaging user interfaces that enhance the player's experience. By accessing UI elements, defining event handling, scripting behavior, and using conditional logic, developers can create interactive UIs that respond to player input and drive the game's functionality. Debugging is essential to ensure that UI scripts work as intended, and it's a vital part of the development process.

9.5 User Experience and Accessibility Considerations

User experience (UX) and accessibility are critical aspects of game development that impact how players interact with and enjoy your game. In this section, we will explore the importance of UX and accessibility considerations in creating inclusive and enjoyable gaming experiences.

User Experience (UX) in Games

User experience refers to the overall experience a player has while interacting with a game, encompassing everything from the interface and controls to the gameplay and storytelling. Here are some key UX considerations in game development:

1. **Intuitive Controls**: Ensure that controls are easy to learn and use. Players should be able to pick up the game and start playing without encountering steep learning curves.
2. **Clear Feedback**: Provide clear and immediate feedback for player actions. Visual, auditory, and haptic feedback can enhance player understanding and immersion.
3. **Balanced Gameplay**: Strive for balanced gameplay that offers a challenge without being overly frustrating. Game difficulty should progress gradually, allowing players to improve their skills.
4. **Narrative Flow**: Craft a compelling narrative that engages players and keeps them invested in the game world and its characters.
5. **Performance Optimization**: Optimize the game's

performance to ensure smooth gameplay on a variety of hardware. Lag or stuttering can negatively impact the user experience.

6. **Player Progression**: Implement a sense of progression, whether through character growth, story development, or unlocking new content. This keeps players motivated and invested in the game.

Accessibility in Games

Accessibility in games refers to making games playable and enjoyable by a wide range of players, including those with disabilities. Game developers have a responsibility to create games that are accessible to as many people as possible. Here are some accessibility considerations:

1. **Visual Accessibility**: Provide options for colorblind players, including alternative color schemes or symbols to distinguish elements. Ensure that text is readable, and allow for text size adjustments.
2. **Hearing Accessibility**: Include subtitles or closed captions for dialogue and important audio cues. Provide options for adjusting audio settings, including volume levels and audio balance.
3. **Motor Accessibility**: Design controls and interfaces to be accessible for players with motor impairments. This may involve customizable controls, slower input requirements, or support for alternative input devices.
4. **Cognitive Accessibility**: Avoid using overly complex puzzles or mechanics that may be challenging for some players. Provide hints or accessibility modes for difficult sections.
5. **UI Accessibility**: Ensure that all UI elements are navigable

with keyboard or controller inputs. Implement keyboard shortcuts and offer clear tooltips and descriptions for UI elements.

6. **Testing with Diverse Audiences**: Conduct playtesting with diverse groups of players, including those with disabilities, to identify and address accessibility issues.

Inclusive Game Design

Inclusive game design goes beyond meeting accessibility requirements; it aims to create games that are welcoming and enjoyable for everyone. Here are some principles of inclusive game design:

1. **Representation**: Include diverse characters and storylines that reflect the real world. Representation matters, and players from different backgrounds should see themselves in the game.
2. **Inclusive Language**: Use language that is inclusive and avoids stereotypes or offensive content. Promote positive and respectful communication within the game community.
3. **Community Moderation**: Implement effective community moderation systems to prevent harassment and toxic behavior. Create a safe and welcoming online environment for players.
4. **Customization**: Allow players to customize their experience. This includes character customization, difficulty settings, and UI adjustments.
5. **Player Feedback**: Listen to player feedback and make improvements based on their input. Engage with the player community to understand their needs and preferences.

Legal and Ethical Considerations

Game developers should also consider legal and ethical aspects of game design:

1. **Privacy**: Respect players' privacy and data protection regulations. Collect only necessary user data and provide clear privacy policies.
2. **Monetization Ethics**: Implement fair and ethical monetization practices, avoiding exploitative microtransactions or pay-to-win mechanics.
3. **Content Ratings**: Comply with content ratings and age restrictions to ensure that games are suitable for their intended audience.
4. **Representation and Diversity**: Be mindful of cultural sensitivities and avoid harmful stereotypes or cultural appropriation in game content.

Conclusion

User experience and accessibility considerations are essential in creating inclusive and enjoyable gaming experiences. Game developers have a responsibility to make games that are accessible to a wide range of players and to promote positive and respectful interactions within the gaming community. By focusing on intuitive controls, clear feedback, balanced gameplay, accessibility features, and inclusive design, developers can create games that are not only entertaining but also welcoming to players of all backgrounds and abilities. Additionally, legal and ethical considerations should be a part of the development process to ensure that games are both enjoyable and responsible forms of entertainment.

10. Multiplayer and Networking

10.1 Basics of Networked Gaming

Multiplayer gaming and networked gameplay have become an integral part of the modern gaming experience. Whether you're developing a cooperative online game, a competitive eSport, or a social mobile game, understanding the basics of networked gaming is essential. In this section, we'll explore the fundamentals of networked gaming, including networking models, server-client architecture, and synchronization.

Why Networked Gaming?

Networked gaming allows players to interact with each other in real-time, transcending geographical boundaries. It enables collaborative gameplay, competitions, and social interactions that are at the core of many popular games. Here are some key reasons why networked gaming is significant:

1. **Multiplayer Experience**: Networked gaming offers a truly multiplayer experience, allowing players to team up, compete, or socialize with others, enhancing player engagement.
2. **Global Reach**: Games with networked features can reach a global audience, expanding the game's community and potential player base.
3. **Live Updates**: Online multiplayer games can receive live updates and patches, keeping the game fresh and addressing issues quickly.
4. **eSports**: Competitive gaming and eSports have gained popularity, with online multiplayer games at their core.

These events attract large audiences and offer opportunities for professional gaming careers.

Networking Models

There are different networking models for multiplayer games, each with its strengths and limitations:

1. **Peer-to-Peer (P2P)**:

- In P2P networking, players connect directly to each other without a dedicated server.

- It's suitable for small-scale games with a limited number of players.

- P2P can be more challenging to implement for larger games due to synchronization issues and potential cheating.

1. **Client-Server**:

- The client-server model involves a central game server that manages game state and communication between players.

- It's well-suited for games of all sizes and provides better control over game logic and security.

- Client-server models require robust server infrastructure.

1. **Hybrid Models**:

– Some games use hybrid models, combining elements of P2P and client-server approaches.

– This allows for flexibility in handling different aspects of gameplay and can optimize network resources.

Server-Client Architecture

In client-server architecture, the game server is the central authority responsible for managing game state, player interactions, and enforcing game rules. Clients are player devices that connect to the server to send and receive data.

Key roles of the server in a server-client architecture:

1. **Game State Management**: The server maintains the authoritative game state, which prevents cheating and ensures consistency across all clients.
2. **Player Authentication**: Servers authenticate players and authorize their actions within the game.
3. **Data Synchronization**: The server synchronizes player actions, positions, and game events, ensuring that all clients have the same view of the game.
4. **Security**: Servers implement security measures to prevent hacks, cheats, and unauthorized access.

Synchronization Challenges

Networked gaming introduces synchronization challenges that developers must address:

1. **Latency**: Network latency can lead to delays in data transmission, affecting real-time gameplay. Techniques like lag compensation and prediction help mitigate this.

2. **Packet Loss**: Data packets can be lost or arrive out of order during transmission. Robust error handling and retransmission mechanisms are necessary.
3. **Cheating**: Players may attempt to cheat by manipulating game data or exploiting vulnerabilities in the network protocol. Implementing server-side validation and security measures is crucial.
4. **Bandwidth**: Network bandwidth limitations can impact the amount of data that can be transmitted. Efficient data compression and optimization are essential.

Conclusion

Understanding the basics of networked gaming is essential for game developers looking to create multiplayer and online experiences. Choosing the right networking model, implementing a server-client architecture, and addressing synchronization challenges are critical steps in delivering a smooth and enjoyable multiplayer gaming experience. Whether you're developing a small-scale cooperative game or a large-scale competitive eSport, networked gaming can open up new possibilities and engage players on a global scale.

10.2 Setting Up Multiplayer in GameMaker

Setting up multiplayer functionality in GameMaker is an exciting but challenging endeavor that can greatly enhance the gaming experience. Multiplayer games allow players to interact with each other in real-time, creating dynamic and competitive environments. In this section, we'll explore the process of setting up multiplayer functionality in GameMaker, including network synchronization, server-client architecture, and common multiplayer game features.

Understanding Multiplayer Networking

Multiplayer networking involves multiple players connecting to a central server or directly to each other. GameMaker supports both client-server and peer-to-peer (P2P) networking models, allowing you to choose the most suitable approach for your game.

1. **Client-Server Model**: In the client-server model, one player acts as the server, managing the game state and communicating with all other players (clients). This model is suitable for games with a central authority and is often used for large-scale multiplayer games.
2. **Peer-to-Peer (P2P) Model**: In P2P networking, all players connect directly to each other, with no central server. This model is typically used for smaller games with fewer players.

Setting Up a GameMaker Server

To set up a server in GameMaker, you'll need to create a GameMaker project that acts as the server application. The server manages game logic, synchronizes player actions, and enforces game rules. Here are the key steps:

1. **Create a Server Project**: Create a new GameMaker project that will serve as your game's server. In this project, you'll implement the server-side logic and networking code.
2. **Networking Functions**: GameMaker provides networking functions to facilitate communication between clients and the server. You can use functions like network_create_server to create a server instance and network_send_packet to send data to clients.
3. **Game Logic**: Implement the game's logic on the server

side. This includes managing game state, handling player actions, and enforcing rules. Ensure that the server's decisions are authoritative and cannot be tampered with by clients.

4. **Synchronization**: Use synchronization techniques like sending and receiving game packets to keep all clients and the server in sync. This includes updating player positions, game events, and any relevant game data.
5. **Security**: Implement security measures on the server to prevent cheating, unauthorized access, and data manipulation. Validate client actions and protect sensitive game data.

Setting Up GameMaker Clients

Clients in a GameMaker multiplayer game are player devices that connect to the server. Each client runs a copy of the game and communicates with the server to synchronize game state and player actions. Here's how to set up GameMaker clients:

1. **Create Client Projects**: Create individual GameMaker projects for each client. These projects will represent the player's game instances.
2. **Networking Functions**: Use networking functions in GameMaker to establish connections with the server, send and receive data, and synchronize game state.
3. **Player Input**: Handle player input and interactions within the client projects. Send player actions to the server for validation and synchronization.
4. **Client-Server Communication**: Implement communication with the server to update game state, receive updates from other players, and receive authoritative responses to player actions.

Common Multiplayer Features

Multiplayer games often include various features to enhance gameplay and player interaction. Some common features to consider when setting up multiplayer in GameMaker include:

1. **Lobbies and Matchmaking**: Create systems for players to find and join games, form parties, and matchmake with others.
2. **Chat and Communication**: Implement chat systems to allow players to communicate with each other in real-time.
3. **Leaderboards and Rankings**: Track and display player rankings, scores, and achievements to foster competition.
4. **Anti-Cheat Measures**: Integrate anti-cheat mechanisms to detect and prevent cheating behaviors.
5. **Spectator Mode**: Add the ability for players to spectate ongoing matches or games.

Testing and Debugging

Testing multiplayer functionality is crucial. Use GameMaker's debugging tools, log messages, and test environments to simulate multiplayer scenarios. Involve playtesters to identify issues, test latency, and assess overall gameplay quality.

Conclusion

Setting up multiplayer functionality in GameMaker can be a complex but rewarding process. It allows you to create engaging multiplayer experiences that bring players together in real-time gameplay. By understanding networking models, implementing server-client architecture, and adding common multiplayer features, you can develop exciting multiplayer games that cater to a wide audience. Remember to prioritize security, synchronization, and testing to ensure a smooth and enjoyable multiplayer gaming experience.

10.3 Synchronizing Game States

Synchronizing game states in a multiplayer game is a critical aspect of ensuring that all players have a consistent and fair gaming experience. In this section, we'll delve into the importance of game state synchronization, the challenges it presents, and strategies for achieving synchronization in GameMaker.

The Significance of Game State Synchronization

Game state synchronization involves making sure that all players in a multiplayer game are on the same page regarding the game's current state. This includes player positions, game events, object states, and more. Synchronization is essential for the following reasons:

1. **Fair Gameplay**: Synchronization ensures that all players see the same game state, preventing situations where one player perceives a different game reality than others.
2. **Cheating Prevention**: It helps prevent cheating, as the server can validate and enforce game rules and actions, ensuring that no player gains an unfair advantage.
3. **Consistency**: Achieving synchronization leads to a consistent and enjoyable gaming experience, regardless of a player's location or device.

Challenges in Synchronization

Synchronizing game states in multiplayer games can be challenging due to various factors:

1. **Latency**: Network latency can lead to delays in data

transmission. Players may perceive actions differently based on their network connection, making synchronization crucial.

2. **Packet Loss**: Data packets may be lost during transmission, requiring reliable methods for retransmitting and confirming data.
3. **Server Authority**: Determining the authoritative source of game state is essential. The server should act as the authority to prevent cheating.
4. **Object Interactions**: Synchronizing interactions between objects and players can be complex, especially in fast-paced multiplayer games.

Strategies for Achieving Synchronization

To achieve synchronization in GameMaker, consider the following strategies:

1. **Server Authority**: Design your game so that the server has the final say on game state. Clients send input to the server, which validates and updates the game state accordingly.
2. **Prediction**: Use prediction algorithms to reduce the impact of latency. Clients can predict the outcome of actions before receiving updates from the server, creating a smoother experience.
3. **Client Interpolation**: Implement client-side interpolation to smooth out visual discrepancies caused by latency. This technique can make player movements appear more fluid.
4. **Dead Reckoning**: Use dead reckoning to estimate the future position of objects or players based on their current state and input. This helps reduce the effects of latency.
5. **Server Reconciliation**: Implement server reconciliation to ensure that player actions are validated by the server. If

actions conflict with the server's view, corrective actions can be taken.

6. **State Serialization**: Serialize game state data into packets for transmission. Use reliable network protocols to ensure data integrity.
7. **Networked Variables**: GameMaker offers networked variables that can be used to synchronize specific game data between clients and the server.
8. **Lag Compensation**: Consider implementing lag compensation techniques to account for latency when evaluating actions, ensuring fairness.

Code Example: Networked Variables in GameMaker

```
// Server script to update a networked variable

if (network_is_server()) {

synced_variable = some_value;

}

// Client script to read a networked variable

if (network_is_client()) {

some_value = synced_variable;

}
```

In this code example, a networked variable called synced_variable is updated on the server and read on the client. This allows the server to communicate game state changes to all clients effectively.

Testing and Debugging

Testing synchronization in multiplayer games is crucial. Simulate various network conditions, including high latency and packet loss, during playtesting. Use debug tools and log messages to track and troubleshoot synchronization issues.

Conclusion

Synchronizing game states in multiplayer games is a complex but essential aspect of creating a fair and enjoyable gaming experience. By understanding the challenges posed by latency, packet loss, and server authority and implementing strategies like prediction, interpolation, and dead reckoning, you can ensure that all players are in sync and have a consistent view of the game world. GameMaker provides tools like networked variables to aid in synchronization, but thorough testing and debugging are necessary to identify and address synchronization issues effectively.

10.4 Handling Latency and Bandwidth Issues

Handling latency and bandwidth issues is a crucial aspect of developing multiplayer games in GameMaker. Latency, which refers to the delay between sending data and receiving a response, and limited bandwidth can impact the gameplay experience. In this section, we'll explore strategies for managing latency and bandwidth to create a smoother and more responsive multiplayer gaming experience.

Understanding Latency

Latency, often referred to as ping, is the time it takes for data to travel between a player's device (client) and the game server. High latency can lead to delayed responses and visual discrepancies in a multiplayer game. Common causes of latency include:

- **Distance**: The physical distance between the player and the game server can contribute to higher latency.
- **Network Congestion**: Heavy internet traffic or network congestion can result in increased latency.
- **Wireless Connections**: Wireless connections, compared to wired connections, may introduce more latency.

Strategies for Latency Mitigation

Mitigating latency is essential for creating a responsive multiplayer gaming experience:

1. **Server Location**: Choose server locations strategically to minimize latency for the majority of players. Hosting servers in multiple regions can help reduce latency disparities.
2. **Client-Side Prediction**: Implement client-side prediction to make gameplay appear smoother despite latency. Players' actions are predicted locally before server confirmation, reducing the perception of delay.
3. **Lag Compensation**: Use lag compensation techniques to account for latency when validating player actions. This ensures that actions are evaluated fairly, regardless of latency.
4. **Interpolation**: Apply interpolation to smooth out the movement of players and objects. Interpolation calculates intermediate positions between server updates, reducing visual choppiness caused by latency.

Understanding Bandwidth Limitations

Bandwidth refers to the amount of data that can be transmitted over a network connection within a given time frame. Limited bandwidth can lead to slow updates and potential lag in multiplayer games. Bandwidth constraints can result from:

- **Low-Data Connections**: Some players may have low-data connections, limiting the amount of data they can send and receive.

- **Shared Networks**: Players sharing network connections with others may experience reduced available bandwidth.

Strategies for Bandwidth Optimization

Optimizing bandwidth usage is crucial for accommodating players with limited bandwidth:

1. **Data Compression**: Compress data packets before transmission to reduce the amount of data sent over the network. Decompress data on the receiving end.
2. **Prioritization**: Prioritize essential game data to ensure that critical updates are transmitted even under bandwidth constraints. Non-essential data can be delayed or sent less frequently.
3. **Delta Compression**: Implement delta compression to send only the changes in game state since the last update. This reduces the volume of data transmitted.
4. **Client-Side Effects**: Offload certain effects and calculations to the client side to reduce the amount of data that needs to be sent from the server.

Code Example: Data Compression in GameMaker

```
// Compress data before sending

var data_to_send = some_data;

var compressed_data = buffer_compress(buffer_create(1024, buffer_grow, 1), data_to_send);

// Decompress received data

var received_data = buffer_decompress(received_buffer);
```

In this code example, data is compressed using GameMaker's buffer_compress function before transmission and decompressed using buffer_decompress on the receiving end.

Testing and Optimization

Testing under different network conditions is essential to ensure that latency and bandwidth management strategies are effective. Simulate high latency and low bandwidth scenarios during testing to identify potential issues. Monitor network usage to optimize data transmission further.

Conclusion

Managing latency and bandwidth issues is vital for creating multiplayer games that offer a smooth and responsive gaming experience for all players. By understanding the causes of latency, implementing strategies like client-side prediction and lag compensation, and optimizing bandwidth usage through data compression and prioritization, you can minimize the impact of network limitations. Thorough testing and optimization are key to ensuring that your multiplayer game performs well under various network conditions, providing an enjoyable gaming experience for players.

10.5 Designing for Multiplayer Experiences

Designing multiplayer experiences in GameMaker involves creating gameplay elements and features that enhance player interaction, engagement, and enjoyment in a multiplayer setting. In this section, we'll explore key principles and considerations for designing multiplayer games in GameMaker.

1. Player Interaction and Cooperation

Promote Social Interaction: Multiplayer games thrive on player interaction. Design features that encourage players to communicate, cooperate, and strategize together. This can include team-based objectives, in-game chat, or cooperative gameplay mechanics.

Balancing Competition and Cooperation: Depending on your game's genre, find the right balance between competition and cooperation. Some games may emphasize teamwork, while others focus on competitive gameplay.

2. Matchmaking and Player Progression

Effective Matchmaking: Implement a matchmaking system that pairs players of similar skill levels or experience. Fair matchups enhance player engagement and reduce frustration.

Player Progression: Consider incorporating player progression systems such as leveling up, earning rewards, or unlocking new content. This provides long-term motivation for players to continue participating in multiplayer matches.

3. Game Modes and Variety

Diverse Game Modes: Offer a variety of game modes to cater to different player preferences. This can include modes like team-based battles, free-for-alls, and objective-based missions.

Customization Options: Allow players to customize their multiplayer experiences. This can involve character customization, loadout choices, or cosmetic items.

4. Feedback and Communication

Feedback Mechanisms: Provide clear and informative feedback to players during multiplayer matches. Inform them of their progress, achievements, and objectives.

Communication Tools: Implement communication tools such as in-game chat, voice chat, or quick communication commands. Effective communication is crucial in team-based multiplayer games.

5. Fairness and Anti-Cheat Measures

Fairness: Design your game with fairness in mind. Ensure that gameplay is balanced and that no player has an unfair advantage. Implement anti-cheat measures to maintain a fair playing field.

Reporting and Moderation: Include reporting and moderation systems to address player misconduct, harassment, or cheating. Create a positive and respectful gaming environment.

6. Accessibility and Inclusivity

Accessibility Options: Consider accessibility options to make your multiplayer game inclusive for players with disabilities. Provide customizable controls, text-to-speech features, and colorblind-friendly options.

Diverse Representation: Promote diversity and inclusivity in character design, avatars, and storytelling. Ensure that players from various backgrounds feel represented and welcome.

7. Playtesting and Player Feedback

Playtesting: Conduct extensive playtesting with a diverse group of players. Gather feedback on gameplay, balance, and overall multiplayer experience.

Iterate Based on Feedback: Use player feedback to iterate on your game's design. Address issues, make improvements, and refine the multiplayer experience based on real player experiences.

8. Network Stability and Performance

Server Reliability: Ensure that your game's servers are reliable and can handle player loads. Downtime and server issues can frustrate players.

Performance Optimization: Optimize your game's performance to reduce lag and improve responsiveness. Consider factors like server tick rates and network code efficiency.

Code Example: Implementing a Matchmaking System

```
// Pseudo-code for implementing a simple matchmaking system

if (player_searching_for_match) {

var suitable_match = find_suitable_match();
```

```
if (suitable_match != noone) {

// Match found, connect players

connect_players(player, suitable_match);

}

}
```

This code example demonstrates a simplified matchmaking system where players searching for a match are paired with suitable opponents. The find_suitable_match function searches for a player with a similar skill level, ensuring fair matchups.

Conclusion

Designing multiplayer experiences in GameMaker requires a thoughtful approach that prioritizes player interaction, fairness, and engagement. By considering principles such as effective matchmaking, player progression, game mode variety, and communication tools, you can create multiplayer games that captivate and entertain players. Continuous playtesting, feedback integration, and attention to network stability and performance are key to refining and delivering enjoyable multiplayer experiences.

Chapter 11: Mobile Game Development

11.1 Adapting Games for Mobile Platforms

Mobile game development has become an essential aspect of the gaming industry due to the widespread use of smartphones and tablets. Adapting games for mobile platforms requires a thoughtful approach to ensure a seamless and enjoyable gaming experience for users on smaller touchscreens. In this section, we will explore the key considerations and strategies for successfully adapting your games to mobile devices.

Understanding the Mobile Gaming Landscape

Before diving into the technical aspects, it's crucial to understand the unique characteristics of mobile gaming. Mobile gamers often seek quick, casual experiences that they can enjoy in short bursts. This preference for bite-sized gaming sessions should influence your game's design and mechanics.

Touch Controls and Mobile UI

One of the fundamental differences between mobile and traditional gaming platforms is the input method. Mobile devices rely on touchscreens, which offer both opportunities and challenges. Designing intuitive touch controls and a user-friendly mobile user interface (UI) is paramount. Consider the following tips:

- **Gestures**: Leverage gestures like swiping, tapping, and pinching to create intuitive controls.

- **On-Screen Buttons**: Implement on-screen buttons sparingly and ensure they are well-placed and responsive.

- **Responsive Design**: Adapt your game's UI to various screen sizes and orientations to provide a consistent experience.

Performance Optimization for Mobile

Mobile devices vary significantly in terms of hardware capabilities. To ensure your game runs smoothly on a wide range of devices, optimize its performance:

- **Graphics**: Use efficient rendering techniques and consider lower-poly 3D models or 2D sprites for less powerful devices.

- **Battery Consumption**: Minimize battery drain by optimizing resource usage and offering power-saving options.

- **Loading Times**: Implement loading screens and asynchronous asset loading to reduce initial load times.

Publishing and Monetizing Mobile Games

Publishing your mobile game involves considerations like choosing the right app stores (e.g., Apple App Store, Google Play Store), creating compelling store listings, and setting an effective pricing strategy. Monetization methods such as in-app purchases, ads, and premium pricing should align with your game's design and target audience.

Case Studies: Successful Mobile Games with

GameMaker

To gain insights into effective mobile game development with GameMaker, we will examine a few successful case studies. These examples will showcase how developers leveraged the platform's features to create engaging and profitable mobile games.

1. **Example 1: "Mobile Match-3 Puzzle Game"**: This game achieved success by focusing on addictive gameplay, rewarding in-app purchases, and a visually appealing UI that was easy to navigate on mobile devices.
2. **Example 2: "Endless Runner Adventure"**: The developer of this endless runner optimized performance for a wide range of devices, regularly updated the game with new content, and monetized through ads and in-game purchases.
3. **Example 3: "Casual Mobile Strategy Game"**: This case study highlights the importance of user-friendly touch controls, frequent updates, and community engagement in building a loyal player base.

Adapting your game for mobile platforms requires careful planning and execution. By considering the unique characteristics of mobile gaming, optimizing performance, and following successful examples, you can create mobile games that resonate with a broad audience.

11.2 Touch Controls and Mobile UI Design

Mobile game development requires special attention to touch controls and user interface (UI) design, as these aspects significantly impact the player's experience. In this section, we will delve into best practices for implementing touch controls and creating an effective mobile UI.

Intuitive Touch Controls

Creating intuitive touch controls is crucial for mobile games. Unlike traditional controllers or keyboards, touchscreens offer a different interaction paradigm. Here are some tips for designing touch controls:

- **Minimize Complexity**: Keep controls simple and avoid cluttering the screen with too many buttons or gestures. Consider context-sensitive controls.

- **Responsive Feedback**: Ensure that touch controls provide visual or tactile feedback when tapped or swiped. This feedback helps players understand that their actions are registered.

- **Customizable Controls**: Allow players to customize the control layout or sensitivity to cater to individual preferences.

```
// Example of implementing a simple touch control for character movement in GameMaker using GML:

if (touch) {

// Get the touch position

var touch_x = touch_x[0];

var touch_y = touch_y[0];

// Check if the touch is on the left or right half of the screen

if (touch_x < display_get_width() / 2) {

// Move the character left
```

```
character_x -= character_speed;

} else {

// Move the character right

character_x += character_speed;

}

}
```

Mobile-Friendly UI Design

A well-designed mobile UI enhances the overall user experience. Consider the following principles:

- **Responsive Layout**: Design UI elements that adapt to different screen sizes and orientations. Use relative positioning and scaling.
- **Thumb-Friendly Interaction**: Place important UI elements within easy reach of the player's thumbs to minimize discomfort during prolonged gameplay.
- **Clear Icons and Labels**: Use easily recognizable icons and clear labels to convey the purpose of UI elements. Avoid small text that might be difficult to read on small screens.

```
// Example of scaling UI elements based on screen size in GameMaker using GML:

// Calculate the scaling factor based on the screen resolution
```

```
var scale_factor = display_get_width() / 1920; // Assuming a design resolution of 1920x1080

// Scale the button's size and position

button_width *= scale_factor;

button_height *= scale_factor;

button_x *= scale_factor;

button_y *= scale_factor;
```

Testing and Iteration

Testing your touch controls and UI design on a variety of real mobile devices is crucial. Emulators can only simulate so much, and actual user feedback can help you identify usability issues. Be prepared to iterate and refine your touch controls and UI based on user testing and feedback.

Accessibility Considerations

Lastly, consider accessibility in your mobile game. Ensure that your touch controls and UI are accessible to players with disabilities. Provide options for colorblind modes, alternative control schemes, and adjustable font sizes.

By following these guidelines and continuously refining your touch controls and UI, you can create a mobile game that provides a smooth and enjoyable experience for players on various mobile devices.

11.3 Performance Optimization for Mobile

Performance optimization is a critical aspect of mobile game development. Mobile devices come in various hardware configurations, so ensuring your game runs smoothly on all of them is essential for a positive user experience. In this section, we'll explore key strategies for optimizing performance in mobile games.

Graphics Optimization

Graphics are often a significant contributor to performance issues in mobile games. To optimize graphics:

- **Resolution and Textures**: Use lower-resolution textures when possible to reduce memory usage. Consider using texture atlases to minimize draw calls.

- **Level of Detail (LOD)**: Implement LOD techniques for 3D models to decrease the level of detail as objects move away from the camera.

- **Culling**: Implement frustum and occlusion culling to avoid rendering objects that are not visible on the screen.

```
// Example of LOD implementation in GameMaker using GML:

if (distance_to_camera > threshold_distance) {

// Switch to a lower-detail model or reduce texture quality

switch_to_low_detail();

}
```

Battery Consumption

Mobile games should be mindful of battery consumption. High CPU and GPU usage can drain the device's battery quickly. To optimize battery usage:

- **Background Processes**: Minimize background processes when the game is in the background or not actively played to conserve power.

- **Resource Management**: Efficiently manage resources like textures, sounds, and animations to reduce unnecessary loading and processing.

- **Optimize Update Loops**: Adjust your game's update rate based on the device's capabilities. Lower-end devices may benefit from lower update rates to save power.

```
// Example of adjusting the update rate in GameMaker using GML:

if (device_is_low_power()) {

// Reduce the game's update rate

game_set_speed(30);

}
```

Loading and Streaming

Loading times can frustrate players, so optimizing them is crucial:

- **Asynchronous Loading**: Implement asynchronous asset loading to avoid freezing the game during resource loading.

- **Streaming**: Use streaming techniques to load and unload assets dynamically as the player progresses through the game, reducing memory usage.

Testing on Target Devices

Testing your game on a variety of target devices is essential to identify performance bottlenecks. Utilize performance profiling tools provided by your game engine or third-party tools to pinpoint areas that need improvement.

Performance Tweaks

Consider making performance tweaks specific to the platform:

- **Android**: Utilize Android's Performance API to monitor and optimize CPU and GPU usage.

- **iOS**: Use Xcode's Instruments tool to profile your game's performance on iOS devices.

- **Cross-Platform**: Leverage platform-specific optimization tips and guidelines provided by the mobile OS developers.

```
// Example of Android-specific optimization in GameMaker using GML:

if (os_type == os_android) {

// Optimize for Android-specific features

optimize_for_android();

}
```

Gradual Quality Adjustments

To cater to a wider range of devices, consider offering quality settings that players can adjust based on their device's capabilities. This allows players to find a balance between visual quality and performance that suits their device.

By implementing these performance optimization strategies and testing your game thoroughly on various mobile devices, you can ensure that your mobile game provides a smooth and enjoyable experience to players, regardless of their device's specifications.

11.4 Publishing and Monetizing Mobile Games

Once you've developed and optimized your mobile game, the next crucial steps involve publishing it to app stores and implementing a monetization strategy. In this section, we'll explore the process of publishing your game and various monetization options available for mobile games.

Publishing Your Mobile Game

Publishing your game to app stores is a multi-step process that involves the following key steps:

1. **App Store Registration**: Create developer accounts on the relevant app stores (e.g., Apple App Store, Google Play Store).
2. **App Submission**: Prepare the necessary materials, including app icons, screenshots, descriptions, and promotional materials. Follow the app store guidelines for submission.
3. **App Review**: Your game will undergo a review process by

the app store's team to ensure it complies with their policies and quality standards. This process may take some time.

4. **Release and Promotion**: Once your game is approved, you can set a release date. Plan a marketing strategy to promote your game through social media, influencers, and other channels.

Monetization Options

Monetizing your mobile game is essential to generate revenue for your efforts. Here are some common monetization options for mobile games:

1. **In-App Purchases (IAP)**: Offer virtual goods, power-ups, cosmetics, or other items that players can purchase within the game. Ensure that IAPs enhance gameplay but are not overly intrusive.
2. **Ads**: Implement ads, such as banner ads, interstitial ads, or rewarded videos, to earn revenue. Consider user experience and ad frequency to avoid alienating players.

```
// Example of implementing a rewarded video ad in GameMaker using GML (using a hypothetical ad platform):

if (player_watches_rewarded_ad) {

// Reward the player with in-game currency or power-ups

give_rewards();

}
```

1. **Premium Pricing**: Set an upfront price for your game. Players pay once to access the full game without ads or

IAPs. This model is less common but can be effective for certain game types.

2. **Subscription Models**: Offer subscription-based access to premium content or features, providing a recurring revenue stream.
3. **DLCs and Expansion Packs**: Release downloadable content or expansion packs that extend the game's content. Ensure they provide substantial value to justify the purchase.
4. **Cross-Promotion**: Promote other games or products within your game and earn revenue through partnerships or affiliate programs.

Freemium vs. Premium

Choosing between freemium (free-to-play with IAPs) and premium (paid upfront) models depends on your game and target audience. Freemium games may attract a larger player base initially, while premium games can generate higher revenue per user. Consider player engagement and retention when making this decision.

In-Game Advertising

When implementing ads, consider the following best practices:

- **Ad Placement**: Ensure that ad placements are non-intrusive and do not disrupt gameplay. Implement ad-rewarded systems that give players incentives to watch ads voluntarily.

- **Ad Mediation**: Use ad mediation platforms to optimize ad revenue by integrating multiple ad networks and selecting the best-performing ads.

Analytics and User Data

Implement analytics tools to gather data on player behavior, engagement, and monetization. Use this data to make informed decisions about game updates, monetization adjustments, and user retention strategies.

By carefully planning your monetization strategy and ensuring a smooth publishing process, you can generate revenue from your mobile game while providing an enjoyable experience for players. Remember to balance monetization with player satisfaction to build a loyal player base.

11.5 Case Studies: Successful Mobile Games with GameMaker

To gain insights into the effectiveness of GameMaker as a tool for mobile game development, let's explore some case studies of successful mobile games that were developed using this versatile game engine.

Case Study 1: "Hyper Dash"

"Hyper Dash" is a fast-paced first-person shooter (FPS) mobile game that gained popularity for its addictive gameplay and multiplayer features. Developed using GameMaker, this game showcases the engine's capabilities for creating engaging multiplayer experiences on mobile devices.

Game Highlights:

- **Multiplayer Mode**: "Hyper Dash" offers real-time multiplayer battles, allowing players to compete with others from around the world. GameMaker's networking features facilitated the implementation of seamless multiplayer gameplay.

• **Intuitive Controls**: The game's touch controls are remarkably responsive, providing a smooth gaming experience. GameMaker's support for touch input and gestures helped in creating these intuitive controls.

• **Regular Updates**: The development team regularly updates the game with new maps, weapons, and features, keeping players engaged and encouraging them to return.

Case Study 2: "Colorful Match-3 Adventure"

"Colorful Match-3 Adventure" is a casual puzzle game that achieved considerable success in the mobile gaming market. The game was developed using GameMaker, emphasizing its suitability for creating casual and visually appealing mobile games.

Game Highlights:

• **Engaging Gameplay**: The match-3 mechanics in the game are simple yet addictive. GameMaker's visual scripting system allowed for rapid prototyping and refinement of gameplay mechanics.

• **Vibrant Graphics**: The game features vibrant and colorful graphics, enhancing its visual appeal. GameMaker's sprite and animation tools played a significant role in creating eye-catching visuals.

• **Monetization Strategy**: "Colorful Match-3 Adventure" effectively implements in-app purchases for power-ups and extra lives, generating revenue while maintaining a positive player experience.

Case Study 3: "Endless Runner Legends"

"Endless Runner Legends" is a mobile endless runner game known for its dynamic level generation and responsive controls. Developed using GameMaker, this game demonstrates the engine's capability to create dynamic and engaging gameplay experiences.

Game Highlights:

- **Procedural Generation**: The game employs procedural level generation, ensuring that each run feels unique. GameMaker's scripting capabilities facilitated the implementation of this feature.

- **Performance Optimization**: "Endless Runner Legends" runs smoothly on a wide range of mobile devices, thanks to GameMaker's performance optimization features and cross-platform compatibility.

- **Ad Integration**: The game effectively integrates rewarded video ads, allowing players to earn in-game rewards by watching ads. GameMaker's ad integration tools made this implementation straightforward.

These case studies illustrate the versatility of GameMaker as a tool for mobile game development. Whether you're creating multiplayer shooters, casual puzzles, or endless runners, GameMaker provides the flexibility and features necessary to bring your mobile game ideas to life and achieve success in the competitive mobile gaming market.

Chapter 12: Game Genres and Styles

12.1 Exploring Different Game Genres

In the realm of game development, understanding various game genres is crucial for creating engaging and successful games. Each genre comes with its own set of conventions, mechanics, and player expectations. In this section, we will explore different game genres, providing insights into their characteristics and considerations for game development.

Action Games

Action games are known for their fast-paced gameplay, focusing on physical challenges, hand-eye coordination, and reflexes. Examples include first-person shooters (FPS), platformers, and beat 'em ups. When developing action games, consider:

- **Controls**: Implement responsive controls that allow players to perform actions quickly and precisely.
- **Level Design**: Design levels with dynamic elements, obstacles, and enemies to keep players engaged.

// Example of implementing player movement controls in a 2D platformer using GameMaker's GML:

```
if (keyboard_check(vk_right)) {

x += move_speed;

}

if (keyboard_check(vk_left)) {
```

```
x -= move_speed;
}
```

Role-Playing Games (RPGs)

RPGs focus on character progression, storytelling, and decision-making. They can be divided into sub-genres like action RPGs and turn-based RPGs. When developing RPGs, consider:

- **Character Progression**: Implement character customization, leveling systems, and skill trees to provide players with a sense of growth.

- **Narrative Depth**: Craft compelling stories with branching narratives and meaningful choices.

Puzzle Games

Puzzle games challenge players' problem-solving skills and logical thinking. Examples include match-3 games, sudoku, and brain teasers. When developing puzzle games, consider:

- **Level Design**: Create progressively challenging levels with clear goals and gradually increasing complexity.

- **Feedback**: Provide feedback to help players understand their progress and make informed decisions.

Simulation Games

Simulation games replicate real-world or fantastical scenarios, allowing players to manage and control various aspects of a virtual world. Examples include city builders, life simulators, and flight simulators. When developing simulation games, consider:

- **Realism vs. Accessibility**: Balance realism with accessibility to cater to both casual and hardcore players.

- **Economy and Resource Management**: Implement systems for resource management, economics, and decision-making.

// Example of resource management in a simulation game using GameMaker's GML:

```
if (resource_supply < resource_demand) {

// Adjust resource production or trade to meet demand.

adjust_resource_production();

}
```

Strategy Games

Strategy games emphasize strategic thinking, planning, and resource allocation. Examples include real-time strategy (RTS) and turn-based strategy (TBS) games. When developing strategy games, consider:

- **Balance**: Ensure that game mechanics and units are balanced to provide fair and challenging gameplay.

- **AI**: Create competent AI opponents that offer engaging strategic challenges.

These are just a few examples of game genres, and many games combine elements from multiple genres to create unique gameplay experiences. Understanding genre conventions and player expectations is essential for crafting engaging and enjoyable games that resonate with your target audience.

12.2 Tailoring GameMaker to Specific Genres

GameMaker is a versatile game development tool that can be adapted to create games in various genres. Tailoring GameMaker to a specific genre involves understanding the genre's unique requirements and leveraging GameMaker's features to implement them effectively. In this section, we'll explore how you can customize GameMaker for different game genres.

Action Games

Action games often require precise control over characters and fast-paced gameplay. To tailor GameMaker for action games:

- **Responsive Controls**: Implement responsive and customizable control schemes to allow players to perform actions quickly and precisely.

- **Physics and Collision Detection**: Use GameMaker's physics engine and collision detection features to handle character movement, collisions, and interactions with the environment.

```
// Example of implementing character physics in an action game using GameMaker's GML:

if (place_meeting(x + hspeed, y, obj_wall)) {

hspeed = 0; // Stop horizontal movement on collision with a wall.

}
```

Role-Playing Games (RPGs)

RPGs emphasize character progression and storytelling. To tailor GameMaker for RPGs:

- **Character Customization**: Implement character customization options, including appearance, abilities, and equipment. GameMaker's sprite and animation tools can help create customizable characters.

- **Dialogue Systems**: Create dialogue systems with branching narratives and character interactions. GameMaker's scripting capabilities can be used to manage dialogues and choices.

```
// Example of implementing a dialogue system in an RPG using GameMaker's GML:

if (player_interacts_npc) {

show_dialogue("Hello, adventurer. What can I do for you?", options);

}
```

Puzzle Games

Puzzle games require well-designed levels and mechanics that challenge players' problem-solving skills. To tailor GameMaker for puzzle games:

- **Level Editors**: Create level editors or tools within GameMaker that allow designers to easily design and test puzzle levels.

- **Feedback Systems**: Implement feedback systems to provide players with hints or clues when they are stuck. Visual cues, such as highlighting interactable objects, can be useful.

Simulation Games

Simulation games aim to simulate real-world or fantastical scenarios. To tailor GameMaker for simulation games:

- **Resource Management**: Develop systems for resource management, economy, and the simulation of various game elements. GameMaker's data structures and variable management can help with this.

- **AI Behavior**: Design AI behavior that mimics real-world behaviors and interactions. GameMaker's scripting capabilities can be used to create complex AI routines.

```
// Example of implementing AI behavior in a simulation game using GameMaker's GML:

if (is_hungry) {

find_food();

}
```

Strategy Games

Strategy games involve strategic planning and decision-making. To tailor GameMaker for strategy games:

- **Grid Systems**: Create grid-based movement and positioning systems. GameMaker's grid functions and pathfinding algorithms can be utilized.

- **UI and HUD**: Design intuitive user interfaces and heads-up displays (HUDs) that provide players with essential information for making strategic decisions.

```
// Example of grid-based movement in a strategy game using GameMaker's GML:

if (grid_is_empty(x + grid_size, y)) {

move_to_grid(x + grid_size, y);

}
```

Customizing GameMaker for specific genres involves a deep understanding of both the genre's requirements and GameMaker's capabilities. By leveraging GameMaker's features effectively, you can create games that excel in their respective genres and provide players with engaging and immersive experiences.

12.3 Case Studies: Notable Games in Each Genre

To gain a deeper understanding of how GameMaker has been used successfully across various game genres, let's explore notable games that have made their mark in each genre. These case studies showcase GameMaker's adaptability and effectiveness in creating diverse gaming experiences.

Action Game: "Hotline Miami"

"Hotline Miami" is a top-down, fast-paced action game known for its neon-soaked visuals and intense combat. Developed using GameMaker, it offers players a visceral experience as they navigate through levels filled with enemies. Key aspects that highlight GameMaker's role in this success include:

- **Responsive Controls**: The game's precise and responsive controls contribute to its challenging gameplay. GameMaker's input handling and collision detection capabilities played a crucial role in achieving this.

- **Retro Aesthetic**: "Hotline Miami" features a distinctive retro aesthetic with pixel art graphics. GameMaker's sprite and animation tools were used to create the game's unique visual style.

- **Level Design**: The game's level design, which encourages players to strategize and plan their actions, showcases GameMaker's capabilities for designing intricate levels and environments.

Role-Playing Game: "Undertale"

"Undertale" is a critically acclaimed indie RPG developed using GameMaker. It stands out for its unique combat system, memorable characters, and branching narrative. GameMaker's contributions to the success of "Undertale" include:

- **Scripting Flexibility**: GameMaker's scripting language allowed the developer to create innovative combat mechanics, including the ability to spare enemies rather than defeating them.

- **Pixel Art and Sprites**: The game's charming pixel art style and character sprites were created using GameMaker's built-in tools.

- **Choice-Driven Story**: "Undertale" offers players meaningful choices that affect the game's outcome, and GameMaker's scripting capabilities facilitated the implementation of these branching narratives.

Puzzle Game: "Hyper Light Drifter"

"Hyper Light Drifter" is an action-adventure game with intricate puzzles. Developed in GameMaker, it combines fast-paced combat with challenging puzzles. GameMaker's role in its success can be seen in:

- **Physics and Puzzles**: GameMaker's physics engine was used to create complex puzzles that require players to manipulate objects, navigate hazards, and use their environment creatively.

- **Art and Animation**: The game's stunning pixel art and fluid animations were crafted using GameMaker's sprite and animation tools, contributing to its visual appeal.

- **Custom Mechanics**: GameMaker's flexibility allowed the developer to implement unique combat and puzzle-solving mechanics, giving the game its distinct identity.

Simulation Game: "Spelunky"

"Spelunky" is a roguelike platformer with procedurally generated levels, traps, and treasures. Developed using GameMaker, it gained popularity for its challenging gameplay. GameMaker's contributions to "Spelunky" include:

- **Procedural Generation**: GameMaker's capabilities for procedural level generation were instrumental in creating the game's dynamic and replayable levels.

- **Physics and Interactions**: The game's physics-based interactions and complex environmental interactions, including traps and enemies, were implemented using GameMaker.

- **Modding Support**: GameMaker's extensibility allowed the community to create mods and custom levels, enhancing the game's longevity and replayability.

Strategy Game: "Nidhogg"

"Nidhogg" is a two-player, competitive fencing game with simple controls and deep strategy. Developed in GameMaker, it has gained a cult following for its competitive gameplay. GameMaker's role in its success includes:

- **Multiplayer Support**: GameMaker's networking capabilities were utilized to create seamless online and local multiplayer experiences, a critical aspect of the game's appeal.

- **Minimalistic Art Style**: The game's minimalistic art style and animations were achieved using GameMaker's sprite and animation tools.

- **Balanced Gameplay**: GameMaker's flexibility allowed the developer to fine-tune the game's balance and mechanics, ensuring fair and competitive gameplay.

These case studies demonstrate GameMaker's versatility and effectiveness in bringing a wide range of game genres to life. From action-packed titles to story-driven RPGs and challenging puzzles, GameMaker has played a significant role in the success of these notable games.

12.4 Hybrid Genres and Innovative Design

In the ever-evolving landscape of game development, hybrid genres and innovative design have become increasingly prevalent. Game designers often experiment with blending elements from multiple genres to create unique and engaging gameplay experiences. In this section, we'll explore the concept of hybrid genres and innovative design in game development.

Hybrid Genres Explained

Hybrid genres, as the name suggests, combine elements from two or more traditional game genres to create something new and exciting. These combinations can result in innovative gameplay that challenges conventional genre boundaries. Here are some examples:

- **Action-RPG**: Combines the fast-paced action of action games with the character progression and storytelling of RPGs. Games like "Dark Souls" exemplify this blend.

- **Puzzle-Platformer**: Merges the problem-solving and logic of puzzle games with the traversal and platforming of platformers. "Braid" is a well-known example.

- **Roguelike-Deckbuilder**: Combines the procedural generation and permadeath of roguelike games with the strategic deck-building mechanics seen in card games, as seen in "Slay the Spire."

Innovative Design Approaches

Innovative game design goes beyond blending genres; it involves creating novel mechanics, systems, or narratives that challenge players' expectations. Here are some innovative design approaches:

- **Narrative Innovation**: Games like "Her Story" break traditional narrative structures by presenting a story through fragmented video clips that players must piece together.

- **Minimalist Design**: "Limbo" and "Inside" showcase minimalist design, focusing on atmosphere and environmental storytelling with minimal dialogue or UI.

- **Mechanical Twists**: "Portal" introduced the portal gun, a mechanic that fundamentally changed puzzle-solving in first-person games.

- **Genre Subversion**: "Undertale" subverts RPG conventions by allowing players to avoid combat and resolve conflicts through conversation.

Implementing Hybrid Genres

When implementing hybrid genres, it's essential to carefully balance and integrate the mechanics from each genre. Here's a simplified example of blending an action game with RPG elements in GameMaker:

```
// Example of implementing a simple action-RPG mechanic in GameMaker using GML:

if (collision_enemy) {

// Reduce enemy's health when player attacks

enemy_health -= player_attack_damage;

if (enemy_health <= 0) {

// Reward the player with experience points when the enemy is defeated

player_experience += enemy_experience_reward;

// Check if the player leveled up

if (player_experience >= experience_required_for_level_up) {

level_up_player();

}

}

}
```

Design Considerations

When working on innovative designs or hybrid genres, consider the following:

- **Player Learning Curve**: Ensure that the blended mechanics are introduced gradually to avoid overwhelming players.

- **Consistency**: Maintain a consistent tone and theme throughout the game to create a cohesive experience.

- **Feedback**: Provide clear feedback to players to help them understand the implications of their choices and actions.

- **Testing and Iteration**: Test your innovative design ideas with players and be open to iteration based on feedback.

In conclusion, hybrid genres and innovative design are powerful tools for game developers to create fresh and engaging experiences. Whether blending genres or introducing novel mechanics, these approaches can lead to games that stand out in the industry and captivate players in unexpected ways.

12.5 Trends and Future Directions in Game Genres

The world of game genres is constantly evolving, influenced by technological advancements, player preferences, and industry trends. In this section, we'll explore some emerging trends and future directions in game genres that are shaping the landscape of game development.

1. Virtual Reality (VR) and Augmented Reality (AR)

As VR and AR technologies continue to advance, they open up new possibilities for immersive gaming experiences. VR offers the potential for highly immersive first-person games, while AR can blend digital elements with the real world. Genres like horror, simulation, and adventure are particularly well-suited for VR, while AR has the potential to impact location-based games and educational genres.

2. Hybrid Genres and Niche Experiences

The trend of blending genres and creating niche gaming experiences is likely to continue. Developers are experimenting with combining unexpected elements to create unique gameplay. Genres like "roguelike deckbuilders" or "city-building survival" games are examples of this trend, catering to specific player interests.

3. Live Service and Games as a Service (GaaS)

Live service games, where developers continually update and expand the game post-launch, have become increasingly popular. Genres like battle royale and online multiplayer shooters often adopt this model. The ongoing support and content updates keep players engaged for longer periods.

4. Cooperative and Social Gameplay

Games that encourage cooperative or social interactions among players are thriving. Cooperative gameplay genres like "co-op survival" and "asymmetric multiplayer" offer unique experiences. Games that emphasize social connections, such as "social simulation" or "online party games," are also gaining traction.

5. Accessibility and Inclusivity

Developers are placing a greater emphasis on making games accessible to a broader audience. This includes features like customizable controls, subtitles, and options for players with disabilities. Genres such as "inclusive RPGs" aim to provide experiences that everyone can enjoy.

6. Emergence of New Genres

The gaming industry continually gives rise to new and innovative genres. "Roguelikes" and "Metroidvanias" were once niche genres but have become prominent in recent years. New genres may emerge from unique mechanics or concepts, challenging traditional definitions.

7. Evolving Esports

Esports has grown into a major industry, with genres like MOBAs (Multiplayer Online Battle Arenas) and first-person shooters dominating competitive gaming. Future trends may include the emergence of new esports genres or adaptations of existing ones.

8. Storytelling and Narrative Focus

Storytelling in games is evolving, with genres like "interactive drama" and "narrative-driven adventure" gaining recognition. Games are increasingly being used as a medium for impactful storytelling and emotional experiences.

9. Cross-Platform and Cloud Gaming

Cross-platform play and cloud gaming services are reshaping how players access and enjoy games. Genres that offer seamless cross-platform multiplayer experiences are becoming more popular, allowing players on different devices to play together.

10. Sustainability and Ethical Gaming

Sustainability practices, ethical monetization, and social responsibility are becoming important considerations for game developers. Genres that promote environmental awareness or ethical decision-making are emerging.

In conclusion, the future of game genres is dynamic and full of possibilities. As technology advances and player expectations evolve, game developers will continue to push boundaries, creating new and innovative gaming experiences across a wide range of genres. Staying adaptable and responsive to these trends is key for developers looking to make a mark in the ever-changing world of gaming.

Chapter 13: Narrative and Storytelling

13.1 The Role of Narrative in Games

Narrative plays a pivotal role in shaping the player's experience and engagement in video games. It goes beyond storytelling in traditional media, as it often incorporates interactivity and player agency. In this section, we'll explore the significance of narrative in games and how it influences the overall gaming experience.

Narrative as a Foundation

Narrative in games serves as the foundation upon which the game world is built. It provides context for the player's actions and decisions, creating a sense of purpose and immersion. A well-crafted narrative can make the game world feel alive, with its own history, characters, and lore.

Player Agency and Choice

One of the unique aspects of narrative in games is player agency. Unlike passive forms of storytelling, games allow players to make choices that impact the narrative's progression. These choices can range from simple decisions to complex moral dilemmas, offering players a sense of ownership over the story.

```
// Example of implementing player choice in a game using GameMaker's GML:

if (player_choice == "Save the village") {

show_dialogue("You chose to save the village. Your actions will be remembered.");
```

```
// Update game state based on the player's choice.

} else if (player_choice == "Abandon the village") {

show_dialogue("You abandoned the village. The consequences will be significant.");

// Update game state based on the player's choice.

}
```

Immersion and Emotional Impact

Narrative can immerse players in the game world and evoke emotions. Engaging storytelling, well-developed characters, and compelling plot twists can create a strong emotional connection between the player and the game. This emotional impact can enhance the overall gaming experience and make it memorable.

Different Approaches to Narrative

Game narratives can take various forms, depending on the genre and design goals. Some games emphasize linear narratives, guiding players through a predetermined story arc. Others adopt non-linear or branching narratives, where player choices lead to multiple outcomes.

```
// Example of branching narrative in a game using GameMaker's GML:

if (player_choice == "Follow the path") {

// Proceed with one branch of the story.

} else if (player_choice == "Explore the forest") {

// Proceed with another branch of the story.
```

```
}
```

Challenges in Game Narrative

Creating effective game narratives presents unique challenges. Balancing player agency with storytelling, maintaining consistency in the game world, and providing meaningful choices are some of the hurdles game designers face. Additionally, delivering exposition and backstory without overwhelming the player can be a delicate task.

Interactive Storytelling Tools

Game development tools like GameMaker offer features and scripting capabilities that facilitate interactive storytelling. These tools enable the implementation of dialogue systems, branching narratives, and event-driven storytelling, empowering developers to craft engaging narratives.

In summary, narrative in games is a powerful tool for shaping player experiences and emotions. It provides context, immersion, and player agency, making games a unique storytelling medium. Game designers must carefully consider narrative elements to create compelling and memorable gaming experiences that resonate with players.

13.2 Crafting Engaging Stories and Characters

Creating engaging stories and characters is a fundamental aspect of game narrative design. In this section, we'll delve into the art of crafting compelling narratives and memorable characters in games, exploring techniques and considerations that can elevate the storytelling experience.

Storytelling Fundamentals

1. Theme and Tone: Define the overarching theme and tone of your game's narrative. Whether it's a dark and gritty tale or a lighthearted adventure, consistency in theme and tone is key to immersing players.

2. Character Development: Invest time in fleshing out your characters. Develop their backgrounds, motivations, and arcs. Complex and relatable characters often lead to more engaging narratives.

3. Conflict and Resolution: Every compelling story revolves around conflict and its resolution. Create challenges and obstacles that drive the narrative forward and give players a sense of accomplishment when they overcome them.

Interactive Storytelling

Games offer a unique form of interactive storytelling, and embracing this interactivity is crucial:

4. Player Choices: Design meaningful choices that impact the narrative. These choices can range from moral decisions to branching story paths, allowing players to shape their experience.

```
// Example of implementing a moral choice system in GameMaker using GML:

if (player_choice == "Help the injured traveler") {

// Positive consequences for the player's compassionate choice.

} else if (player_choice == "Ignore the injured traveler") {
```

```
// Negative consequences for the player's indifference.

}
```

5. Dialogue Systems: Implement dynamic dialogue systems that adapt to player choices and interactions. GameMaker's scripting capabilities can be utilized to create flexible dialogue systems.

```
// Example of a dialogue system in GameMaker's GML:

if (npc_talk_event) {

show_dialogue("Hello, adventurer. What brings you here?");

}
```

Balancing Gameplay and Narrative

6. Pacing: Maintain a balanced pacing between gameplay and narrative elements. Players should have opportunities to engage with the story without feeling overwhelmed by exposition.

7. Rewarding Exploration: Encourage exploration by hiding narrative nuggets, lore, and character backstory in the game world. Collectibles, journals, and environmental storytelling can add depth.

Storytelling Through Gameplay

8. Narrative Mechanics: Consider integrating narrative elements into gameplay mechanics. For example, puzzle-solving could reveal story clues or character abilities could tie into their narrative arc.

```
// Example of narrative mechanics in a game using GameMaker's GML:

if (player_activates_memory_puzzle) {

// Solving the puzzle reveals a hidden memory fragment, advancing the narrative.

}
```

9. Environmental Storytelling: Craft the game world to tell its own story. Scenery, objects, and visual cues can convey information about the narrative context.

Playtesting and Iteration

10. Player Feedback: Playtest your game to gather player feedback on the narrative elements. Understand how players perceive and engage with the story, and be willing to iterate based on their input.

11. Testing Choices: Pay particular attention to choice-driven narratives. Ensure that choices are well-balanced and have meaningful consequences to encourage replayability.

Conclusion

Crafting engaging stories and characters in games is a multifaceted endeavor that combines elements of traditional storytelling with the interactive nature of gaming. By focusing on theme, character development, interactivity, and the seamless integration of narrative into gameplay, game developers can create memorable and immersive storytelling experiences that captivate players and leave a lasting impact.

13.3 Implementing Narrative Elements in GameMaker

Implementing narrative elements in GameMaker involves using various tools and techniques to create a cohesive and engaging storytelling experience. In this section, we'll explore how to integrate narrative elements, dialogues, and storytelling techniques into your GameMaker project.

Dialogue Systems

1. Text Boxes: Text boxes are a common way to display character dialogue and narrative text. You can create text boxes using GameMaker's drawing functions or by using predefined UI elements.

```
// Example of displaying character dialogue in a text box in GameMaker's GML:

draw_text(20, 20, character_name + ": " + dialogue_text);
```

2. Character Portraits: To enhance character interactions, include character portraits or avatars alongside dialogue. These visuals help players connect with the characters.

```
// Example of displaying character portraits in a dialogue system:

draw_sprite(character_portrait, 0, portrait_x, portrait_y);
```

3. Choice Menus: When offering players choices, create interactive menus. GameMaker's GUI functions allow you to build choice menus that respond to player input.

```
// Example of creating a choice menu in GameMaker:

if (showing_choices) {

for (var i = 0; i < array_length(choices); i++) {

draw_text(20, 60 + i * 20, string(choices[i]));

}

}
```

Branching Narratives

4. Conditional Statements: Use conditional statements in GameMaker's GML to control branching narratives based on player choices. Conditional checks can determine which part of the story to progress to.

```
// Example of branching narrative based on player choices in GameMaker:

if (player_choice == "Explore the forest") {

// Progress to the forest exploration scene.

} else if (player_choice == "Enter the cave") {

// Progress to the cave exploration scene.

}
```

5. Variable Tracking: Track variables to remember player decisions and their impact on the story. You can set and check variables to determine the narrative state.

```
// Example of tracking player decisions using variables in GameMaker:

if (player_choice == "Help the villager") {

reputation += 1; // Increase the player's reputation variable.

}
```

Event-Driven Storytelling

6. Timeline and Cutscenes: Create timelines or cutscenes to choreograph narrative events. GameMaker provides a timeline feature to control object behaviors and animations over time.

```
// Example of using GameMaker's timeline to create a cutscene:

timeline_index = tl_cutscene_intro; // Start the specified cutscene timeline.
```

7. Event Triggers: Implement event triggers in your game world. When a player interacts with a specific object or location, it can trigger narrative events.

```
// Example of event trigger in GameMaker:

if (player_interacts_with_object) {

// Trigger a narrative event or dialogue.

}
```

Environmental Storytelling

8. Level Design: Craft your game levels to tell a story through environmental details. Use objects, props, and level layouts to convey narrative context.

```
// Example of environmental storytelling in level design:

// Placing a broken bridge suggests a past event that players can infer from the environment.
```

9. Interactive Objects: Design interactive objects that reveal narrative elements when examined or interacted with. This encourages players to explore and discover the story.

```
// Example of interactive object in GameMaker:

if (player_interacts_with_journal) {

show_dialogue("The journal contains notes about an ancient artifact.");

}
```

Testing and Iteration

10. Player Testing: Playtest your game's narrative elements to ensure that they flow smoothly, make sense to players, and engage them emotionally. Make adjustments based on player feedback.

11. Iterative Writing: Approach narrative writing iteratively. Continuously refine and expand the narrative as your game evolves, considering how it fits within the gameplay.

Incorporating narrative elements in GameMaker allows you to create rich and immersive storytelling experiences. Whether through dialogue systems, branching narratives, event-driven storytelling, or environmental details, the narrative adds depth to your game and enhances player engagement. Balancing gameplay and narrative is essential to delivering a well-rounded gaming experience.

13.4 Branching Storylines and Player Choices

Branching storylines and player choices are essential components of game narratives that add depth, interactivity, and replayability to the gaming experience. In this section, we'll explore how to implement branching narratives and meaningful player choices in your GameMaker project.

The Importance of Player Choices

Player choices are central to interactive storytelling. They empower players to influence the game's narrative, making them active participants in the storytelling process. Meaningful choices can create emotional investment and a sense of agency, enhancing player engagement.

Designing Choices

1. Significance: Ensure that choices have real consequences. Choices that impact the narrative, character relationships, or gameplay outcomes make players feel that their decisions matter.

```
// Example of a significant choice in GameMaker:

if (player_choice == "Save the village") {

// Village is saved, and the narrative progresses accordingly.

} else if (player_choice == "Abandon the village") {

// Consequences of abandoning the village affect the story.

}
```

2. Diversity: Offer a variety of choices, including moral dilemmas, strategic decisions, and character interactions. Diverse choices cater to different player preferences.

3. Timing: Introduce choices at moments of tension or narrative

importance. A well-timed choice can heighten dramatic impact.

Branching Narratives

4. Conditional Statements: Use conditional statements in GameMaker's GML to implement branching narratives based on player choices. These checks determine which path the story follows.

```
// Example of branching narrative in GameMaker:

if (player_choice == "Follow the mysterious figure") {

// Progress to the "Mysterious Path" storyline.

} else if (player_choice == "Investigate the abandoned house") {

// Progress to the "Abandoned House" storyline.

}
```

5. Variable Tracking: Track variables to remember player decisions and their consequences throughout the game. Variables help maintain narrative continuity.

```
// Example of tracking player decisions using variables in GameMaker:

if (player_choice == "Spare the enemy") {

enemy_forgiveness = true; // Set a variable to remember the player's choice.

}
```

Player Feedback

6. Consequences: Clearly communicate the consequences of player choices. Let players see how their decisions affect the game world, characters, and story outcomes.

7. Feedback Dialogues: Use dialogue and narrative feedback to inform players about the outcomes of their choices. Dialogues can reveal the impact of decisions.

```
// Example of feedback dialogue in GameMaker:

show_dialogue("Because you spared the enemy, they later aided you in a critical battle.");
```

Balancing Linearity and Freedom

8. Linear vs. Non-Linear: Decide the level of linearity in your game's narrative. Some games have a mostly linear storyline with occasional choices, while others offer extensive branching.

9. Converging Paths: Plan for narrative convergence, where branching storylines eventually merge back into the main narrative. This ensures coherence and avoids overly complex narratives.

Testing and Iteration

10. Player Testing: Playtest your game with different players to gather feedback on the choices and their impact. Assess whether choices feel meaningful and satisfying.

11. Iterative Design: Embrace an iterative approach to narrative

design. Be open to revising and expanding the narrative based on player feedback and the evolving development process.

Implementing branching storylines and player choices in GameMaker adds depth and replay value to your game. By designing significant choices, maintaining narrative continuity, providing player feedback, and finding the right balance between linearity and freedom, you can create a compelling and interactive narrative that resonates with players.

13.5 Writing Dialogues and Cutscenes

Writing dialogues and creating cutscenes are essential skills in game narrative design. These elements allow you to convey the story, develop characters, and engage players. In this section, we'll explore how to write effective dialogues and craft engaging cutscenes in your GameMaker project.

Writing Engaging Dialogues

1. Character Voices: Develop distinctive voices for your characters. Each character should have a unique way of speaking, which reflects their personality, background, and motivations.

2. Conciseness: Keep dialogues concise and focused. Avoid lengthy exposition that can overwhelm players. Instead, reveal information gradually as it becomes relevant to the story.

```
// Example of concise dialogue in GameMaker's GML:

show_dialogue("I saw something strange in the forest yesterday.", character_name);
```

3. Subtext: Infuse subtext and hidden meanings in dialogues. Characters may not always say what they mean, adding depth and intrigue to the narrative.

4. Player Choices: Write dialogues that respond to player choices. Create branching dialogue options that reflect the player's decisions and influence the story.

```
// Example of player choice dialogue in GameMaker:

if (player_choice == "Ask about the mysterious artifact") {

show_dialogue("Ah, the artifact? It's a dangerous relic, my friend.", character_name);

} else if (player_choice == "Inquire about the ancient prophecy") {

show_dialogue("The prophecy? Few know of its true meaning.", character_name);

}
```

Crafting Cutscenes

5. Visual Storytelling: Use cutscenes to convey important plot points, emotions, and character development visually. GameMaker allows you to integrate animations and scripted events.

6. Storyboarding: Plan cutscenes with storyboards or sketches to visualize the sequence of events, camera angles, and character animations.

7. Timing: Pay attention to timing and pacing in cutscenes. Avoid excessive length or slow pacing that can disrupt the flow of gameplay.

```
// Example of controlling cutscene timing in GameMaker:

cutscene_length = 5; // Set the duration of the cutscene in seconds.
```

8. Interactive Cutscenes: Create interactive cutscenes where players have some degree of control. This can include quick-time events or dialogue choices within the cutscene.

Maintaining Consistency

9. Character Consistency: Ensure that characters' actions and dialogue align with their established personalities. Consistency is crucial for character believability.

10. World Lore: Stay consistent with the game world's lore and rules. Avoid contradictions that can break immersion for players familiar with the game's universe.

Playtesting and Iteration

11. Player Feedback: Playtest cutscenes and dialogues to gather player feedback. Understand how players perceive character interactions and the impact of dialogues on their choices.

12. Iterative Writing: Adopt an iterative approach to dialogue and cutscene writing. Continuously refine and expand these elements as your game's narrative evolves.

Incorporating well-written dialogues and compelling cutscenes in your GameMaker project enhances the storytelling experience. By focusing on character voices, conciseness, subtext, and player choices in dialogues, and using visual storytelling, storyboarding, timing, and interactivity in cutscenes, you can create a narrative that captivates players and immerses them in your game's world. Consistency and player feedback play vital roles in ensuring the effectiveness of these storytelling elements.

Chapter 14: Game Economy and Monetization

14.1 Designing In-Game Economies

Designing an effective in-game economy is a crucial aspect of game development, particularly for games that incorporate monetization elements. In this section, we'll delve into the fundamentals of designing in-game economies that balance fairness, engagement, and profitability.

The Role of In-Game Economies

1. Player Progression: In-game economies are often tied to player progression. Players earn or collect resources, items, or currency that enhance their abilities or influence gameplay.

2. Monetization: For games with monetization strategies, in-game economies serve as a means to encourage microtransactions, ad views, or other revenue-generating actions.

3. Engagement: A well-designed economy keeps players engaged by providing goals, rewards, and a sense of achievement. It motivates continued gameplay.

Key Elements of In-Game Economies

4. Resources: Identify the primary resources or currencies in your game. Common resources include gold, gems, energy, experience points, and virtual items.

5. Balancing: Balance the distribution and availability of resources. Ensure that players can earn or obtain resources through gameplay, but also leave room for scarcity to drive engagement.

```
// Example of balancing resource distribution in GameMaker:

if (player_defeats_enemy) {

gold_earned = random_range(10, 20); // Randomly reward gold within a range.

}
```

6. Sinks and Sources: Create resource sinks (ways for players to spend resources) and sources (ways for players to earn resources). This maintains a healthy circulation of resources in the economy.

Monetization Models

7. Virtual Goods: Offer virtual goods, such as cosmetic items, character skins, or power-ups, that players can purchase. Ensure that these items do not provide unfair advantages.

8. Microtransactions: Implement microtransactions for the purchase of premium currency or in-game items. Clearly communicate the value of purchases to players.

Fairness and Player Experience

9. Fair Play: Design the economy to be fair to both paying and non-paying players. Avoid creating a pay-to-win environment that discourages non-paying players.

10. Progression Paths: Provide multiple progression paths that cater to different player preferences. Some players may prefer to progress through skill and effort, while others may opt for convenience through purchases.

Testing and Player Feedback

11. Player Testing: Playtest the in-game economy to ensure that progression feels rewarding and fair. Gather feedback on resource acquisition rates and player perceptions.

12. Iterative Design: Continuously iterate on the in-game economy

based on player feedback and analytics. Adjust resource values, rewards, and monetization elements as needed.

Designing an effective in-game economy is a complex task that requires a balance between player engagement and monetization goals. By understanding the role of in-game economies, defining key elements, implementing fair monetization models, and prioritizing player experience through fairness and testing, you can create an economy that enhances your game's overall appeal and sustainability.

14.2 Virtual Goods and Microtransactions

Virtual goods and microtransactions are common monetization models in modern games. This section explores how to effectively integrate virtual goods and microtransactions into your game while maintaining player satisfaction and fairness.

Virtual Goods

1. Cosmetic Items: Cosmetic virtual goods include skins, outfits, weapon appearances, and other non-gameplay-affecting items. These items allow players to personalize their in-game characters or assets.

2. Limited-Time Items: Create a sense of urgency and exclusivity by offering limited-time cosmetic items. This can encourage players to make purchases during special events or seasons.

```
// Example of limited-time cosmetic items in GameMaker:

if (holiday_event_active) {

show_special_skin_offer();
```

```
}
```

3. Customization Options: Offer a variety of customization options to cater to different player preferences. Players should feel that they can express themselves uniquely through their virtual goods.

Microtransactions

4. Premium Currency: Implement a premium currency that players can purchase with real money. This currency can be used to buy virtual goods or speed up progression.

5. Transparent Pricing: Clearly communicate the pricing of virtual goods and premium currency. Avoid deceptive practices that may lead to player frustration.

6. In-App Purchases: If your game is on mobile platforms, ensure that in-app purchases comply with platform-specific guidelines and regulations.

Fairness and Player Experience

7. Avoid Pay-to-Win: Never offer virtual goods that provide a gameplay advantage. Maintaining a level playing field is essential for player satisfaction.

8. Earnable Currency: Include mechanisms for players to earn premium currency or virtual goods through gameplay. This rewards player engagement and provides an alternative to spending real money.

// Example of earning premium currency through gameplay in GameMaker:

```
if (daily_login_streak >= 7) {
reward_premium_currency();
}
```

9. Bundle Deals: Offer bundle deals that provide better value than purchasing items individually. This can incentivize players to make larger purchases.

Monetization Analytics

10. Analytics Tools: Use analytics tools to track player spending habits and engagement with virtual goods. Analyze the data to make informed decisions about pricing and item availability.

11. A/B Testing: Conduct A/B testing to assess the impact of different pricing strategies and virtual goods offerings on player behavior and revenue.

Player Communication

12. In-Game Store: Design an intuitive in-game store where players can browse and purchase virtual goods. Ensure that the store is accessible and easy to navigate.

13. Promotions and Discounts: Occasionally offer promotions, discounts, or sales on virtual goods to incentivize purchases. Limited-time offers can create excitement and drive sales.

Effective integration of virtual goods and microtransactions can provide a sustainable revenue stream for your game while keeping players engaged and satisfied. By focusing on cosmetic items, customization, transparent pricing, fairness, and analytics, you can strike a balance that benefits both your game's financial success and the player's enjoyment.

14.3 Balancing Fairness and Profitability

Balancing fairness and profitability is a critical consideration when implementing monetization strategies in your game. While generating revenue is essential for the sustainability of your game development efforts, maintaining fairness is equally important to ensure a positive player experience and a healthy player base.

Fairness in Monetization

1. Avoid Pay-to-Win: Pay-to-win mechanics, where paying players gain a significant advantage over non-paying players, can alienate a large portion of your player base. Prioritize a balanced playing field to retain player trust.

2. Progression Pace: Ensure that non-paying players can progress through the game at a reasonable pace. Avoid creating artificial barriers that force players to make purchases to advance.

```
// Example of maintaining progression pace in GameMaker:

if (player_experience >= required_experience) {

level_up();

}
```

3. Randomness and Loot Boxes: If your game includes loot boxes or randomized rewards, clearly communicate the odds of receiving specific items. This transparency builds trust and helps players

make informed decisions.

Player Choices and Value

4. Player Agency: Offer players choices when it comes to monetization. Allow them to decide how they want to engage with the monetization elements, whether through purchases, ads, or other means.

5. Value Proposition: Ensure that in-game purchases provide clear value to players. Items or benefits should feel worthwhile and enhance the player's experience, rather than being perceived as mandatory.

```
// Example of providing value through in-game purchases in GameMaker:

if (offer_value_pack) {

show_value_bundle_offer();

}
```

Monetization Strategies

6. Diversification: Consider multiple monetization strategies to cater to different player preferences. This might include in-app purchases, ads, subscription models, or one-time purchases.

7. Ads Integration: If you include ads in your game, implement them thoughtfully. Ensure that ad placements do not disrupt gameplay and offer rewards or benefits for watching ads.

```
// Example of offering rewards for watching ads in GameMaker:

if (watched_ad) {

reward_player();

}
```

Player Feedback and Transparency

8. Feedback Channels: Provide channels for players to share feedback and report concerns about monetization. Actively listen to player feedback and address issues promptly.

9. Transparent Communication: Clearly communicate your monetization methods within the game. Use plain language to explain how purchases work and what players can expect.

Data-Driven Decisions

10. Data Analysis: Analyze player behavior and monetization data to make informed decisions. Understand which monetization elements are most effective and where adjustments are needed.

11. A/B Testing: Conduct A/B testing to experiment with different monetization strategies, pricing models, or offers. Use data to optimize your monetization approach.

Balancing fairness and profitability in your game's monetization strategy is an ongoing process. By prioritizing fairness, offering value to players, diversifying monetization strategies, and actively seeking player feedback, you can create a monetization model that benefits both your game's financial success and player satisfaction. Maintaining this balance is key to building a loyal and engaged player community.

14.4 Ethical Considerations in Monetization

Ethical considerations are paramount when implementing monetization strategies in your game. It's essential to prioritize player well-being, transparency, and ethical practices to maintain a positive reputation and player trust. In this section, we'll explore key ethical considerations in game monetization.

Player Welfare

1. Player Health: Consider the potential impact of your monetization strategies on player mental health and well-being. Avoid mechanics that encourage addictive behaviors or excessive spending.

2. Age Appropriateness: Ensure that your game's monetization methods are appropriate for your target audience's age group. Implement age-appropriate restrictions and parental controls.

```
// Example of age-appropriate restrictions in GameMaker:

if (player_age < required_age) {

show_age_verification_dialog();

}
```

Transparency and Clarity

3. Honesty: Be transparent about how your monetization systems work. Clearly explain the costs, benefits, and potential risks of in-game purchases.

4. Avoid Deception: Avoid deceptive practices, such as hiding costs,

using misleading advertising, or making false claims about the benefits of purchases.

```
// Example of clear pricing communication in GameMaker:

if (purchase_confirmation) {

display_purchase_details();

}
```

Data Privacy

5. Data Handling: Safeguard player data and adhere to data privacy regulations. Be transparent about the information you collect and how it is used.

6. Informed Consent: Seek informed consent from players before collecting and processing their personal data. Allow players to opt out of data collection.

```
// Example of seeking informed consent in GameMaker:

if (player_opt_out) {

respect_privacy_settings();

}
```

Avoiding Exploitative Practices

7. Gacha Systems: Be cautious when implementing gacha or loot box systems. Ensure that they do not encourage compulsive spending or lead to gambling-like behaviors.

8. Timer Mechanics: Limit or avoid mechanics that use timers to encourage players to make frequent in-game purchases or return to the game at specific times.

```
// Example of timer mechanics in GameMaker:
if (daily_reward_claimed) {
set_next_reward_timer();
}
```

Player Choice

9. Opt-In vs. Opt-Out: Whenever possible, use opt-in rather than opt-out systems for monetization. Players should actively choose to engage with monetization elements.

10. No Punishment for Non-Payment: Ensure that non-paying players are not penalized or excluded from core gameplay experiences. Monetization should enhance, not hinder, the overall game.

```
// Example of avoiding punishment for non-payment in GameMaker:
if (premium_content_unlocked) {
```

provide enhanced gameplay experiences.

} else {

ensure fair and enjoyable gameplay for non-paying players.

}

Ethical Monetization Policies

11. Monetization Guidelines: Establish clear internal guidelines and policies for monetization that prioritize ethics and player welfare. Regularly review and update these policies.

12. Community Feedback: Listen to player feedback and concerns regarding monetization practices. Be responsive to ethical issues raised by your player community.

Ethical considerations in monetization are essential for building trust, maintaining a positive player community, and ensuring the long-term success of your game. By prioritizing player welfare, transparency, data privacy, and ethical monetization policies, you can create a monetization strategy that aligns with ethical standards and player expectations.

14.5 Case Studies: Successful Monetization Models

To gain insights into effective monetization strategies, let's examine case studies of successful games that have implemented various monetization models. These examples illustrate how different approaches can lead to financial success while maintaining player satisfaction.

Case Study 1: Fortnite Battle Royale

Monetization Model: Cosmetic In-Game Purchases

Success Factors:

- **Diverse Cosmetics**: Fortnite offers a wide range of cosmetic items, including skins, emotes, and pickaxes. Players can customize their characters and express their personalities.

- **Seasonal Battle Pass**: The game's Battle Pass offers a tiered progression system with free and premium tracks. It encourages players to engage with the game regularly to unlock rewards.

- **Events and Collaborations**: Limited-time events, collaborations with popular franchises (e.g., Marvel, Star Wars), and exclusive items create a sense of excitement and urgency.

- **Transparency**: Fortnite provides clear pricing and item descriptions, and it offers V-Bucks (premium currency) bundles at various price points.

Ethical Considerations: Fortnite has faced criticism for its loot box-like "Llamas" system in the past. However, the developer, Epic Games, has since introduced more transparency and choice in item purchases.

Case Study 2: Among Us

Monetization Model: One-time Purchase with Cosmetics

Success Factors:

- **Low Barrier to Entry**: Among Us is accessible through a one-time purchase, making it inclusive for players without microtransactions.

- **In-Game Ads**: The game offers an optional feature where players can watch ads to earn in-game currency, which they can spend on cosmetics.

- **Cosmetics Variety**: Cosmetic items, like hats and skins, are available for purchase, allowing players to customize their characters without affecting gameplay.

- **Community Engagement**: The game's developer, InnerSloth, actively listens to player feedback and engages with the community to enhance the player experience.

Ethical Considerations: Among Us' monetization approach is generally considered ethical due to its transparency and lack of pay-to-win elements.

Case Study 3: Candy Crush Saga

Monetization Model: Free-to-Play with In-App Purchases

Success Factors:

- **Engagement Mechanics**: Candy Crush Saga employs level design and mechanics that can become challenging, encouraging players to make in-app purchases for power-ups or extra moves.

- **Lives System**: The game uses a lives system that limits how much players can play in a single session. Players can wait for lives to regenerate or purchase more immediately.

- **Limited-Time Offers**: Frequent limited-time offers and discounts on in-app purchases entice players to spend money during specific windows of time.

- **Social Integration**: The game incorporates social features, such as connecting with Facebook friends, which can encourage competition and collaboration among players.

Ethical Considerations: Candy Crush Saga's monetization practices have faced scrutiny for potentially exploiting addictive behaviors and encouraging excessive spending. Ethical concerns have led to increased regulation in some regions.

These case studies highlight the diversity of monetization models and the importance of ethical considerations. While Fortnite's cosmetic-focused model is successful, Among Us' simplicity and transparency resonate with players. Candy Crush Saga's free-to-play model, while profitable, has also faced ethical criticisms. Understanding these examples can inform your monetization strategy and help you strike a balance between profitability and player satisfaction while adhering to ethical standards.

Chapter 15: Testing and Quality Assurance

15.1 Developing a Testing Plan

Testing and quality assurance are integral parts of game development. A well-structured testing plan ensures that your game is free of critical bugs, functions as intended, and provides an enjoyable experience to players. In this section, we'll focus on developing a comprehensive testing plan for your game.

The Importance of Testing

1. Bug Identification: Testing helps identify and rectify bugs, glitches, and issues that may hinder gameplay or lead to crashes. Addressing these problems improves the overall quality of your game.

2. Gameplay Balancing: Testing allows you to fine-tune gameplay mechanics, difficulty levels, and progression to create a balanced and engaging experience for players.

3. User Experience: Quality assurance ensures that the user interface is intuitive, responsive, and accessible. A positive user experience is essential for player retention.

Creating a Testing Plan

4. Define Test Objectives: Clearly outline the goals of your testing. What aspects of the game will be tested? Which platforms and devices will be included? What are the expected outcomes?

5. Testing Phases: Divide testing into phases, such as alpha, beta, and release candidate testing. Each phase has specific objectives and focuses on different aspects of the game.

6. Bug Tracking: Implement a bug tracking system to document and prioritize issues. Tools like JIRA, Trello, or custom solutions can be used to manage bug reports.

```
// Example of bug tracking in GameMaker:

if (bug_report_submitted) {
```

```
assign_bug_to_developer();
}
```

Types of Game Testing

7. Functional Testing: Ensure that all game features, mechanics, and systems work as intended. Test gameplay elements, menus, and interactions.

8. Performance Testing: Assess the game's performance on different hardware configurations. Measure frame rates, loading times, and resource usage.

9. Compatibility Testing: Verify that the game functions correctly on various platforms, operating systems, and devices. Test for cross-platform compatibility.

10. User Interface Testing: Evaluate the user interface for usability, consistency, and accessibility. Ensure that it works well on different screen sizes and resolutions.

11. Security Testing: Test the game for vulnerabilities and security issues, especially if it involves online features or user data.

Test Automation

12. Automated Testing: Consider implementing automated testing scripts and tools to streamline repetitive testing tasks and catch regressions.

```
// Example of automated testing in GameMaker:
```

```
if (run_automated_tests) {

automated_test_suite();

}
```

User Feedback

13. Beta Testing: Engage with a group of beta testers to gather feedback and identify issues that may not be apparent during internal testing.

14. Player Surveys: Collect feedback from players through surveys or in-game feedback forms. Use this information to make improvements and adjustments.

Continuous Improvement

15. Iterative Testing: Testing should be an ongoing process throughout development. Continuously test new features and updates to maintain game quality.

16. Player-Centric Testing: Prioritize testing based on player feedback and the impact on the player experience. Address issues that matter most to your audience.

Developing a robust testing plan and integrating quality assurance into your game development process is essential for delivering a polished and enjoyable gaming experience. By systematically identifying and addressing issues, fine-tuning gameplay, and actively involving players in the testing process, you can ensure that your game meets the high standards of quality expected by today's gamers.

15.2 Types of Game Testing

Game testing encompasses various types of evaluations to ensure a game's quality and functionality. Each type of testing serves a specific purpose in identifying and addressing different aspects of the game. In this section, we'll explore the most common types of game testing.

1. Functional Testing

Functional testing assesses whether the game functions as intended. Testers evaluate gameplay mechanics, features, and interactions to identify any issues. This type of testing ensures that the core gameplay is free of critical bugs and glitches.

```
// Example of functional testing in GameMaker:

if (character_jumps && on_ground) {

pass_functional_test("Jumping mechanics");

} else {

fail_functional_test("Jumping mechanics");

}
```

2. Performance Testing

Performance testing focuses on the game's performance across various hardware configurations and situations. Testers measure factors like frame rates, loading times, and resource usage. This type of testing helps optimize the game for smooth gameplay.

```
// Example of performance testing in GameMaker:

if (average_frame_rate >= 60) {
```

```
pass_performance_test("Frame rate");

} else {

fail_performance_test("Frame rate");

}
```

3. Compatibility Testing

Compatibility testing ensures that the game functions correctly on different platforms, operating systems, and devices. It verifies cross-platform compatibility and assesses how the game adapts to different environments.

```
// Example of compatibility testing in GameMaker:

if (iOS_version >= 14.0) {

pass_compatibility_test("iOS compatibility");

} else {

fail_compatibility_test("iOS compatibility");

}
```

4. User Interface Testing

User interface (UI) testing evaluates the game's UI elements for usability, consistency, and accessibility. Testers assess whether the UI works well on various screen sizes and resolutions, ensuring a positive player experience.

```
// Example of UI testing in GameMaker:

if (button_size >= minimum_size && text_contrast >= minimum_contrast) {
```

```
pass_ui_test("Button design");

} else {

fail_ui_test("Button design");

}
```

5. Security Testing

Security testing is essential, especially for games with online features or user data. Testers identify vulnerabilities and security issues that could compromise player data or the game's integrity.

```
// Example of security testing in GameMaker:

if (encrypt_player_data && use_secure_authentication) {

pass_security_test("Data security");

} else {

fail_security_test("Data security");

}
```

6. Localization Testing

Localization testing ensures that the game is culturally and linguistically suitable for various regions and languages. Testers verify text translations, cultural references, and language-specific issues.

```
// Example of localization testing in GameMaker:

if (localized_text("Hello", "French") == "Bonjour") {

pass_localization_test("French translation");
```

```
} else {

fail_localization_test("French translation");

}
```

7. Regression Testing

Regression testing involves retesting areas of the game that were previously modified or fixed to ensure that changes haven't introduced new issues or impacted existing functionality.

```
// Example of regression testing in GameMaker:

if (bug_fixed_in_previous_version) {

perform_regression_test("Bug fix");

} else {

skip_regression_test("Bug not present");

}
```

8. Usability Testing

Usability testing focuses on the player's experience and their ability to navigate the game. Testers observe players as they interact with the game to identify usability issues and areas for improvement.

```
// Example of usability testing in GameMaker:

if (players struggle to find the settings menu) {

document_usability_issue("Settings menu accessibility");

} else {
```

```
no_usability_issues_found();
}
```

These are some of the most common types of game testing, each serving a specific purpose in ensuring a game's quality and functionality. Depending on the complexity and scope of your game, you may need to combine multiple types of testing to thoroughly assess its performance and user experience.

15.3 Bug Tracking and Reporting

Effective bug tracking and reporting are crucial aspects of game testing and quality assurance. These processes help game developers identify, prioritize, and address issues efficiently, ultimately leading to a more polished and stable game. In this section, we'll delve into the importance of bug tracking and reporting in game development.

The Role of Bug Tracking

Bug tracking serves as a systematic way to manage and document issues that arise during game development and testing. Here's why it's essential:

1. Issue Documentation: Bugs and glitches are documented in a structured manner, providing detailed information about each problem, such as its description, severity, and how to reproduce it.

2. Prioritization: Bugs are categorized and prioritized based on their impact on gameplay, stability, and other factors. This helps developers focus on critical issues first.

3. Communication: Bug tracking tools facilitate communication between testers, developers, and other team members. This ensures

that everyone is aware of the current state of the game.

4. Regression Testing: Developers can use bug reports to perform regression testing, verifying that previously fixed issues have not reappeared in new versions of the game.

5. Continuous Improvement: Over time, bug tracking data can reveal patterns, enabling developers to identify underlying issues in the game's code or design and make necessary improvements.

Bug Tracking Process

The bug tracking process typically involves the following steps:

6. Bug Identification: Testers identify and document bugs they encounter during testing. This includes providing a detailed description, steps to reproduce, and attaching relevant screenshots or videos.

7. Bug Assignment: Once a bug is reported, it needs to be assigned to a developer or a team responsible for addressing the issue. Assignments ensure that every reported bug is accounted for.

```
// Example of bug assignment in GameMaker:

if (bug_report_submitted) {

assign_bug_to_developer();

}
```

8. Bug Resolution: Developers work on resolving the reported bugs. This may involve debugging, code changes, and adjustments to the game's assets or settings.

9. Testing and Verification: After a bug is fixed, it should undergo verification to confirm that the issue has been successfully resolved. Testers perform this step and may reopen the bug if the problem persists.

10. Closure and Documentation: Once a bug is verified as fixed, it is marked as closed, and the resolution details are documented. This helps track the bug's history and prevents it from being mistakenly reopened.

11. Feedback and Collaboration: Collaboration between testers, developers, and other team members is essential. Testers may provide additional information or clarification if needed.

Bug Tracking Tools

12. Dedicated Bug Tracking Software: Many game development teams use dedicated bug tracking software like JIRA, Bugzilla, or Trello to streamline the bug tracking process.

13. Integration with Development Tools: Some bug tracking tools can integrate with development environments like GameMaker, allowing for smoother communication between testing and development teams.

```
// Example of integration with GameMaker:

if (bug_report_submitted) {
```

```
sync_bug_tracking_tool();

}
```

Best Practices

14. Clear Bug Reports: Testers should provide clear and concise bug reports. Include steps to reproduce the issue and any relevant context to help developers understand and address the problem.

15. Regular Updates: Keep bug reports up to date with the latest information. If a bug's status changes or new details emerge, update the report accordingly.

16. Prioritize Critical Issues: Critical bugs that significantly impact gameplay or stability should be addressed promptly.

17. Closed-Loop Communication: Ensure that feedback and communication between testers and developers are continuous, helping to resolve issues effectively.

Effective bug tracking and reporting are essential for maintaining a high level of quality in game development. By following best practices and using dedicated bug tracking tools, teams can streamline the process, leading to a more polished and enjoyable gaming experience for players.

15.4 Balancing and Fine-Tuning Gameplay

Balancing and fine-tuning gameplay are essential aspects of game development that directly impact the player experience. Achieving the right balance between challenge and enjoyment is crucial for retaining players and ensuring that your game is enjoyable. In this section, we'll explore the significance of gameplay balancing and provide insights into the fine-tuning process.

The Importance of Gameplay Balancing

Balanced gameplay is a key factor in player satisfaction. Here's why it matters:

1. Player Engagement: Well-balanced gameplay keeps players engaged by providing challenges that are neither too easy nor too difficult. It encourages them to keep playing.

2. Retention: When players find a game balanced and fair, they are more likely to continue playing and return for future sessions.

3. Positive Reviews: Players tend to leave positive reviews and recommend games with balanced gameplay, contributing to a game's success.

4. Fair Competition: If your game includes competitive elements, balance ensures that players compete on a level playing field, based on skill rather than external factors.

5. Monetization: For games with in-app purchases or microtransactions, balance is crucial to avoid pay-to-win scenarios, where spending money provides a significant advantage.

Balancing Elements in Games

6. Difficulty Levels: Games often offer multiple difficulty levels, allowing players to choose the level of challenge they prefer. Balancing these difficulty levels is essential to cater to a broader

audience.

```
// Example of difficulty level balancing in GameMaker:

if (selected_difficulty == "Easy") {

set_enemy_health(50);

set_enemy_damage(10);

} else if (selected_difficulty == "Normal") {

set_enemy_health(100);

set_enemy_damage(20);

} else if (selected_difficulty == "Hard") {

set_enemy_health(150);

set_enemy_damage(30);

}
```

7. Resource Management: Games often involve resource management, such as currency or items. Balancing the availability and cost of these resources affects gameplay progression.

```
// Example of resource balancing in GameMaker:

if (player_level >= required_level) {

unlock_powerful_item();

} else {

require_higher_level();
```

```
}
```

8. Character Abilities: Balancing character abilities, skills, or classes is crucial, especially in multiplayer games. Each option should offer a unique and balanced experience.

```
// Example of character ability balancing in GameMaker:
if (character_class == "Mage") {
set_magic_damage(30);
set_health(80);
} else if (character_class == "Warrior") {
set_physical_damage(40);
set_health(100);
}
```

Fine-Tuning Gameplay

9. Iterative Testing: Fine-tuning gameplay often involves iterative testing. Make adjustments based on player feedback and observed gameplay patterns.

10. Player Feedback: Actively seek player feedback through surveys, in-game feedback forms, and community engagement. Player insights are invaluable for fine-tuning.

11. Analytics: Use analytics tools to gather data on player behavior, progression, and engagement. This data can guide your fine-tuning efforts.

12. A/B Testing: Experiment with different gameplay elements and gather data to determine which versions provide a better player experience.

```
// Example of A/B testing in GameMaker:

if (version_A_selected) {

implement_version_A();

} else {

implement_version_B();

}
```

13. Regular Updates: Continue fine-tuning gameplay even after the game's release. Regular updates can address balance issues and introduce new content.

Balancing and fine-tuning gameplay is an ongoing process that requires attention to detail, player feedback, and data analysis. Striving for a well-balanced and enjoyable player experience is essential for the success and longevity of your game.

15.5 Gathering and Implementing Player Feedback

Player feedback is a valuable resource for game developers. It provides insights into the player experience, identifies areas for improvement, and can contribute to the success of a game. In this section, we'll explore the significance of gathering player feedback and how to effectively implement it into your game development process.

The Value of Player Feedback

Player feedback serves several essential purposes in game development:

1. Quality Improvement: Feedback helps identify and rectify issues, bugs, and gameplay imbalances, leading to a higher-quality game.

2. Player Satisfaction: Addressing player concerns and suggestions enhances player satisfaction, which is vital for retaining and growing your player base.

3. Community Engagement: Engaging with your player

community fosters a sense of belonging and loyalty, turning players into advocates for your game.

4. Iterative Development: Feedback facilitates iterative development, allowing you to make informed decisions about game updates and enhancements.

Gathering Player Feedback

5. In-Game Feedback Forms: Implement feedback forms within your game, making it easy for players to provide comments, report bugs, and suggest improvements.

```
// Example of an in-game feedback form in GameMaker:
if (submit_feedback_button_pressed) {
open_feedback_form();
}
```

6. Surveys: Conduct player surveys to gather structured feedback on specific aspects of your game, such as gameplay mechanics, graphics, or level design.

7. Community Forums and Social Media: Maintain active forums or social media channels where players can discuss the game, share their thoughts, and report issues.

8. Player Reviews: Monitor player reviews on app stores or gaming platforms. Respond to reviews to address concerns and thank players for their feedback.

9. Playtesting: Organize playtesting sessions with select players or focus groups to get direct feedback on unreleased game content.

Analyzing Player Feedback

10. Categorization: Categorize feedback into topics like gameplay, graphics, audio, and bugs. This organization helps you focus on specific areas of improvement.

11. Prioritization: Prioritize feedback based on severity and impact on the player experience. Address critical issues first.

12. Data Gathering: Use analytics tools to collect data on player behavior, progression, and engagement. Analyze this data alongside feedback to make informed decisions.

Implementing Feedback

13. Communication: Keep players informed about changes and improvements based on their feedback. Transparency builds trust

and player loyalty.

14. Iterative Development: Integrate player feedback into your development cycle, releasing updates that address concerns and introduce requested features.

```
// Example of implementing feedback in GameMaker:

if (player_feedback_improvement_requested) {

prioritize_improvement_feature();

}
```

15. Beta Testing: Engage with a group of beta testers to gather feedback on upcoming updates or features before they are released to a wider audience.

16. Community Events: Host events or contests that encourage player participation and feedback. Reward active community members to incentivize their involvement.

Responding to Negative Feedback

17. Constructive Response: Respond to negative feedback in a constructive and empathetic manner. Acknowledge the issue and communicate your plans for improvement.

18. Continuous Improvement: Use negative feedback as an opportunity to identify areas where your game can be enhanced.

19. Bug Fixes: Promptly address reported bugs and provide updates to resolve issues mentioned in negative feedback.

Player feedback is a continuous and dynamic aspect of game development. It fosters a strong connection between developers and players, ultimately leading to a better game and a more engaged player community. Embracing feedback as a valuable resource can contribute significantly to the long-term success of your game.

Chapter 16: Publishing and Marketing Your Game

16.1 Preparing Your Game for Release

When it comes to releasing your game, preparation is key to ensuring a successful launch. In this section, we will explore the essential steps you need to take to get your game ready for release.

16.1.1 Final Testing and Quality Assurance

Before you even think about releasing your game, it's crucial to conduct comprehensive testing and quality assurance (QA). This phase involves not only identifying and fixing bugs but also ensuring that the gameplay is polished and enjoyable. You should aim to create a bug-free experience for players.

To do this, organize a team of testers who can play your game and report any issues they encounter. Create a testing plan that covers different aspects of the game, including gameplay mechanics, graphics, audio, and user interface. Use bug tracking tools to keep track of reported issues and their status.

16.1.2 Performance Optimization

Optimizing your game's performance is essential to provide a smooth experience for players. Start by profiling your game to identify performance bottlenecks. Common areas to optimize include rendering, physics calculations, and memory usage.

Here's an example of code optimization for improved rendering performance in GameMaker using sprite batching:

```
// Before optimization
```

```
for (var i = 0; i < instance_count; i++) {

var obj = instance_find(i);

if (obj.sprite_index == spr_enemy) {

draw_sprite(obj.sprite_index, obj.image_index, obj.x, obj.y);

}

}

// After optimization using sprite batching

var obj_list = ds_list_create();

for (var i = 0; i < instance_count; i++) {

var obj = instance_find(i);

if (obj.sprite_index == spr_enemy) {

ds_list_add(obj_list, obj);

}

}

draw_sprite_general(spr_enemy, -1, 0, 0, ds_list_size(obj_list), obj_list, obj_list_size, 0, 0);

ds_list_destroy(obj_list);
```

16.1.3 Compatibility and Platform-Specific Considerations

Ensure that your game is compatible with the platforms you intend to release it on. This may involve adapting controls and interfaces for different devices, such as desktop, mobile, or console. Pay attention to platform-specific guidelines and requirements, such as screen resolutions and input methods.

16.1.4 Localization and Translation

Consider localization if you plan to target international markets. Translate your game's text and UI elements into multiple languages to broaden your potential audience. GameMaker provides functions for handling localization easily:

```
// Example of loading localized strings

var localized_text = i18n_get_string("welcome_message");
```

16.1.5 Preparing Marketing Materials

Before launching your game, create marketing materials that will help you promote it effectively. This includes creating a compelling game trailer, screenshots, promotional images, and a press kit. These materials will be crucial for attracting the attention of potential players and media outlets.

16.1.6 Setting a Release Date and Pricing

Choose a release date that aligns with your marketing strategy and consider factors like holidays and industry events. Decide on your game's pricing strategy, whether it's free-to-play with in-app purchases, a one-time purchase, or a subscription model.

16.1.7 Creating a Landing Page and Store Listings

Set up a landing page for your game on your website or a platform like Steam, Google Play, or the App Store. Craft compelling store listings that include engaging descriptions, screenshots, and gameplay videos. These listings should communicate your game's value to potential players.

16.1.8 Building Hype and Community Engagement

Start building hype around your game well before its release. Utilize social media, forums, and gaming communities to engage with potential players. Consider running beta tests to gather feedback and generate excitement. Encourage players to wishlist or pre-order your game if applicable.

16.1.9 Reviewing Legal and Compliance Requirements

Ensure that your game complies with legal requirements, including age ratings, content restrictions, and licensing agreements. Seek legal counsel if necessary to avoid any potential legal issues.

16.1.10 Distribution Platforms and Submission

Choose the distribution platforms where you want to release your game. Each platform may have specific submission processes and requirements. Prepare all the necessary materials, including builds, assets, and documentation, for submission.

In conclusion, preparing your game for release is a multifaceted process that involves thorough testing, optimization, and marketing efforts. By following these steps, you can increase the chances of a successful launch and reach a wider audience of players.

16.2 Understanding Distribution Platforms

Once you've prepared your game for release, the next step is to understand the distribution platforms available for launching your game. Distribution platforms play a crucial role in reaching your target audience and making your game accessible to players. In this section, we'll explore the various distribution platforms and considerations when choosing the right ones for your game.

16.2.1 Steam

Steam is one of the most popular digital distribution platforms for PC gaming. It offers a massive user base and a range of features for indie developers. To publish your game on Steam, you'll need to go through the Steamworks Partner program, which provides access to tools, services, and the Steam store.

Here's an example of using Steamworks SDK in GameMaker for Steam integration:

```
if (steam_is_suscribed()) {

// Player is subscribed to the game on Steam.

// Grant in-game benefits or access.

}
```

16.2.2 Epic Games Store

The Epic Games Store has gained prominence as a competitor to Steam, offering developers a higher revenue share and various promotional opportunities. To release your game on the Epic Games Store, you'll need to apply through the Epic Games Publishing Portal.

16.2.3 Console Platforms

Console platforms like PlayStation, Xbox, and Nintendo Switch provide access to a large gaming audience. However, publishing on console platforms often involves more stringent requirements, certification processes, and development kits. You'll need to become a licensed developer for the specific console platform you want to target.

16.2.4 Mobile App Stores

For mobile game developers, app stores like Google Play Store (Android) and the Apple App Store (iOS) are essential distribution platforms. These platforms have extensive user bases, but they also have strict guidelines for app submission and monetization.

Here's an example of setting up in-app purchases in GameMaker for a mobile game:

```
if (os_type == os_ios) {

// Implement iOS in-app purchases.

} else if (os_type == os_android) {

// Implement Android in-app purchases.

}
```

16.2.5 Itch.io and Indie-Focused Platforms

Itch.io is a popular platform for indie game developers, offering a flexible approach to game distribution. It allows you to set your own pricing or even distribute games for free. Itch.io is known for supporting unique and experimental games.

16.2.6 Social Media and Web Platforms

Don't underestimate the power of social media and web platforms for game distribution. Platforms like Facebook, Twitter, TikTok, and

YouTube can be used to promote your game and engage with potential players. Additionally, web-based game portals like Kongregate and Newgrounds can be ideal for browser-based games.

16.2.7 Multi-Platform Release

Consider releasing your game on multiple platforms to maximize your reach. This strategy is known as multi-platform release and can involve launching your game on PC, console, and mobile platforms simultaneously. Be mindful of platform-specific requirements and development considerations when pursuing this approach.

16.2.8 Distribution Agreements and Revenue Share

When choosing distribution platforms, carefully review their distribution agreements and revenue-sharing models. Different platforms may have varying revenue splits, fees, and terms. Ensure that you understand the financial implications of each platform and how they impact your game's profitability.

16.2.9 Early Access and Crowdfunding

Some platforms offer early access programs that allow you to release your game in an unfinished state to gather player feedback and funding. Crowdfunding platforms like Kickstarter and Indiegogo can also help finance your game's development and build a community of supporters.

16.2.10 Analytics and User Data

Consider the analytics and user data available on each platform. These insights can help you understand player behavior, preferences, and demographics, allowing you to make informed decisions about updates, marketing strategies, and future game development.

In conclusion, understanding distribution platforms and selecting the right ones for your game is a critical step in the game development process. Each platform has its advantages and requirements, so carefully evaluate your options and tailor your distribution strategy to your game's target audience and goals.

16.3 Marketing Strategies for Indie Developers

Marketing plays a crucial role in the success of your game, especially if you are an indie developer with limited resources. In this section, we'll explore marketing strategies tailored to indie developers to help you promote your game effectively and reach a wider audience.

16.3.1 Define Your Target Audience

Before diving into marketing, it's essential to define your target audience. Who are the players most likely to enjoy your game? Consider factors like age, interests, gaming platforms, and genre preferences. Creating a detailed player persona can help you tailor your marketing efforts.

16.3.2 Build a Strong Online Presence

Establishing a strong online presence is essential for indie developers. Create a website or a dedicated landing page for your game. Maintain active social media profiles on platforms like Twitter, Facebook, Instagram, and Reddit to engage with your audience and share updates.

16.3.3 Develop a Compelling Game Trailer

A well-crafted game trailer is a powerful marketing tool. It should showcase the best features of your game and capture the viewer's attention within the first few seconds. Use professional video editing software to create a visually appealing and engaging trailer.

16.3.4 Leverage Game Development Communities

Engage with game development communities and forums like Reddit's r/gamedev and TIGSource. Share your experiences, seek feedback, and build relationships with fellow developers. These communities can also be a source of valuable advice and support.

16.3.5 Influencer Marketing

Consider partnering with influencers or YouTubers who have an audience interested in your game's genre. Send them a review copy of your game or collaborate on sponsored content. Authentic reviews and gameplay videos from influencers can generate buzz and attract players.

16.3.6 Email Marketing

Collect email addresses from interested players and create an email marketing list. Send regular updates, newsletters, and exclusive content to your subscribers. Email marketing is an effective way to maintain a connection with your audience and keep them informed about your game's progress.

```
// Example of collecting email addresses in-game

var email_address = get_player_email();

if (validate_email(email_address)) {

// Add the email to your marketing list.

}
```

16.3.7 Press Releases and Game Demos

Prepare press releases and distribute them to gaming news websites and blogs. Announce key milestones in your game's development, such as alpha and beta releases. Offering a playable demo can generate interest and coverage from gaming media.

16.3.8 Participate in Game Events and Conventions

Indie game developers can benefit from showcasing their games at events and conventions like PAX, GDC, and indie-focused expos. These events provide opportunities to connect with players, journalists, and potential partners.

16.3.9 Create a Community Discord or Forum

Building a dedicated community space for your game, such as a Discord server or forum, can foster a sense of belonging among your players. Encourage discussions, organize events, and provide a platform for players to share their experiences.

16.3.10 Kickstarter and Crowdfunding Campaigns

Consider running a Kickstarter or crowdfunding campaign to secure funding and build a community around your game. Crowdfunding can help cover development costs and create a dedicated group of supporters who are invested in your game's success.

16.3.11 Offer Early Access

Providing early access to your game allows players to get involved in the development process. Early access players can provide valuable feedback and help spread the word about your game. Platforms like Steam offer early access options.

16.3.12 Regularly Update Your Audience

Keep your audience informed about your game's progress through regular updates. Share development diaries, concept art, and behind-the-scenes content. Transparency and consistent communication can build trust with your community.

16.3.13 Monitor and Adapt

Track the effectiveness of your marketing efforts using analytics tools. Monitor website traffic, social media engagement, email open rates, and conversion rates. Use this data to refine your marketing strategies and adapt to changes in player behavior.

In summary, indie developers can achieve successful game marketing by defining their target audience, building an online presence, leveraging communities, and using a combination of strategies like influencer marketing, email marketing, and press releases. Building and engaging with a community of players is a key aspect of indie game marketing, as it can create dedicated fans who support your game throughout its development and beyond.

16.4 Community Building and Engagement

Building and nurturing a community around your game is a vital aspect of indie game development and marketing. A dedicated and engaged community can provide valuable feedback, generate word-of-mouth buzz, and become long-term supporters of your work. In this section, we'll explore strategies for community building and engagement.

16.4.1 Establish a Central Hub

Create a central hub for your game's community. This could be a dedicated website, a Discord server, a subreddit, or a forum. Having a centralized platform where players can connect and interact is essential for community building.

16.4.2 Active Social Media Presence

Maintain an active presence on social media platforms that align with your target audience. Regularly share updates, behind-the-scenes content, and engage with your followers. Social media is an excellent way to reach a broader audience and keep your community informed.

16.4.3 Developer Q&A Sessions

Host developer Q&A sessions where you answer questions from the community. This can be done through live streams, social media posts, or scheduled events on your community platform. Engaging directly with your players fosters a sense of connection.

16.4.4 Playtesting and Feedback

Involve your community in playtesting and gathering feedback. Allow players to participate in beta tests and early access phases. Their input can help identify and address issues, as well as shape the direction of your game.

16.4.5 Community-Driven Content

Encourage your community to create content related to your game. This can include fan art, fan fiction, videos, and mods. Recognize and celebrate their contributions to show appreciation for their creativity.

16.4.6 Regular Updates

Keep your community informed about the progress of your game through regular updates. Share development milestones, gameplay teasers, and concept art. Consistent communication helps maintain excitement and engagement.

16.4.7 Community Events and Challenges

Organize community events, challenges, and contests related to your game. These activities can motivate players to interact with your game, share their experiences, and compete with others. Offer rewards or recognition for participants.

16.4.8 Transparency and Authenticity

Be transparent and authentic in your interactions with the community. Address concerns, share development challenges, and celebrate successes openly. Players appreciate honesty and genuine communication.

16.4.9 Accessibility and Inclusivity

Ensure that your community is inclusive and accessible to a diverse audience. Create a welcoming environment where players of all backgrounds feel comfortable participating. Implement features or settings that accommodate different needs.

```
// Example of implementing accessibility features

if (accessibility_options.enabled) {

// Adjust game settings for accessibility.

}
```

16.4.10 Reward Loyalty

Recognize and reward loyal community members. This could involve giving them early access to updates, exclusive content, or special in-game items. Acknowledging their support builds a strong sense of community loyalty.

16.4.11 Moderation and Code of Conduct

Implement clear community guidelines and a code of conduct to ensure a positive and respectful environment. Have a moderation team in place to address any issues promptly and maintain a friendly atmosphere.

16.4.12 Cross-Promotion

Explore cross-promotion opportunities with other indie developers or gaming communities that share similar interests. Collaborative efforts can introduce your game to new audiences and strengthen your community.

16.4.13 Feedback Implementation

Show your community that their feedback matters by actively implementing suggestions and improvements from players. When they see their ideas come to life in the game, it reinforces their sense of ownership and involvement.

In conclusion, community building and engagement are integral to the success of indie game development. By creating a welcoming and active community around your game, you can harness the collective enthusiasm and creativity of your players to not only improve your game but also ensure its long-term success. Building a loyal and engaged player base is an ongoing process that requires dedication and genuine interaction.

16.5 Post-Launch Support and Updates

Your responsibilities as a game developer don't end when you launch your game; in fact, they've only just begun. Post-launch support and updates are essential for maintaining player satisfaction, addressing issues, and keeping your game relevant. In this section, we'll explore the importance of post-launch support and strategies for effective updates.

16.5.1 Bug Fixes and Technical Support

One of the primary aspects of post-launch support is addressing bugs and technical issues that players encounter. Promptly identify and fix game-breaking bugs and crashes to ensure a smooth player experience. Provide technical support channels for players to report issues.

```
// Example of a bug fix in GameMaker

if (bug_detected) {

// Fix the bug and release a patch.

}
```

16.5.2 Balancing and Gameplay Tuning

Analyze player feedback and gameplay data to fine-tune your game's balance. Adjust difficulty levels, tweak character abilities, and optimize gameplay mechanics based on player experiences. Balancing updates can enhance player satisfaction.

16.5.3 Content Updates

Regularly adding new content to your game can keep players engaged and interested. Consider introducing new levels, characters, weapons, or features. Content updates provide players with fresh experiences and reasons to return to your game.

```
// Example of adding new content in GameMaker

if (new_level_released) {

// Include new level assets and gameplay.

}
```

16.5.4 Community Feedback Integration

Continue to engage with your community and integrate their feedback into updates. Address player suggestions and concerns, demonstrating your commitment to improving the game based on their input.

16.5.5 Event-Based Updates

Coordinate special in-game events or themed updates tied to holidays, seasons, or real-world events. Event-based updates can create excitement and encourage players to return to your game during specific times.

16.5.6 Performance Optimization

Optimize your game's performance through updates. Address issues related to frame rate drops, loading times, and memory usage. Performance improvements contribute to a better player experience.

16.5.7 Communication

Maintain open communication with your player community through regular updates, newsletters, and social media. Keep players informed about upcoming changes, events, and improvements. Transparent communication fosters trust.

16.5.8 Monetization Updates

If your game includes monetization elements such as in-app purchases or downloadable content (DLC), consider introducing new monetization options or expanding your game's economy. However, ensure that any monetization updates are fair and don't disrupt the gameplay balance.

16.5.9 Cross-Platform Updates

If your game is available on multiple platforms, synchronize updates across all platforms to provide a consistent experience for players. Cross-platform updates can include bug fixes, new content, and gameplay improvements.

16.5.10 Long-Term Roadmap

Maintain a long-term development roadmap that outlines your plans for the game's future. Share this roadmap with your community to provide transparency and generate excitement about upcoming updates and features.

16.5.11 Quality Assurance

Thoroughly test each update before release to avoid introducing new bugs or issues. Implement a rigorous quality assurance process to ensure that updates enhance, rather than disrupt, the player experience.

16.5.12 Player Feedback Channels

Continue to offer channels for player feedback and bug reporting even after the initial launch. Actively monitor these channels and respond to player inquiries and issues promptly.

In summary, post-launch support and updates are essential for the long-term success and sustainability of your game. Regularly addressing technical issues, fine-tuning gameplay, adding new content, and engaging with your player community are all key components of effective post-launch support. By demonstrating your commitment to the game and its community, you can maintain player interest and satisfaction over time, ultimately leading to a more successful and enduring game.

Chapter 17: Expanding Your Skills with Extensions

17.1 Using and Creating GameMaker Extensions

GameMaker allows developers to extend its capabilities by using and creating extensions. In this section, we will explore the concept of extensions, how to use them in your projects, and even how to create your own extensions to enhance GameMaker's functionality.

17.1.1 What Are GameMaker Extensions?

GameMaker extensions are packages of code and resources that add new features or functionality to your GameMaker projects. These extensions can be created by the GameMaker community or by you to customize and extend the engine's capabilities. Extensions can include code scripts, shaders, assets, and even custom functions that you can use in your projects.

17.1.2 Using Existing Extensions

To use existing extensions in your GameMaker project, you need to import them. Here's a step-by-step guide on how to do it:

1. **Download the Extension**: First, download the extension file, usually provided in a ".yymp" format.
2. **Import the Extension**: In your GameMaker project, go to the "Extensions" tab, right-click, and select "Import Extension Package." Choose the downloaded extension file.
3. **Configure Extension Properties**: Once imported, you can configure the extension's properties and settings. This

might include specifying required assets or setting up variables.

4. **Use Extension Functions**: You can now use the functions and features provided by the extension in your game. Refer to the extension's documentation for details on how to use it.

```
// Example of using a custom extension function

if (extension_function_exists("my_extension", "awesome_function")) {

var result = my_extension_awesome_function(argument0, argument1);

}
```

17.1.3 Creating Your Own Extensions

Creating your own GameMaker extensions allows you to add custom functionality tailored to your project's specific needs. Here's a high-level overview of the process:

1. **Plan Your Extension**: Clearly define the functionality you want to add through your extension. Create a design document outlining the features, scripts, and assets your extension will include.
2. **Write the Code**: Write the necessary code scripts in GML to implement your extension's functionality. This can include new functions, data structures, or algorithms.
3. **Organize Assets**: If your extension requires assets like sprites, sounds, or shaders, organize them in a separate folder within your extension package.
4. **Package the Extension**: Package your extension into a

".yymp" file using GameMaker's extension packaging tools. Specify the extension's metadata, dependencies, and any required resources.

5. **Test Thoroughly**: Before sharing or using your extension in a project, thoroughly test it to ensure it works as expected and doesn't introduce errors or conflicts.
6. **Share or Import**: You can choose to share your extension with the GameMaker community or import it into your projects following the same steps as mentioned earlier for using existing extensions.

17.1.4 Extending GameMaker's Capabilities

Extensions can be used to extend GameMaker's capabilities in various ways:

- **Custom Functions**: Add new functions and scripts that perform specific tasks or calculations for your game.

- **Asset Libraries**: Include custom assets like sprites, sounds, or backgrounds that are essential for your project.

- **Shaders**: Create custom shaders to achieve unique visual effects or optimize rendering.

- **Data Structures**: Define custom data structures or containers tailored to your game's data needs.

- **Third-Party Integrations**: Integrate third-party APIs or libraries to enable features like online multiplayer or analytics.

- **Gameplay Enhancements**: Implement gameplay systems or mechanics that go beyond what GameMaker offers by default.

Extensions open up endless possibilities for game development, allowing you to tailor GameMaker to your specific project requirements and creative vision.

17.1.5 Case Studies: Successful Projects Using Extensions

To inspire your extension development journey, here are some case studies of successful GameMaker projects that utilized extensions to enhance their gameplay, graphics, and overall player experience:

- **Hyper Light Drifter**: This indie action-adventure game used custom extensions for its dynamic lighting and particle effects, contributing to its visually striking and immersive world.

- **Spelunky**: The procedural level generation and physics in Spelunky were achieved through custom extensions, enabling the creation of its challenging and endlessly replayable levels.

- **Undertale**: Undertale used extensions to implement unique combat mechanics, dialog systems, and character interactions, leading to its innovative gameplay and storytelling.

- **Hotline Miami**: The fast-paced action and intense visuals of Hotline Miami were made possible by extensions that provided advanced sprite manipulation and shader effects.

In conclusion, GameMaker extensions offer a powerful way to expand the capabilities of the engine and tailor it to your game's specific needs. Whether you're using existing extensions or creating your own, extensions can be a game-changer in enhancing gameplay, graphics, and overall player experience. Experiment, iterate, and leverage extensions to bring your creative ideas to life in your GameMaker projects.

17.2 Integration with Third-Party Tools

Integration with third-party tools is a crucial aspect of game development with GameMaker. These tools can expand your project's capabilities, streamline your workflow, and enhance the overall development process. In this section, we will explore the importance of integrating third-party tools and how to do it effectively.

17.2.1 The Role of Third-Party Tools

Third-party tools can serve a variety of purposes in your GameMaker project:

- **Asset Creation**: Tools like Adobe Photoshop, GIMP, or Aseprite are essential for creating sprites, textures, and other graphical assets.

- **Sound and Music**: Audio editing software such as Audacity or Adobe Audition can help you create and edit sound effects and music for your game.

- **Version Control**: Version control systems like Git and platforms like GitHub are crucial for collaboration, tracking changes, and managing your project's source code.

- **Project Management**: Project management tools like Trello, Jira, or Asana help you plan, track tasks, and stay organized throughout development.

- **Code Editors**: Text editors like Visual Studio Code or Sublime Text can be used for writing and editing GML code, providing features like syntax highlighting and debugging.

- **Physics Engines**: You can integrate third-party physics engines like Box2D or LiquidFun to implement realistic physics in your game.

- **Analytics and Monetization**: Services like Google Analytics or ad networks like AdMob are essential for tracking player behavior and monetizing your game.

17.2.2 Setting Up Third-Party Tools

To integrate third-party tools effectively, follow these general steps:

1. **Installation**: Install the third-party tool on your development machine, following the tool's official documentation.
2. **Configuration**: Configure the tool according to your project's needs. This may involve setting up preferences, profiles, or project-specific settings.
3. **Integration with GameMaker**: Depending on the tool, you may need to establish a connection or interaction between the tool and your GameMaker project. This can involve importing assets, connecting to APIs, or configuring export settings.

```
// Example of using an API key for integration
```

```
var api_key = "YOUR_API_KEY";

http_set_custom_header("Authorization", "Bearer " + api_key);
```

1. **Testing**: Test the integration thoroughly to ensure that data and assets are transferred correctly between GameMaker and the third-party tool.
2. **Documentation**: Document the integration process for your team, including any setup instructions, configurations, or code snippets required.

17.2.3 Common Third-Party Integrations

Here are some common types of third-party integrations and tools used in GameMaker development:

- **Texture Packer**: Tools like TexturePacker help you create sprite sheets and optimize texture atlases for efficient rendering in GameMaker.

- **Physics Engines**: GameMaker supports integration with popular physics engines like Box2D and LiquidFun to add realistic physics interactions to your game.

- **Networking Libraries**: Integrating networking libraries or middleware can enable online multiplayer functionality or data synchronization with servers.

- **Ads and Monetization**: You can integrate ad networks like AdMob, Chartboost, or Unity Ads to monetize your game through in-game advertisements.

- **Analytics**: Implementing analytics tools like Google Analytics or GameAnalytics helps you track player behavior, gather data, and make informed decisions for game optimization.

- **Social Media**: Integrating social media APIs allows players to share achievements or progress on platforms like Facebook or Twitter.

- **Cloud Services**: Services like Firebase can be used for real-time multiplayer, cloud storage, and user authentication.

17.2.4 Benefits of Third-Party Integrations

Integrating third-party tools offers several benefits for your GameMaker project:

- **Efficiency**: These tools can streamline various aspects of development, from asset creation to code editing and project management.

- **Quality**: Specialized third-party tools often provide features and capabilities that can enhance the quality of your game's assets and code.

- **Collaboration**: Tools like version control systems enable collaboration with team members and facilitate code sharing and merging.

- **Data and Insights**: Integrating analytics and monetization tools allows you to gather valuable data about player behavior and optimize your game accordingly.

- **Monetization**: Ad networks and monetization platforms help you generate revenue from your game through ads or in-app purchases.

- **Enhanced Functionality**: Third-party physics engines, networking libraries, and other middleware can add advanced functionality to your game.

In conclusion, integrating third-party tools is a fundamental aspect of successful GameMaker development. These tools expand your project's capabilities, improve efficiency, and enable you to create high-quality games. Whether you need to create assets, manage code, implement analytics, or add advanced features, third-party integrations can be a game-changer in your game development journey.

17.3 Extending GameMaker's Capabilities

GameMaker's flexibility extends beyond its core features, thanks to its extensibility through scripting and code. In this section, we'll delve into advanced scripting techniques and strategies to extend GameMaker's capabilities for your game development needs.

17.3.1 Advanced Scripting with GML

GameMaker Language (GML) is the scripting language that powers GameMaker. To extend GameMaker's capabilities, you'll often need to write custom scripts. Here are some advanced scripting techniques:

- **Custom Data Structures**: Create your own data structures using arrays, lists, or grids to manage complex data efficiently.

```
// Example of a custom data structure

var player_inventory = ds_map_create();

ds_map_add(player_inventory, "item", "sword");

ds_map_add(player_inventory, "quantity", 3);
```

- **Object-Oriented Programming (OOP)**: Implement OOP principles in GML by using objects as classes and instances as objects. This allows you to organize code in a more structured way.

```
// Example of an OOP approach

// Create a "Player" object as a class

player_class = function() {

this.hp = 100;

this.attack = function() {

// Attack logic

}

}

// Create instances of the "Player" class

player_instance_1 = new player_class();

player_instance_2 = new player_class();
```

- **Function Libraries**: Create libraries of reusable functions to modularize your code and make it more maintainable. This can include functions for pathfinding, input handling, or custom math operations.

```
// Example of a function library

/// @function custom_math_add

/// @param {real} a

/// @param {real} b

/// @return {real}

var custom_math_add = function(a, b) {

return a + b;

}
```

- **Optimization Techniques**: Optimize your scripts for performance by minimizing unnecessary calculations and loops. Profiling tools in GameMaker can help identify bottlenecks.

```
// Example of loop optimization

for (var i = 0; i < array_length_1d(my_array); i++) {

// Code to execute

}
```

17.3.2 Extending GameMaker's Events

GameMaker's event system is powerful, but you can extend it further using custom events and user-defined event systems. Here's how:

- **Custom Events**: Create custom events within objects to handle specific behaviors or interactions unique to your game.

```
// Example of a custom event

// In an object's Create event

event_user(1); // Calls custom event 1

// In the object's custom event 1

// Custom logic for this event
```

- **User-Defined Event Systems**: Implement a custom event system using variables or data structures to manage complex sequences of events.

```
// Example of a user-defined event system

var current_event = 0;

// In the Step event

switch (current_event) {

case 0:

// Event 0 logic

break;

case 1:

// Event 1 logic

break;
```

```
// Add more cases for additional events

}
```

17.3.3 Advanced Scripting Techniques

To truly extend GameMaker's capabilities, consider these advanced scripting techniques:

- **Dynamic Resource Creation**: Use scripting to create objects, instances, or resources dynamically during runtime, allowing for procedural content generation or adaptive gameplay.

```
// Example of dynamic instance creation

var new_enemy = instance_create(x, y, obj_enemy);

new_enemy.speed = random_range(2, 5);
```

- **DLL Integration**: GameMaker allows you to integrate dynamic link libraries (DLLs) written in other languages, enabling access to external functionality.

```
// Example of DLL integration

external_define("example.dll", dll_cdecl, dll_int, "example_function");

external_define("example.dll", dll_cdecl, dll_void, "another_function");

external_load("example.dll");

var result = external_define("example_function", argument0, argument1);
```

```
external_free("example.dll");
```

- **Networking and Multiplayer**: Create multiplayer games by implementing networking code using sockets or GameMaker's built-in networking functions.

```
// Example of multiplayer synchronization

if (network_connect(ip_address, port)) {

// Connected to the server

network_send_message(my_message);

}
```

- **Real-time Shader Programming**: Utilize shaders to create real-time visual effects by writing shader code directly within GameMaker.

```
// Example of applying a shader

shader_set(my_shader);

draw_self();

shader_reset();
```

- **Advanced AI and Pathfinding**: Implement sophisticated AI behavior and pathfinding algorithms to create intelligent game entities.

```
// Example of advanced AI logic

if (can_see_player()) {

// Implement advanced chasing or decision-making behavior
```

```
}
```

17.3.4 Debugging and Optimization

As you extend GameMaker's capabilities with advanced scripting, debugging and optimization become crucial. Use GameMaker's debugging tools, such as the Debugger and Profiler, to identify and resolve issues in your code. Optimize your scripts and resource management to ensure smooth gameplay and performance.

17.3.5 Version Control and Collaboration

When working with advanced scripting and extending GameMaker's capabilities, version control systems like Git are invaluable. They allow you to track changes, collaborate with team members, and manage code branches effectively.

In conclusion, extending GameMaker's capabilities through advanced scripting techniques empowers you to create complex and innovative games. Whether it's through custom scripts, event systems, or advanced programming, GameMaker provides the flexibility you need to bring your creative ideas to life. However, remember to balance creativity with optimization and debugging to ensure your game runs smoothly and efficiently.

17.4 Sharing and Collaborating within the Community

Collaboration and sharing within the GameMaker community can be incredibly beneficial for your game development journey. In this section, we'll explore how to connect with other developers, share resources, and leverage the power of community-driven development.

17.4.1 GameMaker Community Platforms

The GameMaker community spans various platforms where developers come together to share knowledge, collaborate, and seek help. Here are some key community platforms:

- **GameMaker Community Forum**: The official GameMaker forum is a hub for discussions, tutorials, and collaboration. It's a great place to ask for assistance and share your knowledge.

- **Reddit (r/gamemaker)**: The GameMaker subreddit is a lively community where developers share projects, ask questions, and provide feedback.

- **Discord Servers**: Many GameMaker Discord servers cater to specific interests or game genres. Joining these servers allows you to engage in real-time discussions and collaboration.

- **Indie Game Development Communities**: Platforms like IndieDB and itch.io have dedicated communities where you can showcase your games and interact with other indie developers.

17.4.2 Sharing Resources

Sharing resources within the GameMaker community can benefit both you and fellow developers. Here's how you can contribute:

- **Open-Source Projects**: Share your open-source GameMaker projects on platforms like GitHub. This allows others to learn from your code and even contribute to your projects.

- **Tutorials and Guides**: Create tutorials and guides on topics you're knowledgeable about. Share them on forums, blogs, or YouTube to help newcomers and fellow developers.

- **Asset Sharing**: Share your game assets, such as sprites, sound effects, or scripts, on forums or asset marketplaces. Some developers offer assets for free, while others sell them.

- **Collaborative Projects**: Join collaborative projects initiated by the community. Contributing to such projects can help you gain experience and expand your network.

- **Feedback and Playtesting**: Offer to playtest and provide feedback on other developers' games. They may return the favor and help you improve your games.

17.4.3 Collaborative Development

Collaborating with other GameMaker developers can lead to exciting projects and shared knowledge. Here are ways to engage in collaborative development:

- **Game Jams**: Participate in Game Jams, which are time-limited events where developers create games based on a theme. Collaborate with others or join existing teams.

- **Online Teams**: Join or create online development teams. Platforms like itch.io and Game Jolt have sections dedicated to team recruitment.

- **Local Meetups**: If possible, attend local game development meetups or events. Networking with developers in your area can lead to valuable collaborations.

- **GitHub Collaboration**: Use GitHub for collaborative game development. Create repositories for your projects and invite collaborators to work together on code and assets.

17.4.4 GameMaker Marketplace

The GameMaker Marketplace is a platform for buying and selling GameMaker assets, scripts, extensions, and tools. It's a great way to monetize your creations and find resources to enhance your projects. If you have assets or tools to share, consider listing them on the marketplace.

17.4.5 Developer Communities

Joining developer communities, whether online or local, can provide opportunities for collaboration, knowledge sharing, and support. Engaging with these communities allows you to learn from others, receive feedback, and find potential collaborators.

17.4.6 Code Reviews and Feedback

When collaborating within the GameMaker community, consider participating in code reviews and providing constructive feedback. Code reviews help improve code quality, while feedback can help developers identify and address issues in their projects.

17.4.7 Game Jams

Participating in Game Jams is a fantastic way to collaborate with other developers and create small games within a limited time frame. Game Jams encourage creativity, experimentation, and the rapid development of prototypes.

17.4.8 Showcasing Your Work

Share your game projects and progress on community platforms, social media, and game development forums. Showcasing your work not only garners feedback but also builds anticipation and interest in your games.

17.4.9 Learning Opportunities

Engaging with the GameMaker community provides continuous learning opportunities. By observing others' projects, asking questions, and receiving feedback, you can improve your skills and stay updated with the latest developments in GameMaker.

17.4.10 Contributing to Community Projects

Consider contributing to community-driven projects, such as open-source GameMaker extensions or collaborative games. Contributing to such projects can help you gain recognition within the community and broaden your skill set.

In summary, the GameMaker community is a valuable resource for developers at all levels. Whether you're seeking help, sharing resources, collaborating on projects, or simply learning from others, active participation in the community can greatly enhance your game development journey. Sharing your knowledge and experiences can benefit not only you but also fellow developers looking to achieve their game development goals.

17.5 Case Studies: Successful Projects Using Extensions

In this section, we'll explore real-world case studies of successful game development projects that have leveraged GameMaker extensions to enhance their gameplay, graphics, and overall player experience. These case studies highlight the creative ways in which developers have extended GameMaker's capabilities to create standout games.

17.5.1 Hyper Light Drifter

Hyper Light Drifter is an indie action-adventure game developed by Heart Machine. This critically acclaimed title showcases the power of GameMaker extensions in creating visually striking and immersive worlds.

Use of Extensions:

- *Dynamic Lighting*: Hyper Light Drifter utilizes custom extensions for dynamic lighting effects. These extensions allow for real-time lighting changes, creating a visually captivating and atmospheric game world.

Impact:

- The game's dynamic lighting significantly enhances its visual appeal and immerses players in its mysterious and dark world.

- The use of extensions allowed for the creation of complex lighting scenarios, contributing to the game's unique art style.

17.5.2 Spelunky

Spelunky is a roguelike platformer created by Derek Yu. Its procedurally generated levels and physics-based gameplay were made possible through GameMaker extensions.

Use of Extensions:

- *Procedural Level Generation*: Spelunky employs extensions to generate its levels procedurally. This approach ensures that each playthrough is unique and challenging.

- *Physics Engine*: The game integrates a custom physics engine through extensions to handle character movement and interactions with the environment.

Impact:

- The use of procedural generation keeps the game fresh and replayable, making it a favorite among players who enjoy challenging gameplay.

- By integrating a physics engine, Spelunky delivers a realistic and responsive gaming experience, enhancing immersion.

17.5.3 Undertale

Undertale, developed by Toby Fox, is celebrated for its innovative gameplay and storytelling. Extensions played a pivotal role in achieving these unique features.

Use of Extensions:

- *Unique Combat Mechanics*: Extensions were used to implement the game's innovative combat mechanics, which involve interacting with enemies in unconventional ways, such as through dialogue or sparing them.

- *Branching Storylines*: Extensions were employed to create branching storylines and character interactions based on player choices, offering a personalized gaming experience.

Impact:

- Undertale's distinctive combat and storytelling mechanics set it apart from traditional RPGs, contributing to its critical acclaim.

- The extensions enabled complex branching narratives, making players feel that their decisions truly impact the game world.

17.5.4 Hotline Miami

Hotline Miami is a fast-paced top-down shooter known for its intense action and retro-inspired visuals. GameMaker extensions were used to achieve its vibrant and dynamic gameplay.

Use of Extensions:

- *Sprite Manipulation*: Extensions allowed for advanced sprite manipulation, enabling fluid character animations and seamless transitions.

- *Shader Effects*: The game utilized extensions to implement shader effects for its neon-soaked, psychedelic visuals.

Impact:

- Hotline Miami's smooth and visually engaging gameplay owes much to the extensions used for sprite manipulation and shaders.
- The integration of these extensions contributed to the game's distinct aesthetic, which became a defining feature of the series.

In conclusion, these case studies demonstrate the versatility of GameMaker extensions and how they can be used to create innovative and visually stunning games. Game developers have leveraged extensions to push the boundaries of what is possible within the GameMaker engine, resulting in critically acclaimed titles that continue to captivate players worldwide. Whether it's dynamic lighting, procedural generation, unique combat mechanics, or striking visual effects, GameMaker extensions have played a pivotal role in shaping the success of these games.

18. Working with 3D in GameMaker

18.1 Basics of 3D Game Development

Adding 3D elements to your GameMaker projects can open up new possibilities for gameplay and visual experiences. While GameMaker primarily focuses on 2D game development, it does offer some basic 3D functionality that you can leverage to create depth and immersion in your games.

18.1.1 Understanding 3D in GameMaker

In GameMaker, 3D elements are generally limited to simple 3D transformations and rendering. While it's not a fully-fledged 3D game engine like Unity or Unreal Engine, GameMaker can handle certain 3D tasks, which can be useful for specific game mechanics or visual effects.

3D Transformations

You can manipulate objects in 3D space by changing their position, rotation, and scale. Here's a brief overview of how to perform basic 3D transformations:

- **Position**: Use the x, y, and z properties to set the position of an object in 3D space. For example, x = 100, y = 50, z = 10 would place an object 100 units to the right, 50 units down, and 10 units closer to the camera.

```
// Move an object in 3D space

x += 5; // Move 5 units to the right
```

```
y -= 2; // Move 2 units up

z += 1; // Move 1 unit closer to the camera
```

- **Rotation**: You can rotate objects around their axes using the image_angle, rotation_x, rotation_y, and rotation_z properties. For example, to rotate an object 90 degrees around the X-axis:

```
// Rotate an object around the X-axis

rotation_x += 90; // Rotate 90 degrees
```

- **Scale**: Change an object's size in 3D space using the image_xscale, image_yscale, and image_zscale properties. For uniform scaling, set all three properties to the same value:

```
// Scale an object uniformly in 3D space

image_xscale = 2; // Double the size

image_yscale = 2; // Double the size

image_zscale = 2; // Double the size
```

3D Rendering

GameMaker allows you to render objects in 3D space using a basic perspective projection. The projection matrix, accessible through the d3d_set_projection function, defines how 3D objects are projected onto the 2D screen.

```
// Set a basic perspective projection

d3d_set_projection(proj_ortho, 45, aspect_ratio, 0.1, 10000);
```

- proj_ortho: Specifies a perspective projection.
- 45: The field of view angle (in degrees).
- aspect_ratio: The aspect ratio of the screen.
- 0.1: The near clipping plane (objects closer than this won't be rendered).
- 10000: The far clipping plane (objects farther than this won't be rendered).

18.1.2 Use Cases for 3D in GameMaker

While GameMaker's 3D capabilities are limited, there are several use cases where you can leverage 3D elements to enhance your 2D games:

3D Visual Effects

You can use 3D transformations to create visual effects like parallax scrolling, depth effects, or the illusion of 3D movement. For example, you can make a background object gradually appear larger as it moves closer to the camera, creating a sense of depth.

3D-Like Gameplay

Implement gameplay mechanics that involve 3D-like interactions, such as jumping between platforms in a 2D game that gives the impression of vertical depth.

3D User Interface

Create 3D user interface elements or menus that react to player interactions, providing a unique and immersive experience.

Cinematics and Cutscenes

Use 3D rotations and sçaling to create dynamic camera movements and dramatic cutscenes in your games.

Minigames or Bonus Levels

Include minigames or bonus levels with 3D elements that deviate from the primary 2D gameplay.

18.1.3 Limitations of 3D in GameMaker

While GameMaker's 3D capabilities offer versatility, it's important to be aware of their limitations:

- **Performance**: GameMaker's 3D performance is limited compared to dedicated 3D engines. Complex 3D scenes may lead to reduced frame rates.

- **Lack of Advanced Features**: GameMaker lacks advanced 3D features such as advanced lighting, shadow mapping, and physics simulation commonly found in full-fledged 3D engines.

- **Art and Design Challenges**: Integrating 3D elements into a 2D game may require careful art and level design to maintain a consistent visual style.

In summary, GameMaker's 3D capabilities provide a bridge between 2D and 3D game development, offering opportunities to enhance your games with depth and visual effects. While it may not replace dedicated 3D engines, understanding the basics of 3D transformations and rendering can open up creative possibilities for your GameMaker projects.

18.2 Creating 3D Models and Textures

In GameMaker, incorporating 3D models and textures is a fundamental aspect of working with 3D elements. While GameMaker primarily focuses on 2D game development, it allows you to import and use 3D models and textures to enhance your games. In this section, we'll explore the process of creating and incorporating 3D assets into your GameMaker projects.

18.2.1 3D Model Creation

Creating 3D models is typically done using specialized 3D modeling software such as Blender, Maya, or 3ds Max. These software tools allow you to design and sculpt 3D objects, characters, and environments with precision. Once you have created a 3D model, you can export it in a compatible format for GameMaker.

Exporting 3D Models

GameMaker supports the import of 3D models in various formats, including .obj and .fbx. To export a 3D model from your modeling software for GameMaker, follow these general steps:

1. Open your 3D modeling software.
2. Load the model you want to export.
3. Navigate to the export or save menu.

4. Select the appropriate file format (e.g., .obj, .fbx).
5. Configure export settings, such as scale and orientation.
6. Export the model to your desired directory.

Importing 3D Models into GameMaker

Once you have exported a 3D model, you can import it into your GameMaker project. Follow these steps:

1. In GameMaker, open your project.
2. In the resource tree, right-click on the "3D Models" folder and select "Import 3D Model."
3. Browse to the directory where you exported your 3D model and select the model file.
4. Configure import settings, such as scale and position.
5. Click "Import" to add the 3D model to your project.

18.2.2 3D Texture Creation

Textures are essential for adding visual detail and realism to 3D models. You can create textures using graphic design software like Adobe Photoshop or specialized texture creation software such as Substance Painter. These tools enable you to design textures that can be applied to your 3D models.

Texture Mapping

Texture mapping is the process of applying a 2D image (the texture) onto a 3D model's surface. This process gives the model its visual appearance and can include colors, patterns, and details.

To create textures for your 3D models, follow these steps:

1. Open your preferred texture creation software.
2. Create a new texture document with the desired dimensions and resolution.
3. Design the texture by painting or applying patterns and details.
4. Save the texture in a common image format (e.g., .png, .jpg).

Texture UV Mapping

In 3D modeling, textures are applied using UV mapping, which defines how a 2D texture aligns with the 3D model's surfaces. UV mapping involves unwrapping the 3D model to create a 2D representation (UV map) that corresponds to the model's surface. This UV map is then used to position and apply the texture accurately.

Importing Textures into GameMaker

Once you have created textures for your 3D models, you can import them into GameMaker for use in your 3D scenes. Follow these steps:

1. In GameMaker, open your project.
2. In the resource tree, right-click on the "Sprites" folder (or a relevant folder) and select "Import Sprite."
3. Browse to the directory where you saved your texture image and select the image file.
4. Configure import settings, such as transparency and texture group.
5. Click "Import" to add the texture to your project as a sprite.

18.2.3 Applying Textures to 3D Models

Once you have imported both your 3D model and its associated textures into GameMaker, you can apply the textures to the model's surfaces. This process involves assigning the imported textures to the model's materials and specifying how they should be mapped to the model's UV coordinates.

Material Creation

In GameMaker, materials are used to define how a 3D model's surfaces should appear, including the textures to be used. To apply textures to a 3D model, you need to create materials that reference the imported textures. Follow these steps:

1. In the resource tree, right-click on the "Materials" folder and select "Create Material."
2. Configure the material's settings, including its name and properties.
3. Under the "Textures" section, assign the appropriate texture(s) to the material's slots (e.g., diffuse, normal, specular).
4. Adjust material properties such as color, transparency, and shininess.

Assigning Materials to 3D Models

Once you have created materials with assigned textures, you can apply these materials to specific parts of your 3D model. This process involves selecting the model and specifying which material should be used for each part.

1. Select the 3D model in your project's resource tree.

2. In the properties panel, locate the "Materials" section.
3. For each part of the model (e.g., individual meshes or groups of vertices), select the material to be applied.

By assigning materials to different parts of your 3D model, you can control how textures are mapped and displayed on its surfaces.

In summary, creating and incorporating 3D models and textures into GameMaker can expand your game development possibilities by adding depth and realism to your projects. While GameMaker's 3D capabilities are not as advanced as dedicated 3D engines, you can still create visually appealing 3D elements within your 2D games. Understanding the process of exporting, importing, and applying 3D models and textures is a valuable skill for enhancing your GameMaker projects.

18.3 Implementing 3D Environments

Creating 3D environments in GameMaker can add depth and immersion to your games. While GameMaker primarily focuses on 2D game development, you can leverage its 3D capabilities to design and render 3D environments. In this section, we'll explore the process of implementing 3D environments in your GameMaker projects.

18.3.1 Working with 3D Objects

To build a 3D environment, you need 3D objects that represent elements of the environment, such as buildings, terrain, or props. These objects are typically created in 3D modeling software and imported into GameMaker, as discussed in the previous section.

Placing 3D Objects

Once you have imported your 3D objects into GameMaker, you can place them within your game world. This involves positioning and orienting the objects to create the desired environment. Use the x, y, and z properties to set the position of 3D objects in 3D space and the rotation_x, rotation_y, and rotation_z properties to adjust their orientation.

```
// Positioning a 3D object

obj_building.x = 100; // X-coordinate

obj_building.y = 0; // Y-coordinate

obj_building.z = 20; // Z-coordinate

// Rotating a 3D object

obj_tree.rotation_x = 0; // Rotation around X-axis (pitch)

obj_tree.rotation_y = 90; // Rotation around Y-axis (yaw)

obj_tree.rotation_z = 0; // Rotation around Z-axis (roll)
```

Grouping and Organization

In complex 3D environments, it's essential to organize 3D objects efficiently. You can group related objects together using parent-child relationships or containers. This simplifies management and manipulation, especially when dealing with large environments.

18.3.2 Camera Control

Camera control is crucial for defining the player's perspective within a 3D environment. GameMaker provides tools for setting up and controlling the camera to achieve various camera angles and movements.

Camera Setup

To set up the camera for a 3D environment, you can use the d3d_set_projection function to configure the camera's properties:

```
d3d_set_projection(proj_perspective, fov, aspect_ratio, near_clip, far_clip);
```

- proj_perspective: Specifies a perspective projection.
- fov: The field of view angle (in degrees).
- aspect_ratio: The aspect ratio of the screen.
- near_clip: The near clipping plane (objects closer than this won't be rendered).
- far_clip: The far clipping plane (objects farther than this won't be rendered).

Camera Movement

Implementing camera movement allows players to explore the 3D environment from different angles. You can control the camera's position and orientation based on player input or scripted events. Here's a simple example of how to move the camera:

```
// Camera movement

var move_speed = 5;

var rotate_speed = 2;
```

```
// Move the camera forward and backward

if (keyboard_check(ord("W"))) {

camera_move_z(move_speed);

}

if (keyboard_check(ord("S"))) {

camera_move_z(-move_speed);

}

// Rotate the camera left and right

if (keyboard_check(ord("A"))) {

camera_rotate_z(rotate_speed);

}

if (keyboard_check(ord("D"))) {

camera_rotate_z(-rotate_speed);

}
```

Camera Modes

You can implement different camera modes to provide varied perspectives in your 3D environment. For example, you can switch between first-person and third-person views or use fixed cameras for cinematic sequences. Each camera mode requires setting up the camera and controlling its position and orientation accordingly.

18.3.3 Lighting and Shading

Lighting plays a crucial role in rendering realistic 3D environments. GameMaker allows you to incorporate lighting and shading effects to enhance the visual quality of your 3D scenes.

Light Sources

You can add various light sources to your 3D environment, such as directional lights, point lights, or spotlights. Light sources affect how 3D objects are illuminated and shaded. GameMaker provides functions to control the properties of light sources, including their position, intensity, and color.

```
// Create a point light

var light = d3d_light_create();

d3d_light_define(light, lt_point);

d3d_light_position(light, x, y, z);

d3d_light_color(light, c_white);

d3d_light_intensity(light, 1.0);
```

Shaders

Shaders are powerful tools for achieving advanced lighting and shading effects in your 3D environments. You can write custom shaders or use pre-built shader programs to simulate various materials and lighting conditions. GameMaker supports both GLSL and HLSL shaders.

18.3.4 Collision Detection

Implementing collision detection in a 3D environment is essential to ensure that players and objects interact with the environment realistically. GameMaker provides collision functions to handle collisions between 3D objects and the environment.

Collision Events

You can create collision events in GameMaker to define specific interactions between 3D objects and the environment. For example, when a player-controlled 3D character collides with a wall, you can trigger actions like stopping the character's movement or playing a sound effect.

```
// Collision event with a wall object

if (collision_wall) {

// Stop the character's movement

speed = 0;

// Play a collision sound effect

audio_play_sound(snd_collision, 1, false);

}
```

18.3.5 Optimization

Optimizing your 3D environment is crucial to maintain good performance. Large 3D environments with many detailed objects can strain the hardware, leading to reduced frame rates. Here are some optimization techniques:

Level of Detail (LOD)

Implement LOD systems that reduce the complexity of distant objects. Use simpler 3D models or lower-resolution textures for objects in the background to improve performance.

Occlusion Culling

Implement occlusion culling techniques to prevent rendering objects that are not visible to the camera. This reduces the number of objects the game needs to render, improving performance.

Efficient Models and Textures

Optimize 3D models by reducing the number of polygons and using efficient textures. Texture atlases and texture compression can also save memory and improve performance.

In summary, implementing 3D environments in GameMaker involves creating and placing 3D objects, controlling the camera, incorporating lighting and shading, handling collision detection, and optimizing performance. While GameMaker's 3D capabilities are not as extensive as dedicated 3D engines, they offer flexibility for creating visually appealing and immersive 3D experiences within your 2D games. Understanding these concepts and techniques will help you make the most of GameMaker's 3D features in your game development projects.

18.4 Lighting and Rendering Techniques

Lighting and rendering play a significant role in creating visually appealing 3D environments in GameMaker. Properly implemented lighting can enhance the atmosphere, realism, and mood of your game. In this section, we'll delve into various lighting and rendering techniques you can use to improve the visual quality of your 3D scenes.

18.4.1 Types of Lighting

GameMaker offers several types of lighting that you can use to illuminate your 3D environments:

1. Ambient Lighting

Ambient lighting provides a base level of illumination across the entire scene, simulating indirect or scattered light. It ensures that objects are not completely in the dark, even in areas not directly lit by other light sources. You can configure ambient lighting using the d3d_set_ambient_lighting function:

```
// Set ambient lighting

d3d_set_ambient_lighting(c_gray);
```

2. Directional Lighting

Directional lighting, also known as sunlight or moonlight, simulates light coming from a distant source. It affects all objects uniformly and can cast shadows. You can configure directional lighting using the d3d_light_define_directional function:

```
// Define directional light

var light = d3d_light_define_directional();

d3d_light_direction(light, -1, -1, -1); // Light direction vector

d3d_light_color(light, c_white);
```

```
d3d_light_intensity(light, 1.0);
```

3. Point Lighting

Point lights simulate light originating from a specific point in space and radiating in all directions. They create realistic light falloff and can cast shadows. You can configure point lighting using the d3d_light_define_point function:

```
// Define point light

var light = d3d_light_define_point();

d3d_light_position(light, x, y, z); // Light position

d3d_light_range(light, 300); // Light range

d3d_light_color(light, c_yellow);

d3d_light_intensity(light, 1.0);
```

4. Spot Lighting

Spot lights simulate focused beams of light, such as flashlights or torches. They have a position, direction, and cone angle. Spot lights can cast shadows and create dramatic effects. You can configure spot lighting using the d3d_light_define_spot function:

```
// Define spot light

var light = d3d_light_define_spot();

d3d_light_position(light, x, y, z); // Light position

d3d_light_direction(light, dir_x, dir_y, dir_z); // Light direction vector
```

d3d_light_range(light, 200); // Light range

d3d_light_color(light, c_white);

d3d_light_intensity(light, 1.0);

d3d_light_spot_angle(light, 45); // Cone angle (in degrees)

18.4.2 Shadows

Shadows add depth and realism to your 3D scenes by simulating how objects block and cast shadows on one another. GameMaker offers shadow casting and receiving capabilities, primarily for point and spot lights.

Enabling Shadows

To enable shadow casting for a light source, use the d3d_light_enable_shadow function:

// Enable shadow casting for a point light

d3d_light_enable_shadow(light, true);

Shadow Receivers

By default, objects can receive shadows cast by light sources. Ensure that the objects you want to cast and receive shadows have the appropriate settings enabled. Additionally, you can control the shadow quality using the d3d_set_shadow_quality function:

// Set shadow quality

d3d_set_shadow_quality(1); // High quality

Shadow Mapping

GameMaker utilizes shadow mapping techniques to create shadows. This involves rendering the scene from the light's perspective (shadow map) and using that information to determine which areas are in shadow. Shadow mapping can be computationally intensive, so optimizing your scenes is essential for maintaining good performance.

18.4.3 Reflections

Reflections can add a layer of realism to your 3D environments, especially when dealing with reflective surfaces like water, mirrors, or shiny objects. Achieving reflections in GameMaker typically involves using reflective shaders or rendering techniques.

Environment Mapping

Environment mapping is a technique where you capture the surroundings of a reflective object and use it as a texture to simulate reflections. GameMaker supports environment mapping through shaders, allowing you to apply reflective surfaces to objects dynamically.

Screen-Space Reflections (SSR)

Screen-Space Reflections is another technique that simulates reflections by analyzing the screen space and reflecting objects based on the visible content. SSR can be computationally expensive but provides dynamic and accurate reflections.

18.4.4 Post-Processing Effects

Post-processing effects can dramatically impact the visual quality of your 3D scenes. These effects are applied after rendering the scene and can include:

- **Bloom**: Adds a soft glow to bright areas.
- **Depth of Field**: Blurs objects that are out of focus.
- **Motion Blur**: Simulates motion blur for fast-moving objects.
- **Color Grading**: Adjusts the color tone and mood of the scene.

You can implement these effects using shaders and the post-processing pipeline in GameMaker.

18.4.5 Particle Systems

Particle systems can enhance the visual quality of your 3D environments by adding effects like fire, smoke, rain, or sparks. GameMaker provides a built-in particle system that you can use to create and control dynamic visual effects within your scenes.

```
// Create a particle system

var ps = part_system_create();

// Define particle properties

part_system_depth(ps, depth);

part_type_sprite(part_type, sprite_index);

part_type_alpha1(part_type, 1);
```

```
part_type_color1(part_type, c_red);

part_type_speed(part_type, 1, 2);

part_type_direction(part_type, 0, 360);

part_type_life(part_type, 30, 60);

part_type_size(part_type, 1, 2);

// Emit particles

part_particles_create(ps, x, y, part_type, 10);
```

In summary, implementing lighting and rendering techniques in GameMaker is crucial for creating visually stunning 3D environments. By mastering these techniques, you can enhance the atmosphere, realism, and overall quality of your 3D game worlds. Whether it's configuring different types of lighting, enabling shadows, simulating reflections, applying post-processing effects, or utilizing particle systems, these tools provide you with creative ways to make your 3D scenes come to life.

18.5 Performance Considerations in 3D Games

Optimizing the performance of your 3D games is crucial to ensure a smooth and enjoyable player experience. While GameMaker provides 3D capabilities, it's essential to be mindful of performance considerations, as 3D rendering can be computationally intensive. In this section, we'll explore various performance optimization techniques for 3D games in GameMaker.

18.5.1 Level of Detail (LOD)

Level of Detail (LOD) is a technique that involves using lower-polygon models or lower-resolution textures for distant objects. By reducing the detail of objects as they move farther from the camera, you can significantly improve rendering performance. GameMaker supports LOD systems, allowing you to swap between different levels of detail for objects based on their distance from the camera.

Implementing LOD

To implement LOD in GameMaker, you can create multiple versions of an object with varying levels of detail and use scripts or logic to switch between them based on the object's distance from the camera. For example, you can use the d3d_set_lod_level function to set the LOD level for an object:

```
// Set LOD level for an object

d3d_set_lod_level(obj_tree, 1); // High-detail version
```

18.5.2 Occlusion Culling

Occlusion culling is a technique that prevents rendering objects that are not visible to the camera. By avoiding the rendering of hidden objects, you can significantly reduce the workload on the graphics hardware and improve performance.

Implementing Occlusion Culling

GameMaker provides functions and features for implementing occlusion culling. You can use the d3d_start_culling and d3d_end_culling functions to define a culling region and exclude objects outside that region from rendering. Additionally, you can use bounding volumes (such as spheres or boxes) to determine whether an object is within the culling region.

```
// Start occlusion culling

d3d_start_culling();

// Define culling region or bounding volumes

// Render objects

d3d_end_culling();
```

18.5.3 Efficient Models and Textures

Efficiency in 3D models and textures can significantly impact performance. Here are some considerations:

Model Optimization

- **Polygon Count**: Reduce the number of polygons in your 3D models, especially for objects that are less visible or not central to the gameplay.

- **Mesh Simplification**: Use mesh simplification algorithms to automatically reduce the complexity of 3D models.

- **LOD Models**: Create multiple LOD versions of your models and switch between them based on distance.

Texture Optimization

- **Texture Atlases**: Combine multiple textures into a single texture atlas to reduce the number of texture switches during rendering.

- **Texture Compression**: Use texture compression formats (e.g., DXT, ETC) to reduce texture memory usage.

- **Mipmapping**: Generate mipmaps for textures to improve rendering quality and performance at various distances.

18.5.4 Batching and Draw Calls

Reducing the number of draw calls (the commands to render an object) can significantly improve rendering performance. GameMaker allows you to batch objects together, reducing the number of draw calls required to render them.

Object Batching

You can batch objects together using the d3d_model_batch function. This function allows you to group multiple instances of the same object into a single batch, reducing draw calls.

```
// Batch objects together

d3d_model_batch(obj_tree);
```

Dynamic Batching

GameMaker also supports dynamic batching, which automatically combines objects that share similar properties (e.g., same model and texture) into batches during runtime. This can be particularly helpful when you have many instances of the same object.

18.5.5 Shader Optimization

Shaders can provide advanced rendering effects but can also impact performance. Optimizing shaders is essential to ensure they run efficiently.

Shader Complexity

- **Simplify Shaders**: Keep shaders as simple as possible to reduce computation time.
- **Avoid Expensive Operations**: Minimize expensive operations like ray tracing or complex simulations in shaders.

Shader Caching

GameMaker caches compiled shaders for reuse. Take advantage of shader caching to avoid recompiling shaders every frame.

18.5.6 Testing and Profiling

Profiling your game to identify performance bottlenecks is crucial. GameMaker provides built-in profiling tools that allow you to monitor CPU and GPU usage, draw calls, and memory usage.

Profiling Tools

- **Profiler**: Use GameMaker's built-in profiler to monitor CPU and GPU usage and identify performance hotspots.
- **Debug Mode**: Enable Debug Mode to see real-time performance statistics in the development environment.

In summary, optimizing the performance of your 3D games in GameMaker involves careful consideration of factors such as level of detail, occlusion culling, efficient models and textures, reducing draw calls, shader optimization, and profiling. By implementing these techniques and fine-tuning your game, you can achieve smooth and responsive 3D gameplay experiences that captivate your players while maintaining good performance on a variety of hardware configurations.

19. Legal and Ethical Aspects

In the world of game development, legal and ethical considerations are vital to ensuring that your games are not only entertaining but also compliant with laws and ethical standards. This chapter explores the legal and ethical aspects that game developers should be aware of when creating and publishing their games.

19.1 Copyrights and Intellectual Property in Games

Understanding copyright and intellectual property (IP) laws is crucial in the game development industry. Copyright law protects original creative works, including video games, from being copied or used without permission. Here are some key aspects to consider:

19.1.1 Copyright Ownership

In most cases, the person or entity that creates a game owns the copyright to it. This includes the game's code, art, music, and any other original content. However, when multiple individuals or entities collaborate on a game, it's essential to establish clear agreements regarding copyright ownership to avoid disputes.

19.1.2 Fair Use

Fair use is a legal doctrine that allows the limited use of copyrighted material without permission for purposes such as commentary, criticism, parody, or education. Game developers should be aware of fair use principles when including copyrighted material in their games, but it's essential to consult legal counsel to determine if a particular use qualifies as fair use.

19.1.3 Licensing and Permissions

To use copyrighted material in your game, you may need to obtain licenses or permissions from the copyright holders. This applies to using music, artwork, characters, or any other content created by someone else. Failing to secure the necessary permissions can lead to legal issues.

19.1.4 Open Source and Public Domain

Open source software and public domain assets can be valuable resources for game developers. However, it's crucial to review the licenses associated with open source code and assets to ensure compliance with their terms. Public domain assets are not protected by copyright and can be freely used.

19.1.5 Protecting Your Own IP

While respecting the IP of others, you should also take steps to protect your own game's IP. This may involve registering copyrights, trademarks, or patents for your game, characters, or unique game mechanics.

19.1.6 Game Cloning and Intellectual Property Infringement

Game cloning, where developers create games that closely resemble existing successful games, can raise legal and ethical concerns. While game mechanics themselves are not typically protected by copyright, copying the unique look and feel of a game can lead to intellectual property infringement claims.

It's essential to strike a balance between drawing inspiration from existing games and creating something original to avoid legal disputes and ethical dilemmas. Conducting thorough research and consulting with legal experts can help you navigate these issues.

19.1.7 User-Generated Content

Many games allow players to create and share their content within the game, such as custom levels, characters, or mods. Developers must establish clear terms of service and guidelines for user-generated content to protect their IP rights and maintain a safe and respectful gaming environment.

19.1.8 Licensing Models and Revenue Sharing

Game developers often consider various licensing models, such as free-to-play, premium, or subscription-based, when releasing their games. Each model comes with its legal and ethical considerations, including revenue sharing with platforms and partners. Developers should carefully review the terms and agreements associated with their chosen licensing model to ensure fairness and compliance.

19.1.9 Ethical Considerations in Game Design

Beyond legal aspects, ethical considerations in game design have gained significant attention. Developers should be mindful of the impact their games have on players and society. Some ethical considerations include:

19.1.10 Addiction and Monetization

Designing games that exploit addictive tendencies or employ aggressive monetization practices can lead to negative player experiences and ethical concerns. Striking a balance between profitability and player well-being is essential.

19.1.11 Representation and Diversity

Games should strive for diversity and inclusive representation of different cultures, genders, and backgrounds. Avoiding harmful stereotypes and promoting positive portrayals can contribute to a more inclusive gaming industry.

19.1.12 Player Safety

Ensuring the safety of players, especially in online multiplayer environments, is crucial. Implementing measures to prevent harassment, bullying, and other harmful behaviors should be a priority for developers.

19.1.13 Privacy and Data Protection

Games that collect and store user data must adhere to privacy regulations and protect user information. Developers should be transparent about data collection practices and obtain informed consent from players.

19.1.14 Content Ratings and Age Appropriateness

Providing accurate content ratings and age-appropriate experiences helps players and parents make informed decisions. Misrepresenting the content of a game can lead to ethical concerns and regulatory issues.

19.1.15 Responsible Marketing and Promotion

Game developers should engage in responsible marketing practices and avoid deceptive or manipulative tactics. Truthful advertising and avoiding predatory practices in monetization are ethical considerations in marketing games.

In summary, game developers must navigate a complex landscape of legal and ethical considerations. Understanding copyright and IP laws, respecting the rights of others, protecting your own IP, and adhering to ethical principles in game design and marketing are essential steps to ensure that your games are not only successful but also compliant with legal and ethical standards. Consulting with legal experts and staying informed about industry trends and regulations is crucial for responsible game development.

19.2 Navigating Legal Issues in Game Development

Game developers often encounter various legal challenges throughout the development and publishing process. Navigating these legal issues requires a solid understanding of intellectual property, contracts, and industry regulations. This section explores some common legal issues in game development and offers guidance on how to address them.

19.2.1 Intellectual Property (IP) Protection

Protecting your intellectual property is a top priority in game development. This includes safeguarding your game's code, art, music, characters, and other original content. To protect your IP:

- **Copyright Registration**: Consider registering your game and its components with relevant copyright offices. Registration provides legal evidence of your ownership.

- **Trademarking**: If you have unique branding elements, such as logos or character names, consider trademark registration to protect them from unauthorized use.

- **Non-Disclosure Agreements (NDAs)**: Use NDAs when discussing your game with potential collaborators, contractors, or partners to ensure they don't share your confidential information.

19.2.2 Contracts and Agreements

Contracts are essential in game development to define roles, responsibilities, and rights. Common contracts include:

- **Development Contracts**: Contracts between developers and publishers or clients that outline project scope, payment terms, and IP ownership.

- **Collaboration Agreements**: When working with a team, define each member's contributions and how revenue will be shared.

- **End-User License Agreements (EULAs)**: EULAs set terms and conditions for players, including how the game can be used and any restrictions.

- **Distribution Agreements**: When publishing on platforms or stores, understand the terms and revenue splits, and negotiate if necessary.

- **Music Licensing**: If using licensed music, obtain proper licenses and permissions from music rights holders.

19.2.3 Game Cloning and Copyright Infringement

Game cloning, where developers create games that closely mimic existing games, can lead to copyright infringement claims. To avoid legal issues:

- **Analyze Existing Games**: Before starting development, research similar games to understand their mechanics and unique features. Ensure your game offers distinct gameplay experiences.

- **Legal Consultation**: If you're uncertain about potential infringement, consult with legal experts to assess the risks and make necessary adjustments.

19.2.4 User-Generated Content and Moderation

Games that allow user-generated content (UGC) should establish clear guidelines for what's acceptable. Implement moderation to prevent offensive or infringing content from reaching players. UGC platforms should have:

- **Terms of Service (ToS)**: Develop ToS that define acceptable content, penalties for violations, and a dispute resolution process.

- **Moderation Tools**: Implement automated and manual moderation tools to review and filter UGC.

- **Reporting Mechanisms**: Provide players with a way to report inappropriate content.

19.2.5 Privacy and Data Protection

Collecting player data requires adherence to privacy regulations like the General Data Protection Regulation (GDPR) or the Children's Online Privacy Protection Act (COPPA). Ensure compliance by:

- **Privacy Policies**: Create and prominently display a privacy policy that explains what data is collected and how it's used.

- **User Consent**: Obtain informed consent from players before collecting any personal information.

- **Data Security**: Implement robust security measures to protect player data from breaches.

- **Data Deletion**: Allow players to request the deletion of their data when requested.

19.2.6 Accessibility Compliance

Ensure your game complies with accessibility standards, such as the Web Content Accessibility Guidelines (WCAG) or local regulations. Consider:

- **Accessible Design**: Design your game to be playable by individuals with disabilities, including options for adjustable text size, color schemes, and control schemes.

- **Testing**: Regularly test your game with individuals who have disabilities to identify and address accessibility issues.

- **Documentation**: Provide accessibility information in your game's documentation and marketing materials.

19.2.7 International and Regulatory Compliance

Game developers must comply with international laws and regulations. Consider:

- **Age Ratings**: Obtain age ratings and comply with regional content guidelines (e.g., ESRB in North America, PEGI in Europe).

- **Taxation**: Understand tax regulations for digital goods and in-app purchases in various countries.

- **Cultural Sensitivity**: Be aware of cultural differences and sensitivities when designing and marketing your game globally.

19.2.8 Dispute Resolution

In the event of disputes with partners, collaborators, or players, having dispute resolution mechanisms in place can prevent costly legal battles. Consider:

- **Arbitration Clauses**: Include clauses in contracts that require disputes to be resolved through arbitration rather than litigation.

- **Mediation**: Explore mediation as an alternative to arbitration or court proceedings.

In summary, game developers must be well-versed in legal matters to protect their IP, create binding contracts, address privacy and accessibility requirements, and comply with international regulations. Legal consultation and thorough documentation are essential for navigating these complex legal issues successfully.

19.3 Ethical Considerations in Game Design

Ethical considerations in game design are crucial for creating games that not only entertain but also promote positive experiences and avoid harm to players. Game developers should be mindful of various ethical aspects during the design and development process. Here are some key ethical considerations:

19.3.1 Addiction and Monetization

Responsible Monetization

Game developers should prioritize player well-being over excessive profits. Implementing fair and ethical monetization practices can help prevent player addiction and dissatisfaction. Examples of responsible monetization practices include:

- **Avoiding Pay-to-Win**: Do not sell in-game advantages that unbalance gameplay.
- **Transparent Microtransactions**: Clearly communicate the cost and benefits of in-game purchases to players.
- **Limiting Spending**: Allow players to set spending limits or disable microtransactions.

Player Engagement

While it's essential to keep players engaged, developers must avoid manipulative practices that exploit players' time and money. Designing games that encourage healthy play and meaningful experiences can enhance player satisfaction.

19.3.2 Representation and Diversity

Inclusive Design

Game developers should strive to create inclusive and diverse game worlds that reflect the richness of human experiences. Promote diversity in character design, storytelling, and world-building to ensure players from various backgrounds feel represented and welcome.

Avoiding Harmful Stereotypes

Be cautious not to perpetuate harmful stereotypes or biases in game design. Avoid using offensive or discriminatory content that can alienate or harm certain groups of players.

19.3.3 Player Safety

Ensuring player safety in online games is a top priority. Developers should implement robust systems to prevent harassment, bullying, and abusive behavior. Some measures include:

- **Reporting and Blocking**: Provide tools for players to report and block abusive individuals.
- **Moderation**: Implement moderation systems to identify and address toxic behavior.
- **Code of Conduct**: Establish clear and enforceable codes of conduct for online interactions.

19.3.4 Privacy and Data Protection

Respecting player privacy and data protection laws is essential. Game developers must be transparent about data collection practices, obtain informed consent, and safeguard player data from breaches or misuse. Key considerations include:

- **Privacy Policies**: Clearly communicate what data is collected and how it will be used in a privacy policy.

- **Data Security**: Implement robust security measures to protect player data.

- **Data Minimization**: Collect only the necessary data for the game's functionality.

19.3.5 Content Ratings and Age-Appropriateness

Providing accurate content ratings and age-appropriate experiences is essential. Misrepresenting the content of a game can lead to ethical concerns and regulatory issues. Developers should:

- **Provide Clear Ratings**: Ensure content ratings accurately reflect the game's content, and follow industry-standard rating systems.

- **Age Gates**: Implement age gates to restrict access to mature content for underage players.

19.3.6 Responsible Marketing and Promotion

Developers should engage in responsible marketing practices and avoid deceptive or manipulative tactics. Truthful advertising and avoiding predatory practices in monetization are ethical considerations in marketing games. Key practices include:

- **Honest Advertising**: Represent the game accurately in marketing materials and advertisements.

- **Avoiding Exploitative Tactics**: Refrain from tactics that create false urgency or exploit players' emotions to make purchases.

19.3.7 Social and Environmental Impact

Game developers should consider the broader social and environmental impact of their work. This includes:

- **Sustainability**: Minimize the environmental impact of game development and distribution, such as reducing carbon emissions.

- **Community Engagement**: Build and engage with a positive and respectful player community.

- **Support for Social Causes**: Consider using your platform to support social and charitable causes.

19.3.8 Testing and Feedback

During development, actively seek player feedback and conduct testing to identify and address potential ethical issues. Listening to player concerns and making necessary improvements can lead to a more ethical and player-centric game.

In conclusion, ethical considerations in game design are essential for creating games that promote positive experiences, inclusivity, and player well-being. Game developers should be mindful of addiction and monetization practices, representation and diversity, player safety, privacy and data protection, content ratings, responsible marketing, social and environmental impact, and the importance of testing and feedback. By prioritizing these ethical considerations, developers can contribute to a healthier and more ethical gaming industry.

19.4 Community Standards and Player Conduct

Establishing community standards and promoting positive player conduct is crucial for maintaining a healthy gaming environment. Game developers have a responsibility to foster a sense of respect, fairness, and inclusivity among their player communities. In this section, we explore the importance of community standards and strategies for managing player conduct.

19.4.1 Defining Community Standards

Community standards are a set of guidelines and rules that outline expected behavior within the game's community. Developers should establish clear and concise standards that promote a positive and respectful atmosphere. Some key elements of community standards include:

- **Respectful Communication**: Encourage players to communicate respectfully, avoiding harassment, hate speech, and personal attacks.

- **Fair Play**: Emphasize fair competition and discourage cheating, exploiting, or hacking.

- **Inclusivity**: Promote inclusivity by prohibiting discrimination based on race, gender, religion, or any other personal characteristics.

- **Privacy and Safety**: Ensure that players' privacy and safety are respected, and provide mechanisms for reporting and addressing safety concerns.

19.4.2 Communicating Community Standards

Once community standards are defined, it's essential to effectively communicate them to the player base. Strategies for communicating community standards include:

- **In-Game Notifications**: Display community standards and guidelines prominently within the game.

- **Terms of Service (ToS)**: Include community standards in the game's ToS, which players must agree to when creating an account or installing the game.

- **Community Guidelines Page**: Create a dedicated web page or forum section where players can reference and discuss community standards.

19.4.3 Enforcing Community Standards

Enforcing community standards is a crucial step in maintaining a positive gaming environment. Developers should establish a system for reporting violations and consequences for misconduct. Enforcement strategies include:

- **Reporting Mechanisms**: Implement easy-to-use reporting tools that allow players to report inappropriate behavior.

- **Moderation Teams**: Employ moderation teams to review and address reports promptly.

- **Consistent Enforcement**: Ensure that community standards are enforced consistently and fairly for all players.

- **Progressive Discipline**: Consider a progressive discipline approach, where penalties escalate for repeat offenders.

19.4.4 Promoting Positive Conduct

In addition to enforcing rules, developers can take proactive measures to encourage positive player conduct:

- **Rewards for Good Behavior**: Implement reward systems that incentivize positive behavior, such as helpfulness or sportsmanship.

- **Community Events**: Organize community events and initiatives that promote cooperation and camaraderie among players.

- **Education and Awareness**: Raise awareness about the importance of positive conduct through in-game messages, community newsletters, or social media.

19.4.5 Handling Toxicity

Toxic behavior can be challenging to address but is crucial for maintaining a healthy community. Strategies for handling toxicity include:

- **Chat Filters**: Implement chat filters to automatically block or censor offensive language.

- **Temporary Bans**: Use temporary bans as a consequence for disruptive behavior, with the option for appeals.

- **Permanent Bans**: Reserve permanent bans for severe or repeated misconduct.

19.4.6 Community Feedback

Listen to the feedback and concerns of your player community. Encourage open communication and consider player input when making decisions related to community standards and conduct management.

19.4.7 Regular Review and Updates

Community standards should not be static. Regularly review and update them based on changing player dynamics, emerging issues, and feedback. Keeping community standards relevant ensures that they continue to foster a positive gaming environment.

19.4.8 Promoting Inclusivity

Promoting inclusivity within the gaming community is a core ethical principle. Developers should actively work to create an environment where players of all backgrounds feel welcome and respected. Consider initiatives such as:

- **Diverse Representation**: Ensure that the game's characters and storylines reflect diversity.

- **Accessibility Features**: Implement accessibility features that accommodate players with disabilities.

- **Diversity and Inclusion Training**: Provide training for community moderators and staff on diversity and inclusion topics.

In conclusion, community standards and managing player conduct are integral aspects of game development. Developers have a responsibility to foster a positive and inclusive gaming environment by defining clear community standards, effectively communicating them, enforcing them fairly, and proactively promoting positive player conduct. By prioritizing these aspects, developers can contribute to a thriving and respectful player community.

19.5 Promoting Diversity and Inclusion in Games

Promoting diversity and inclusion in games is not only a moral imperative but also a way to create more enriching and representative gaming experiences. Game developers play a vital role in fostering a gaming industry that welcomes players from all backgrounds. In this section, we explore strategies and considerations for promoting diversity and inclusion in games.

19.5.1 Representation Matters

Representation in games is a critical aspect of diversity and inclusion. Players should see themselves reflected in the games they play. Here are some key considerations:

- **Character Diversity**: Create a diverse range of characters in terms of gender, race, ethnicity, sexual orientation, and abilities. Avoid stereotypes and ensure that characters have depth and agency.

- **Storytelling**: Develop narratives that explore diverse perspectives and experiences. Incorporate themes that resonate with a broad audience.

- **Inclusive Language**: Use inclusive language and avoid derogatory terms or slurs in game content, dialogues, and interactions.

19.5.2 Accessibility

Accessibility is another essential aspect of inclusion. Developers should aim to make their games accessible to players with disabilities. Consider the following:

- **Customizable Controls**: Allow players to customize controls, including options for different input devices and button remapping.

- **Text-to-Speech and Speech-to-Text**: Implement text-to-speech and speech-to-text features to assist players with hearing or speech impairments.

- **Visual and Audio Options**: Provide visual cues for important audio information and subtitles or captions for dialogue and sound effects.

19.5.3 Cultural Sensitivity

Respect for diverse cultures is paramount in promoting inclusion. Game developers should be mindful of cultural differences and potential sensitivities. Consider these guidelines:

- **Research**: When portraying cultures other than your own, conduct thorough research to ensure accurate and respectful representation.

- **Consultation**: If possible, consult with individuals from the culture you are depicting to gain insights and avoid stereotypes.

- **Avoid Appropriation**: Be cautious about appropriating elements from cultures without proper understanding or permission.

19.5.4 Inclusive Gameplay

Inclusive gameplay ensures that players of various skill levels and backgrounds can enjoy the game. Consider the following:

- **Difficulty Levels**: Offer multiple difficulty levels to accommodate both novice and experienced players.

- **Tutorials and Onboarding**: Provide comprehensive tutorials and onboarding experiences to help newcomers understand the game mechanics.

- **Assistive Features**: Implement assistive features, such as aim assist or auto-drive, to aid players who may struggle with certain aspects of gameplay.

19.5.5 Representation Behind the Scenes

Diversity and inclusion should extend to the development teams themselves. Encourage diversity in hiring and decision-making roles within your development studio. Diverse teams bring a broader range of perspectives and experiences to the creative process.

19.5.6 Inclusivity in Marketing and Community Building

Inclusivity should also be reflected in your game's marketing materials and community-building efforts. Consider the following:

- **Inclusive Advertising**: Create marketing materials that showcase the diversity of players and characters in your game.

- **Community Guidelines**: Establish community guidelines that explicitly prohibit discriminatory or exclusionary behavior.

- **Moderation**: Enforce moderation policies that address harassment and discrimination in community spaces, both in-game and online.

19.5.7 Diversity and Inclusion Training

Consider providing diversity and inclusion training for your development team and community moderators. Training can increase awareness of potential biases and help create a more inclusive environment.

19.5.8 Feedback and Continuous Improvement

Encourage feedback from players and the community regarding diversity and inclusion in your game. Act on feedback to make improvements and demonstrate your commitment to inclusivity.

19.5.9 Collaboration and Partnerships

Collaborate with organizations and initiatives that promote diversity and inclusion in the gaming industry. Partnering with advocacy groups or participating in diversity-focused events can help raise awareness and foster inclusivity.

In conclusion, promoting diversity and inclusion in games is a multifaceted endeavor that encompasses representation, accessibility, cultural sensitivity, inclusive gameplay, diversity behind the scenes, and inclusivity in marketing and community building. By actively addressing these considerations, game developers can contribute to a more inclusive and welcoming gaming industry where players from all backgrounds feel valued and represented.

20.1 Emerging Trends in Game Development

The field of game development is constantly evolving, driven by technological advancements, changing player preferences, and industry innovations. Staying up-to-date with emerging trends is essential for developers looking to create successful and relevant games. In this section, we explore some of the emerging trends in game development.

20.1.1 Virtual Reality (VR) and Augmented Reality (AR)

Virtual reality and augmented reality have gained momentum in recent years. VR immerses players in entirely virtual worlds, while AR overlays digital content onto the real world. These technologies offer exciting opportunities for new game experiences, such as interactive storytelling, immersive simulations, and location-based AR games.

Developers interested in VR and AR should invest in the necessary hardware and familiarize themselves with development platforms like Oculus, HTC Vive, or ARKit/ARCore for mobile AR.

20.1.2 Cloud Gaming

Cloud gaming platforms have the potential to revolutionize the industry by enabling players to stream games from remote servers, eliminating the need for high-end gaming hardware. Services like Google Stadia, Microsoft's xCloud, and NVIDIA GeForce Now are gaining popularity. Developers can leverage cloud gaming to reach a broader audience and focus on game optimization for various devices and network conditions.

20.1.3 Cross-Platform Play

Cross-platform play, where players on different gaming platforms can play together, is becoming increasingly important. Game developers are implementing this feature to create a more inclusive and connected player base. Ensuring compatibility between consoles, PC, and mobile devices can be a significant advantage.

20.1.4 Game Streaming and Content Creation

Streaming platforms like Twitch and YouTube Gaming continue to grow, providing opportunities for game developers to engage with players directly. Developers can benefit from streamers and content creators who showcase their games, reaching wider audiences and building a dedicated fanbase.

20.1.5 User-Generated Content

Games that allow players to create and share their content are gaining popularity. Titles like Minecraft and Roblox empower players to design their levels, characters, and experiences. Developers can tap into this trend by providing tools and platforms for user-generated content, fostering community-driven creativity.

20.1.6 Artificial Intelligence (AI)

AI is enhancing various aspects of game development, including character behaviors, procedural content generation, and player analytics. Game developers are using AI to create more dynamic and engaging experiences. Machine learning algorithms can adapt gameplay based on player preferences, making each playthrough unique.

20.1.7 Blockchain and NFTs

Blockchain technology and non-fungible tokens (NFTs) are entering the gaming space. NFTs can represent in-game assets, skins, or collectibles that players can buy, sell, or trade. Blockchain can also enhance player ownership and security of in-game assets.

20.1.8 Live Services and Continuous Updates

Live services, where games receive continuous updates, events, and content expansions, are becoming the norm. Developers are shifting from one-time purchases to ongoing revenue models. Keeping players engaged and invested in the long term is essential for success in this model.

20.1.9 Sustainability and Ethical Game Development

Environmental sustainability and ethical game development practices are gaining importance. Developers are exploring ways to reduce the carbon footprint of game development and address ethical concerns in monetization, representation, and player well-being.

20.1.10 Indie and Small-Scale Development

Indie game development continues to flourish, with many successful indie titles gaining recognition. The democratization of game development tools and distribution platforms allows smaller teams and solo developers to create unique and innovative games.

In conclusion, staying informed about emerging trends in game development is crucial for developers looking to create successful and relevant games. Whether it's embracing new technologies like VR and AR, exploring cloud gaming, fostering cross-platform play, or focusing on ethical and sustainable practices, adapting to these trends can lead to exciting opportunities and successful game projects.

20.2 GameMaker's Place in the Evolving Industry

As the game development industry continues to evolve, GameMaker has maintained its relevance and adaptability. GameMaker, a versatile game engine known for its user-friendly interface and accessibility, has found its place in various aspects of the industry. In this section, we explore GameMaker's role and contributions to the evolving landscape of game development.

20.2.1 Indie Game Development

GameMaker has been a favorite among indie developers for years. Its user-friendly drag-and-drop interface, along with its built-in scripting language (GML), makes it accessible to solo developers and small teams with limited resources. Many successful indie games, such as "Undertale" and "Hyper Light Drifter," were created using GameMaker.

20.2.2 Rapid Prototyping

GameMaker's rapid development capabilities are well-suited for prototyping game concepts quickly. Game designers and developers can use it to test and iterate on ideas, experiment with gameplay mechanics, and create playable prototypes before committing to a full development cycle. This agility is essential in the fast-paced game industry.

```
// Example: Rapidly prototyping a character movement script

if keyboard_check(vk_left)
```

```
{
x -= move_speed;
}
if keyboard_check(vk_right)
{
x += move_speed;
}
```

20.2.3 Educational Tool

GameMaker serves as an excellent educational tool for aspiring game developers. Its user-friendly interface allows educators to teach game design and development concepts effectively. Many educational institutions use GameMaker to introduce students to game development, providing a solid foundation for future careers in the industry.

20.2.4 GameMaker Studio 2

The release of GameMaker Studio 2 brought significant improvements and modernization to the engine. It introduced enhanced features, better performance, and improved export options. GameMaker Studio 2's visual scripting system, the Drag and Drop (DnD) interface, and the updated GameMaker Language (GML) make it a powerful choice for both beginners and experienced developers.

20.2.5 Cross-Platform Compatibility

GameMaker allows developers to export their games to multiple platforms, including PC, consoles, mobile devices, and the web. This cross-platform compatibility is invaluable in an industry where reaching a broad audience is essential for success. Developers can create a game once and publish it on various platforms with relative ease.

```
// Example: Exporting a game for multiple platforms

if os_type == os_windows

{

game_set_windows();

}

else if os_type == os_macos

{

game_set_macos();

}

else if os_type == os_ios

{

game_set_ios();

}
```

20.2.6 Continued Community Support

GameMaker boasts a dedicated and active user community. The GameMaker Community Forums and online resources provide a platform for developers to seek help, share knowledge, and collaborate on projects. This supportive community contributes to GameMaker's longevity and relevance.

20.2.7 Expanding Beyond 2D

While GameMaker has traditionally been associated with 2D game development, it has made strides in supporting 3D game development. With the introduction of 3D capabilities in GameMaker Studio 2, developers can create 3D games, opening up new possibilities for the engine.

```
// Example: Creating a 3D object in GameMaker

var cube = d3d_model_create();

d3d_primitive_begin(pr_trianglelist);

// Define cube vertices and faces

d3d_vertex_position(0, 0, 0);

// Define other vertices and faces...

d3d_primitive_end();
```

20.2.8 GameMaker's Role in Game Jams

Game jams, events where developers create games within a short timeframe, often rely on GameMaker due to its ease of use and rapid prototyping capabilities. Game jams foster creativity and innovation, and GameMaker's accessibility allows participants to focus on game design rather than complex coding.

20.2.9 Mobile Game Development

GameMaker's support for mobile game development has also made it a valuable tool in the industry. As mobile gaming continues to grow, GameMaker provides developers with the means to create engaging mobile titles.

```
// Example: Implementing touch controls for a mobile game

if device_mouse_check_button_pressed(mb_left)

{

// Handle touch input...

}
```

In conclusion, GameMaker remains a relevant and versatile game development engine in the evolving industry. Its accessibility, educational value, cross-platform capabilities, and support for both 2D and 3D game development make it a valuable choice for developers of all levels of expertise. As the industry continues to change, GameMaker continues to adapt and empower developers to bring their creative visions to life.

20.3 Advancements in Game Technology

The game development industry is heavily influenced by advancements in technology. In this section, we'll explore some of the key technological trends and innovations that are shaping the future of game development.

20.3.1 Real-Time Ray Tracing

Real-time ray tracing is a cutting-edge rendering technique that simulates the behavior of light in a virtual environment. It enhances visual fidelity by accurately modeling the reflection, refraction, and scattering of light. Games that incorporate ray tracing can achieve stunning levels of realism, making them visually impressive.

```
// Example: Enabling ray tracing in a game engine

Engine.EnableRayTracing();
```

20.3.2 High Refresh Rate Displays

High refresh rate displays, such as 120Hz, 144Hz, or even 240Hz monitors, are becoming more common. These displays offer smoother and more responsive gameplay experiences, making them particularly attractive for competitive and fast-paced games. Game developers are optimizing their titles to take full advantage of these displays.

```
// Example: Implementing variable refresh rate support

if (Display.SupportsVariableRefreshRate())

{

Display.EnableVariableRefreshRate();

}
```

20.3.3 Cloud-Based Gaming

Cloud-based gaming services are on the rise, allowing players to stream games from remote servers. This technology eliminates the need for powerful gaming hardware, making high-quality gaming accessible on a wider range of devices. Game developers are exploring ways to adapt their games for cloud-based platforms.

20.3.4 Machine Learning and AI

Machine learning and artificial intelligence are being used in various aspects of game development. AI-driven NPCs can exhibit more complex and human-like behaviors, enhancing gameplay experiences. Machine learning can also be applied to procedural content generation, creating dynamic and adaptive game worlds.

```
# Example: Implementing AI behavior with machine learning

if enemy.health < 25 and player.health > 50:

enemy.retreat()

else:

enemy.attack()
```

20.3.5 Virtual Reality (VR) and Augmented Reality (AR)

VR and AR technologies are evolving rapidly. VR headsets are becoming more affordable and capable, while AR is finding applications in location-based games and interactive experiences. Game developers are exploring new ways to create immersive VR and AR content.

20.3.6 Quantum Computing

Although quantum computing is still in its infancy, it holds promise for solving complex problems in game development. Quantum computers can potentially optimize game simulations, physics calculations, and AI pathfinding, leading to more realistic and dynamic gameplay.

```
// Example: Quantum computing for optimized pathfinding

operation QuantumPathfinding(map: Qubit[]) : Result {

// Quantum pathfinding algorithm

// ...

return Result.Zero;

}
```

20.3.7 5G Connectivity

The rollout of 5G networks promises faster and more stable internet connections, which can benefit online multiplayer and cloud gaming experiences. Developers are taking advantage of 5G to create seamless and low-latency multiplayer gameplay.

```
// Example: Implementing 5G support for multiplayer games

if (Network.Is5GConnected())

{

Network.Enable5GFeatures();

}
```

20.3.8 Haptic Feedback

Haptic feedback technology is enhancing player immersion by providing tactile sensations through controllers and devices. Games are incorporating haptic feedback to make interactions more tactile and engaging, adding a new dimension to gameplay experiences.

```
// Example: Configuring haptic feedback for controller input
Controller.ConfigureHapticFeedback(HapticPattern.Explosion);
```

20.3.9 Quantum Dots and OLED Displays

Quantum dot and OLED displays offer improved color accuracy and contrast ratios, enhancing the visual quality of games. These displays are becoming more common in high-end gaming monitors and VR headsets, providing players with more vibrant and immersive visuals.

20.3.10 Blockchain and NFT Integration

Blockchain technology and non-fungible tokens (NFTs) are finding their way into gaming. Developers are exploring how blockchain can be used to create verifiable ownership of in-game assets and unique collectibles, opening up new possibilities for monetization and player engagement.

In conclusion, advancements in technology continue to shape the game development industry. From cutting-edge rendering techniques like real-time ray tracing to the adoption of high refresh rate displays and the integration of machine learning and AI, game developers are leveraging these innovations to create more immersive and engaging experiences for players. Staying informed about these technological trends is essential for developers looking to push the boundaries of game development in the future.

20.4 Community and Educational Impact

The game development community plays a pivotal role in shaping the industry's future. It influences trends, fosters innovation, and provides valuable resources and knowledge to aspiring developers.

Additionally, education in game development is essential for nurturing the next generation of talent. In this section, we explore the impact of the community and education on the game development landscape.

20.4.1 Open Source and Collaborative Development

Open source game development has gained popularity, allowing developers to collaborate on projects and share resources. Communities such as GitHub provide platforms for open source game development, enabling developers to contribute to and learn from a global network of peers.

```
# Example: Collaborative development on an open source game project

git clone https://github.com/open-source-game/project.git
```

20.4.2 Crowdsourcing and Crowdfunding

Crowdsourcing and crowdfunding platforms like Kickstarter and IndieGoGo have empowered developers to fund their projects and build communities around their games. This approach allows developers to engage directly with their audience and receive valuable feedback during development.

```
<!—Example: Crowdfunding campaign for a game project—>

<a href="https://www.kickstarter.com/projects/game-project/game-title">Support Our Game on Kickstarter</a>
```

20.4.3 Game Jams and Hackathons

Game jams and hackathons provide opportunities for developers to come together and create games within a short time frame. These events foster creativity, experimentation, and skill development. Many innovative game concepts have originated from game jams.

```
// Example: Participating in a game jam

const gameJamStartDate = new Date('2023-02-10T12:00:00Z');

const gameJamEndDate = new Date('2023-02-13T12:00:00Z');

if (currentDate >= gameJamStartDate && currentDate <= gameJamEndDate) {

joinGameJam();

}
```

20.4.4 Online Learning and Tutorials

Online platforms like YouTube, Udemy, and Coursera offer a wealth of game development tutorials and courses. These resources allow aspiring developers to learn at their own pace and gain valuable skills in various aspects of game development, from programming to design.

```
<!—Example: Enrolling in an online game development course—>

<a href="https://www.udemy.com/course/game-development-for-beginners">Enroll in Game Development Course</a>
```

20.4.5 Game Development Schools and Degrees

Many universities and educational institutions offer specialized game development programs and degrees. These formal education pathways provide in-depth knowledge and hands-on experience, preparing students for careers in the game industry.

```
<!—Example: Applying to a game development degree program—>
```

```
<a href="https://www.university.edu/game-development-degree">Apply for Game Development Degree</a>
```

20.4.6 Mentorship and Knowledge Sharing

Experienced developers often mentor newcomers and share their knowledge within the community. Mentorship programs, online forums, and social media platforms facilitate knowledge sharing, helping individuals grow in their game development journey.

```
// Example: Joining a game development mentorship program

const mentorshipProgram = 'GameDevMentor';

if (mentorshipProgram.isOpenForApplications()) {

applyForMentorship();

}
```

20.4.7 Diversity and Inclusion Initiatives

Efforts to promote diversity and inclusion in the game development community have gained traction. Initiatives, conferences, and organizations aim to create a more inclusive and welcoming environment for underrepresented groups, fostering a diverse talent pool in the industry.

```
<!—Example: Supporting a diversity and inclusion initiative—>

<a href="https://www.diversity-in-gaming.org">Support Diversity in Gaming</a>
```

20.4.8 Game Development Competitions

Competitions and showcases, such as the Independent Games Festival (IGF) and the Global Game Jam, provide platforms for developers to showcase their work and gain recognition. These events encourage innovation and creativity within the industry.

```
// Example: Preparing a game for a game development competition

const competitionDeadline = new Date('2023-05-15T23:59:59Z');

if (currentDate <= competitionDeadline) {

polishGameForCompetition();

}
```

20.4.9 Industry Conferences and Events

Industry conferences and events, such as the Game Developers Conference (GDC) and E3, bring together professionals from all facets of game development. These gatherings provide opportunities for networking, knowledge exchange, and the unveiling of industry trends and innovations.

```
<!—Example: Attending a game development conference—>

<a href="https://www.gdc.com">Register for Game Developers Conference</a>
```

20.4.10 Game Development Communities

Online and local game development communities create spaces for developers to connect, collaborate, and share their experiences. These communities offer forums, social media groups

20.5 Looking Ahead: The Next Generation of GameMaker Developers

The future of game development with GameMaker holds exciting prospects for aspiring developers who are ready to embrace innovation, adapt to evolving trends, and contribute to the ever-growing community. In this section, we'll explore the potential paths and opportunities for the next generation of GameMaker developers.

20.5.1 Cross-Disciplinary Collaboration

Future GameMaker developers can benefit from cross-disciplinary collaboration. Game development increasingly involves skills from various domains, including art, music, programming, and design. Collaborating with experts in these areas can lead to more polished and engaging games.

```
// Example: Collaborating with an artist for game assets

const artist = findArtistForCollaboration();

if (artist.isAvailable()) {

startCollaborationWithArtist(artist);

}
```

20.5.2 Continued Learning and Adaptation

The game development landscape is dynamic, with new tools and technologies emerging regularly. Future GameMaker developers should prioritize continued learning and adaptability. Staying updated on industry trends and acquiring new skills will be essential for success.

<!—Example: Enrolling in a lifelong learning program for game development—>

<a **href**="https://www.gamedevlearning.org">Join Lifelong Learning for Game Developers</**a**>

20.5.3 Entrepreneurship and Indie Development

GameMaker offers a gateway to indie game development and entrepreneurship. Future developers can leverage platforms like Steam, itch.io, and the Epic Games Store to publish their games independently. Entrepreneurial skills will be valuable for marketing and monetizing their creations.

<!—Example: Launching an indie game on a digital distribution platform—>

<a href="https://www.steamworks.com/indie-publishing">Publish Your Indie Game on Steam</**a**>

20.5.4 Specialization and Niche Markets

Future GameMaker developers can specialize in niche markets or genres. Focusing on a particular area of expertise, such as mobile puzzle games or VR experiences, can help developers stand out in a competitive market.

```
// Example: Specializing in educational games for children

const nicheMarket = 'EducationalGamesForChildren';

if (developer.isPassionateAboutEducation() && nicheMarket.hasOpportunities()) {

specializeInNicheMarket(nicheMarket);
```

```
}
```

20.5.5 Game Development as a Service

Game development services, such as asset creation, sound design, and QA testing, offer opportunities for future developers to contribute to the industry. Providing specialized services to other developers can be a viable career path.

```
<!—Example: Offering game sound design services—>

<a href="https://www.gamedevsounddesign.com">Provide Sound Design Services for Game Developers</a>
```

20.5.6 Game Development Education

Experienced GameMaker developers can become educators and mentors to the next generation. Teaching game development in schools, colleges, or through online courses can be a rewarding way to share knowledge and inspire new talent.

```
// Example: Becoming a game development instructor

const educationalInstitution = 'GameDevAcademy';

if (developer.hasTeachingPassion() && educationalInstitution.isHiring()) {

becomeGameDevInstructor(educationalInstitution);

}
```

20.5.7 Game Development Ethics

Future GameMaker developers should prioritize ethical considerations in game development. Addressing issues like diversity, inclusion, representation, and responsible monetization will contribute to a more ethical and sustainable industry.

```
<!—Example: Joining an ethics committee for game development—>

<a href="https://www.gameethics.org">Become a Member of the Game Development Ethics Committee</a>
```

20.5.8 Innovation and Experimentation

Innovation and experimentation will be at the core of future GameMaker development. Trying out new ideas, mechanics, and storytelling techniques can lead to groundbreaking games that push the boundaries of the medium.

```
// Example: Experimenting with unconventional gameplay mechanics

if (developer.isPassionateAboutInnovation()) {

experimentWithUnconventionalGameplay();

}
```

20.5.9 Sustainable Development Practices

Sustainability in game development is gaining importance. Future GameMaker developers can adopt eco-friendly practices, reduce carbon footprints, and create games that raise awareness about environmental issues.

```
// Example: Developing a sustainable game with a green message

const sustainabilityInitiative = 'EcoFriendlyGames';

if (developer.isPassionateAboutSustainability()) {

createSustainableGameWithInitiative(sustainabilityInitiative);
```

}

20.5.10 Community Engagement

Engaging with the GameMaker community and contributing to its growth will be crucial for future developers. Sharing knowledge, participating in discussions, and collaborating on projects within the community can lead to valuable connections and opportunities.

<!—Example: Becoming an active member of the GameMaker community—>

<a href="https://www.gamemakercommunity.org">Join the GameMaker Community and Start Contributing**</a>**

In conclusion, the future of game development with GameMaker is brimming with possibilities. The next generation of developers can shape the industry through collaboration, adaptability, entrepreneurship, specialization, ethical considerations, and innovation. By embracing these opportunities, future GameMaker developers can make a lasting impact on the world of gaming.

www.ingramcontent.com/pod-product-compliance
Lightning Source LLC
LaVergne TN
LVHW090259210926
848480LV00001B/79
9798224908905